Free Video   **Free Video**

Essential Test Tips Video from Trivium Test Prep

Dear Customer,

Thank you for purchasing from Trivium Test Prep! We're honored to help you prepare for your ACCUPLACER exam.

To show our appreciation, we're offering a **FREE** *ACCUPLACER Essential Test Tips* **Video by Trivium Test Prep.*** Our video includes 35 test preparation strategies that will make you successful on the ACCUPLACER. All we ask is that you email us your feedback and describe your experience with our product. Amazing, awful, or just so-so: we want to hear what you have to say!

To receive your **FREE** *ACCUPLACER Essential Test Tips* **Video,** please email us at 5star@triviumtestprep.com. Include "Free 5 Star" in the subject line and the following information in your email:

1. The title of the product you purchased.

2. Your rating from 1 – 5 (with 5 being the best).

3. Your feedback about the product, including how our materials helped you meet your goals and ways in which we can improve our products.

4. Your full name and shipping address so we can send your **FREE** *ACCUPLACER Essential Test Tips* **Video**.

If you have any questions or concerns please feel free to contact us directly at 5star@triviumtestprep.com.

Thank you!

– Trivium Test Prep Team

*To get access to the free video please email us at 5star@triviumtestprep.com, and please follow the instructions above.

ACCUPLACER
Study Guide 2021-2022
English and Math Exam Prep with Practice Test
Questions for the ACCUPLACER Examination

Table of Contents

Introduction i

PART I: MATHEMATICS   1

ONE: Arithmetic................. 3

Types of Numbers............................. 3

Scientific Notation............................ 5

Positive and Negative Numbers 5

Order of Operations 7

Decimals and Fractions 7

Percentages 10

Rounding and Estimation 11

Comparison of Rational Numbers... 12

Answer Key 13

TWO: Quantitative Reasoning, Algebra, and Statistics 17

Units of Measurement 17

Ratios 19

Proportions 19

Exponents and Radicals 20

Algebraic Expressions...................... 22

Operations with Expressions 22

Linear Equations 25

Linear Inequalities........................... 30

Properties of Shapes 33

Three-Dimensional Shapes.............. 43

Describing Sets of Data................... 45

Probability...................................... 48

Answer Key 53

THREE: Advanced Algebra and Functions.... 65

Quadratic Equations........................ 65

Absolute Value Equations and Inequalities 69

Functions.. 70

Polynomial Functions...................... 75

Rational Functions 76

Radical Functions............................ 78

Exponential and Logarithmic Functions.................... 78

Trigonometry.................................. 81

Equality, Congruence, and Similarity................................. 87

Transformations of Geometric Figures........................... 90

Answer Key 95

PART II: READING   107

FOUR: Reading............ 109

The Main Idea 109

Supporting Details 113

The Author's Purpose 114

Organization and
Text Structures 115

The Audience.............................. 116

Evaluating Arguments 117

Drawing Conclusions 119

Tone and Mood 120

Meaning of Words and Phrases..... 122

Figurative Language..................... 123

Elements of Fiction 125

Answer Key 129

PART III: WRITING   131

FIVE: Language Skills 133

Parts of Speech 133

Constructing Sentences 142

Punctuation 146

Avoiding Common
Usage Errors 150

Answer Key 157

SIX: Writing 159

Types of Essays............................ 159

Writing a Thesis Statement............161

Structuring the Essay 162

Supporting Evidence 165

Writing Well 166

Example Essays 169

PART IV: TEST YOUR KNOWLEDGE   173

SEVEN: Mathematics Practice Test.................. 175

Arithmetic.................................. 175

Quantitative Reasoning,
Algebra, and Statistics 178

Advanced Algebra
and Functions 182

Answer Key 185

EIGHT: Reading Practice Test.................. 193

Answer Key 203

NINE: Writing Practice Test.................. 209

Selected-Response 209

The Essay.................................... 218

Answer Key 219

Introduction

Congratulations on choosing to take the ACCUPLACER! By purchasing this book, you've taken the first step toward preparing for your college and career goals. This guide will provide you with a detailed overview of the ACCUPLACER, so you know exactly what to expect on test day. We'll take you through all the concepts covered on the test and give you the opportunity to test your knowledge with practice questions. Even if it's been a while since you last took a major test, don't worry; we'll make sure you're more than ready!

What is the ACCUPLACER?

The ACCUPLACER is a collection of multiple-choice tests used to determine student readiness for college. It will help you and your academic advisors choose which classes are right for you as you get ready for academic work at the university level.

There are ten tests that comprise the ACCUPLACER; they cover reading, writing, mathematics, and English as a second language. Not every student takes all ten tests; check with your college and advisors to determine your requirements.

The ACCUPLACER is a diagnostic test; it is not scored, and there is no way to pass or fail it. This computer-based test adapts to the student's skill level: a student's response to a question determines the difficulty level of the next one.

What's on the ACCUPLACER?

The ACCUPLACER assesses basic reading comprehension, writing, and arithmetic skills. Students who answer basic questions correctly will encounter more difficult ones: college-level mathematics including algebra, coordinate geometry, and trigonometry, and college-level grammar and reading skills questions.

Today, most schools use the *Next-Generation ACCUPLACER* placement tests to measure mathematics, reading, and writing. In 2016, the College Board made a few changes to those placement tests, adding some questions, featuring paired passages in the Reading Placement Test, focusing more on organization and development in the Writing Placement Test, and aligning the tests with the SAT suite.

A student may take any or all of the tests outlined below:

What's on the ACCUPLACER?		
TEST	CONCEPTS	NUMBER OF QUESTIONS
Math: Arithmetic Placement Test	Operations with whole numbers, fractions, decimals, percentages, number comparisons and equivalents	20 questions
Math: Quantitative Reasoning, Algebra, and Statistics Placement Test	Rational numbers; ratios and proportions; exponents; algebraic expressions; linear equations, applications, and graphs; probability and sets; descriptive statistics; geometry for pre-algebra and Algebra 1	20 questions
Math: Advanced Algebra and Functions Placement Test	Linear equations, applications, and graphs; factoring; quadratics; functions; radical, rational, polynomial, exponential, and logarithmic equations; geometry concepts for Algebra 1 and Algebra 2; trigonometry	20 questions
Reading Placement Test	Main and supporting ideas, drawing inferences, rhetoric, vocabulary, identifying details	20 questions
Writing Placement Test	Expression of ideas (development, organization, and effective language use); conventions of Standard English (sentence structure, usage, punctuation)	25 questions
WritePlacer (essay)	Effective, organized writing with supported and well-developed ideas, strong sentence structure, and few mechanical errors	1 essay (300 – 600 words)
ESL—Language use	Grammar and usage	20 questions
ESL—Listening	Comprehension of spoken English	20 questions
ESL—Reading Skills	Comprehension of English-language reading (short and mid-length passages)	20 questions
ESL—Sentence Meaning	Comprehension of English-language sentences	20 questions

How is the ACCUPLACER Scored?

The ACCUPLACER is a diagnostic test used to determine a student's readiness for college-level coursework or whether developmental or transitional courses are required before enrolling. Therefore, it is not possible to pass or fail it.

The ACCUPLACER is computer adaptive: it is administered by computer, and a student's response to one question determines the difficulty level of the next. If you answer a question incorrectly, the next question will be easier; if you answer a question correctly, you will then be presented with one of higher difficulty. You will receive your results immediately.

How is the ACCUPLACER Administered?

The ACCUPLACER is a multiple-choice test administered by computer. The ESL – Listening section may be administered as a conversation. The exam is not timed. Students must directly contact their college counseling office in order to arrange to take the ACCUPLACER. Your institution's test center will provide information about accommodation for disabilities, required identification or materials, and any options for taking the test remotely.

About This Guide

This guide will help you master the most important test topics and develop critical test-taking skills. We have built features into our books to prepare you for your tests and increase your score. Along with a detailed summary of the test's format, content, and scoring, we offer an in-depth overview of the content knowledge required to pass the test. In the review you'll find sidebars that provide interesting information, highlight key concepts, and review content so that you can solidify your understanding of the exam's concepts. You can also test your knowledge with sample questions throughout the text and practice questions that reflect the content and format of the ACCUPLACER. We're pleased you've chosen Accepted, Inc. to be a part of your journey!

PART I
Mathematics

CHAPTER ONE

Arithmetic

T his chapter provides a review of the basic yet critical components of mathematics such as manipulating fractions, comparing numbers, and using units. These concepts will provide the foundation for more complex mathematical operations in later chapters.

Types of Numbers

Numbers are placed in categories based on their properties.

- ▶ A **NATURAL NUMBER** is greater than 0 and has no decimal or fraction attached. These are also sometimes called counting numbers {1, 2, 3, 4, ...}.

- ▶ **WHOLE NUMBERS** are natural numbers and the number 0 {0, 1, 2, 3, 4, ...}.

- ▶ **INTEGERS** include positive and negative natural numbers and 0 {..., –4, –3, –2, –1, 0, 1, 2, 3, 4, ...}.

- ▶ A **RATIONAL NUMBER** can be represented as a fraction. Any decimal part must terminate or resolve into a repeating pattern. Examples include –12, $-\frac{4}{5}$, 0.36, 7.$\overline{7}$, 26 $\frac{1}{2}$, etc.

- ▶ An **IRRATIONAL NUMBER** cannot be represented as a fraction. An irrational decimal number never ends and never resolves into a repeating pattern. Examples include $-\sqrt{7}$, π, and 0.34567989135...

- ▶ A **REAL NUMBER** is a number that can be represented by a point on a number line. Real numbers include all the rational and irrational numbers.

- ▶ An **IMAGINARY NUMBER** includes the imaginary unit i, where $i = \sqrt{-1}$ Because $i^2 = -1$, imaginary numbers produce a negative value when squared. Examples of imaginary numbers include $-4i$, $0.75i$, $i\sqrt{2}$ and $\frac{8}{3}i$.

▶ A **COMPLEX NUMBER** is in the form $a + bi$, where a and b are real numbers. Examples of complex numbers include $3 + 2i$, $-4 + i$, $\sqrt{3} - i\sqrt[3]{5}$ and $\frac{5}{8} - \frac{7i}{8}$. All imaginary numbers are also complex.

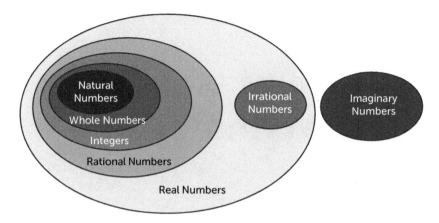

Figure 1.1. Types of Numbers

The **FACTORS** of a natural number are all the numbers that can multiply together to make the number. For example, the factors of 24 are 1, 2, 3, 4, 6, 8, 12, and 24. Every natural number is either prime or composite. A **PRIME NUMBER** is a number that is only divisible by itself and 1. (The number 1 is not considered prime.) Examples of prime numbers are 2, 3, 7, and 29. The number 2 is the only even prime number. A **COMPOSITE NUMBER** has more than two factors. For example, 6 is composite because its factors are 1, 6, 2, and 3. Every composite number can be written as a unique product of prime numbers, called the **PRIME FACTORIZATION** of the number. For example, the prime factorization of 90 is 90 = $2 \times 3^2 \times 5$. All integers are either even or odd. An even number is divisible by 2; an odd number is not.

EXAMPLES

1. Classify the following numbers as natural, whole, integer, rational, or irrational. (The numbers may have more than one classification.)

   [A] 72

   [B] $-\frac{2}{3}$

   [C] $\sqrt{5}$

2. Determine the real and imaginary parts of the following complex numbers.

   [A] 20

   [B] $10 - i$

   [C] $15i$

Scientific Notation

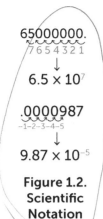

Figure 1.2. Scientific Notation

SCIENTIFIC NOTATION is a method of representing very large and small numbers in the form $a \times 10^n$, where a is a value between 1 and 10, and n is a nonzero integer. For example, the number 927,000,000 is written in scientific notation as 9.27×10^8. Multiplying 9.27 by 10 eight times gives 927,000,000. When performing operations with scientific notation, the final answer should be in the form $a \times 10^n$.

When adding and subtracting numbers in scientific notation, the power of 10 must be the same for all numbers. This results in like terms in which the a terms are added or subtracted and the 10^n remains unchanged. When multiplying numbers in scientific notation, multiply the a factors, and then multiply that answer by 10 to the sum of the exponents. For division, divide the a factors and subtract the exponents.

DID YOU KNOW?
When multiplying numbers in scientific notation, add the exponents. When dividing, subtract the exponents.

EXAMPLES

3. Simplify: $(3.8 \times 10^3) + (4.7 \times 10^2)$

4. Simplify: $(8.1 \times 10^{-5})(1.4 \times 10^7)$

Positive and Negative Numbers

POSITIVE NUMBERS are greater than 0, and **NEGATIVE NUMBERS** are less than 0. Both positive and negative numbers can be shown on a **NUMBER LINE**.

Figure 1.3. Number Line

The **ABSOLUTE VALUE** of a number is the distance the number is from 0. Since distance is always positive, the absolute value of a number is always positive. The absolute value of a is denoted $|a|$. For example, $|-2| = 2$ since -2 is two units away from 0.

Positive and negative numbers can be added, subtracted, multiplied, and divided. The sign of the resulting number is governed by a specific set of rules shown in Table 1.1.

Table 1.1. Operations with Positive and Negative Numbers

ADDING REAL NUMBERS		SUBTRACTING REAL NUMBERS	
Positive + Positive = Positive	7 + 8 = 15	Negative − Positive = Negative	−7 − 8 = −7 + (−8) = −15
Negative + Negative = Negative	−7 + (−8) = −15	Positive − Negative = Positive	7 − (−8) = 7 + 8 = 15
Negative + Positive OR Positive + Negative = Keep the sign of the number with larger absolute value	−7 + 8 = 1 7 + −8 = −1	Negative − Negative = Change the subtraction to addition and change the sign of the second number; then use addition rules.	−7 − (−8) = −7 + 8 = 1 −8 − (−7) = −8 + 7 = −1

MULTIPLYING REAL NUMBERS		DIVIDING REAL NUMBERS	
Positive × Positive = Positive	8 × 4 = 32	Positive ÷ Positive = Positive	8 ÷ 4 = 2
Negative × Negative = Positive	−8 × (−4) = 32	Negative ÷ Negative = Positive	−8 ÷ (−4) = 2
Positive × Negative OR Negative × Positive = Negative	8 × (−4) = −32 −8 × 4 = −32	Positive ÷ Negative OR Negative ÷ Positive = Negative	8 ÷ (−4) = −2 −8 ÷ 4 = −2

EXAMPLES

5. Add or subtract the following real numbers:

   [A] −18 + 12

   [B] −3.64 + (−2.18)

   [C] 9.37 − 4.25

   [D] 86 − (−20)

6. Multiply or divide the following real numbers:

   [A] $\left(\frac{10}{3}\right)\left(-\frac{9}{5}\right)$

   [B] $\frac{-64}{-10}$

   [C] (2.2)(3.3)

   [D] −52 ÷ 13

Order of Operations

The ORDER OF OPERATIONS is simply the order in which operations are performed. Multiplication and division, and addition and subtraction, are performed together from left to right. So, performing multiple operations on a set of numbers is a four-step process. **PEMDAS** is a common way to remember the order of operations:

1. **P**arentheses: Calculate expressions inside parentheses, brackets, braces, etc.

2. **E**xponents: Calculate exponents and square roots.

3. **M**ultiplication: Calculate any remaining multiplication and division in order from left to right.

4. **D**ivision: Calculate any remaining multiplication and division in order from left to right.

5. **A**ddition: Calculate any remaining addition and subtraction in order from left to right.

6. **S**ubtraction: Calculate any remaining addition and subtraction in order from left to right.

Always work from left to right within each step when simplifying expressions.

EXAMPLES

7. Simplify: $2(21 - 14) + 6 \div (-2) \times 3 - 10$

8. Simplify: $-(3)^2 + 4(5) + (5 - 6)^2 - 8$

9. Simplify: $\dfrac{(7 - 9)^3 + 8(10 - 12)}{4^2 - 5^2}$

Decimals and Fractions
DECIMALS

A DECIMAL is a number that contains a decimal point. A decimal number is an alternative way of writing a fraction. The place value for a decimal includes TENTHS (one place after the decimal), HUNDREDTHS (two places after the decimal), THOUSANDTHS (three places after the decimal), etc.

Table 1.2. Place Values		
1,000,000	10^6	millions
100,000	10^5	hundred thousands
10,000	10^4	ten thousands
1,000	10^3	thousands

Table 1.2. Place Values (continued)		
100	10^2	hundreds
10	10^1	tens
1	10^0	ones
.		decimal
$\frac{1}{10}$	10^{-1}	tenths
$\frac{1}{100}$	10^{-2}	hundredths
$\frac{1}{1000}$	10^{-3}	thousandths

Decimals can be added, subtracted, multiplied, and divided:

▶ To add or subtract decimals, line up the decimal point and perform the operation, keeping the decimal point in the same place in the answer.

▶ To multiply decimals, first multiply the numbers without the decimal points. Then, sum the number of decimal places to the right of the decimal point in the original numbers and place the decimal point in the answer so that there are that many places to the right of the decimal.

▶ When dividing decimals move the decimal point to the right in order to make the divisor a whole number and move the decimal the same number of places in the dividend. Divide the numbers without regard to the decimal. Then, place the decimal point of the quotient directly above the decimal point of the dividend.

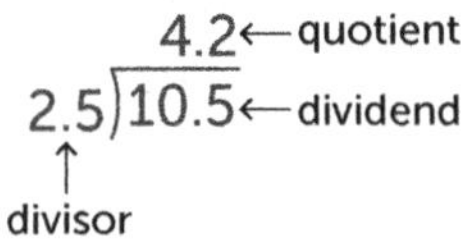

$$2.5 \overline{)10.5}$$

4.2 ← quotient
10.5 ← dividend
↑ divisor

Figure 1.4. Division Terms

EXAMPLES

10. Simplify: 24.38 + 16.51 − 29.87

11. Simplify: (10.4)(18.2)

12. Simplify: 80 ÷ 2.5

FRACTIONS

A **FRACTION** is a number that can be written in the form $\frac{a}{b}$, where b is not equal to 0. The a part of the fraction is the **NUMERATOR** (top number) and the b part of the fraction is the **DENOMINATOR** (bottom number).

If the denominator of a fraction is greater than the numerator, the value of the fraction is less than 1 and it is called a **PROPER FRACTION** (for example, $\frac{3}{5}$ is a proper fraction). In an **IMPROPER FRACTION**, the denominator is less than the numerator and the value of the fraction is greater than 1 ($\frac{8}{3}$ is an improper fraction). An improper fraction can be written as a **MIXED NUMBER**, which has a whole number part and a proper fraction part. Improper fractions can be converted to mixed numbers by dividing the numerator by the denominator, which gives the whole number part, and the remainder becomes the numerator of the proper fraction part. (For example, the improper fraction $\frac{25}{9}$ is equal to mixed number $2\frac{7}{9}$ because 9 divides into 25 two times, with a remainder of 7.)

Conversely, mixed numbers can be converted to improper fractions. To do so, determine the numerator of the improper fraction by multiplying the denominator by the whole number, and then adding the numerator. The final number is written as the (now larger) numerator over the original denominator.

> **DID YOU KNOW?**
> To convert mixed numbers to improper fractions:
> $$a\frac{m}{n} = \frac{n \times a + m}{n}$$

Fractions with the same denominator can be added or subtracted by simply adding or subtracting the numerators; the denominator will remain unchanged. To add or subtract fractions with different denominators, find the **LEAST COMMON DENOMINATOR (LCD)** of all the fractions. The LCD is the smallest number exactly divisible by each denominator. (For example, the least common denominator of the numbers 2, 3, and 8 is 24.) Once the LCD has been found, each fraction should be written in an equivalent form with the LCD as the denominator.

To multiply fractions, the numerators are multiplied together and denominators are multiplied together. If there are any mixed numbers, they should first be changed to improper fractions. Then, the numerators are multiplied together and the denominators are multiplied together. The fraction can then be reduced if necessary. To divide fractions, multiply the first fraction by the reciprocal of the second.

Any common denominator can be used to add or subtract fractions. The quickest way to find a common denominator of a set of values is simply to multiply all the values together. The result might not be the least common denominator, but it will allow the problem to be worked.

> **DID YOU KNOW?**
> $$\frac{a}{b} \pm \frac{c}{b} = \frac{a + c}{b}$$
> $$\frac{a}{b} \times \frac{c}{d} = \frac{ac}{bd}$$
> $$\frac{a}{b} \div \frac{c}{d} = \left(\frac{a}{b}\right)\left(\frac{d}{c}\right) = \frac{ad}{bc}$$

EXAMPLES

13. Simplify: $2\frac{3}{5} + 3\frac{1}{4} - 1\frac{1}{2}$

14. Simplify: $\frac{7}{8} \times 3\frac{1}{3}$

15. Simplify: $4\frac{1}{2} \div \frac{2}{3}$

CONVERTING BETWEEN FRACTIONS and DECIMALS

A fraction is converted to a decimal by using long division until there is no remainder and no pattern of repeating numbers occurs.

A decimal is converted to a fraction using the following steps:

▶ Place the decimal value as the numerator in a fraction with a denominator of 1.

▶ Multiply the fraction by $\frac{10}{10}$ for every digit in the decimal value, so that there is no longer a decimal in the numerator.

▶ Reduce the fraction.

EXAMPLES

16. Write the fraction $\frac{7}{8}$ as a decimal.

17. Write the fraction $\frac{5}{11}$ as a decimal.

18. Write the decimal 0.125 as a fraction.

Percentages

A **PERCENT** (or percentage) means per hundred and is expressed with a percent symbol (%). For example, 54% means 54 out of every 100. A percent can be converted to a decimal by removing the % symbol and moving the decimal point two places to the left, while a decimal can be converted to a percent by moving the decimal point two places to the right and attaching the % sign. A percent can be converted to a fraction by writing the percent as a fraction with 100 as the denominator and reducing. A fraction can be converted to a percent by performing the indicated division, multiplying the result by 100, and attaching the % sign.

The equation for finding percentages has three variables: the part, the whole, and the percent (which is expressed in the equation as a decimal). The equation, as shown below, can be rearranged to solve for any of these variables.

▶ part = whole × percent

▶ percent = $\frac{\text{part}}{\text{whole}}$

▶ whole = $\frac{\text{part}}{\text{percent}}$

This set of equations can be used to solve percent word problems. All that's needed is to identify the part, whole, and/or percent, and then to plug those values into the appropriate equation and solve.

19. Change the following values to the indicated form:

   [A] 18% to a fraction

   [B] $\frac{3}{5}$ to a percent

   [C] 1.125 to a percent

   [D] 84% to a decimal

20. In a school of 650 students, 54% of the students are boys. How many students are girls?

PERCENT CHANGE

Percent change problems involve a change from an original amount. Often percent change problems appear as word problems that include discounts, growth, or markups. In order to solve percent change problems, it's necessary to identify the percent change (as a decimal), the amount of change, and the original amount. (Keep in mind that one of these will be the value being solved for.) These values can then be plugged into the equations below:

▶   amount of change = original amount × percent change

▶   percent change = $\dfrac{\text{amount of change}}{\text{original amount}}$

▶   original amount = $\dfrac{\text{amount of change}}{\text{percent change}}$

DID YOU KNOW?
Key terms associated with percent change problems include *discount*, *sales tax*, and *markup*.

EXAMPLES

21. An HDTV that originally cost $1,500 is on sale for 45% off. What is the sale price for the item?

22. A house was bought in 2000 for $100,000 and sold in 2015 for $120,000. What was the percent growth in the value of the house from 2000 to 2015?

Rounding and Estimation

ROUNDING is a way of simplifying a complicated number. The result of rounding will be a less precise value with which it is easier to write or perform operations. Rounding is performed to a specific place value, for example the thousands or tenths place.

The rules for rounding are as follows:

1. Underline the place value being rounded to.

DID YOU KNOW?
Estimation can often be used to eliminate answer choices on multiple-choice tests without having to work the problem to completion.

2. Locate the digit one place value to the right of the underlined value. If this value is less than 5, then keep the underlined value and replace all digits to the right of the underlined value with 0. If the value to the right of the underlined digit is greater than or equal to 5, then increase the underlined digit by one and replace all digits to the right of it with 0.

ESTIMATION is when numbers are rounded and then an operation is performed. This process can be used when working with large numbers to find a close, but not exact, answer.

EXAMPLES

23. Round the number 138,472 to the nearest thousands.

24. The populations of five local towns are 12,341, 8975, 9431, 10,521, and 11,427. Estimate the total population to the nearest 1000 people.

Comparison of Rational Numbers

Rational numbers can be ordered from least to greatest (or greatest to least) by placing them in the order in which they fall on a number line. When comparing a set of fractions, it's often easiest to convert each value to a common denominator. Then, it's only necessary to compare the numerators of each fraction.

DID YOU KNOW?
Drawing a number line can help when comparing numbers: the final list should go in order from left to right (least to greatest) or right to left (greatest to least) on the line.

When working with numbers in multiple forms (for example, a group of fractions and decimals), convert the values so that the set contains only fractions or only decimals. When ordering negative numbers, remember that the negative numbers with the largest absolute values are farthest from 0 and are therefore the smallest numbers. (For example, –75 is smaller than –25.)

EXAMPLES

25. Order the following numbers from greatest to least: $-\frac{2}{3}$, 1.2, 0, –2.1, $\frac{5}{4}$, –1, $\frac{1}{8}$

26. Order the following numbers from least to greatest: $\frac{1}{3}$, $-\frac{5}{6}$, $1\frac{1}{8}$, $\frac{7}{12}$, $-\frac{3}{4}$, $-\frac{3}{2}$.

Answer Key

1. [A] **The number is natural, whole, an integer, and rational.**

   [B] **The fraction is rational.**

   [C] **The number is irrational.** (It cannot be written as a fraction, and written as a decimal is approximately 2.2360679...)

2. A complex number is in the form of $a + bi$, where a is the real part and bi is the imaginary part.

   [A] $20 = 20 + 0i$

   The real part is 20, and there is no imaginary part.

   [B] $10 - i = 10 - 1i$

   The real part is 10, and −1i is the imaginary part.

   [C] $15i = 0 + 15i$

   The real part is 0, and the imaginary part is 15i.

3. $(3.8 \times 10^3) + (4.7 \times 10^2)$

   To add, the exponents of 10 must be the same.

   $3.8 \times 10^3 = 3.8 \times 10 \times 10^2 = 38 \times 10^2$

   Add the a terms together.

   $38 \times 10^2 + 4.7 \times 10^2 = 42.7 \times 10^2$

   Write the number in proper scientific notation.

   $= \mathbf{4.27 \times 10^3}$

4. $(8.1 \times 10^{-5})(1.4 \times 10^7)$

   Multiply the a factors and add the exponents on the base of 10.

   $8.1 \times 1.4 = 11.34$

   $-5 + 7 = 2$

   $= 11.34 \times 10^2$

   Write the number in proper scientific notation.

   $= \mathbf{1.134 \times 10^3}$

5. [A] Since $|-18| > |12|$, the answer is negative: $|-18| - |12| = 6$. So the answer is **−6**.

   [B] Adding two negative numbers results in a negative number. Add the values: **−5.82**.

   [C] The first number is larger than the second, so the final answer is positive: **5.12**.

   [D] Change the subtraction to addition, change the sign of the second number, and then add: $86 - (-20) = 86 + (+20) = \mathbf{106}$.

6. [A] Multiply the numerators, multiply the denominators, and simplify: $\frac{-90}{15} = \mathbf{-6}$.

   [B] A negative divided by a negative is a positive number: **6.4**.

   [C] Multiplying positive numbers gives a positive answer: **7.26**.

   [D] Dividing a negative by a positive number gives a negative answer: **−4**.

7. $2(21 - 14) + 6 \div (-2) \times 3 - 10$

   Calculate expressions inside parentheses.

   $= 2(7) + 6 \div (-2) \times 3 - 10$

   There are no exponents or radicals, so perform multiplication and division from left to right.

   $= 14 + 6 \div (-2) \times 3 - 10$

   $= 14 + (-3) \times 3 - 10$

   $= 14 + (-9) - 10$

   Perform addition and subtraction from left to right.

   $= 5 - 10 = \mathbf{-5}$

8. $-(3)^2 + 4(5) + (5 - 6)^2 - 8$

   Calculate expressions inside parentheses.

$= -(3)^2 + 4(5) + (-1)^2 - 8$

Simplify exponents and radicals.

$= -9 + 4(5) + 1 - 8$

Perform multiplication and division from left to right.

$= -9 + 20 + 1 - 8$

Perform addition and subtraction from left to right.

$= 11 + 1 - 8$

$= 12 - 8 = \mathbf{4}$

9. Simplify: $\dfrac{(7-9)^3 + 8(10-12)}{4^2 - 5^2}$

Calculate expressions inside parentheses.

$= \dfrac{(-2)^3 + 8(-2)}{4^2 - 5^2}$

Simplify exponents and radicals.

$= \dfrac{-8 + (-16)}{16 - 25}$

Perform addition and subtraction from left to right.

$= \dfrac{-24}{-9}$

Simplify.

$= \dfrac{\mathbf{8}}{\mathbf{3}}$

10. $24.38 + 16.51 - 29.87$

Align the decimals and apply the order of operations left to right.

$\begin{array}{r} 24.38 \\ +\ 16.51 \\ \hline = 40.89 \end{array} \rightarrow \begin{array}{r} 40.89 \\ -\ 29.87 \\ \hline = \mathbf{11.02} \end{array}$

11. $(10.4)(18.2)$

Multiply the numbers ignoring the decimals.

$104 \times 182 = 18{,}928$

The original problem includes two decimal places (one in each number), so move the decimal point in the answer so that there are two places after the decimal point.

$18{,}928 \rightarrow \mathbf{189.28}$

Estimating is a good way to check the answer: $10.4 \approx 10$, $18.2 \approx 18$, and $10 \times 18 = 180$.

12. $80 \div 2.5$

Move both decimals one place to the right (multiply by 10) so that the divisor is a whole number.

$80 \rightarrow 800$

$2.5 \rightarrow 25$

Divide normally.

$800 \div 25 = \mathbf{32}$

13. $2\frac{3}{5} + 3\frac{1}{4} - 1\frac{1}{2}$

Change each fraction so it has a denominator of 20, which is the LCD of 5, 4, and 2.

$2 + 3 - 1 = 4$

$\dfrac{12}{20} + \dfrac{5}{20} - \dfrac{10}{20} = \dfrac{7}{20}$

Combine to get the final answer (a mixed number).

$\mathbf{4\frac{7}{20}}$

14. $\frac{7}{8} \times 3\frac{1}{3}$

Change the mixed number to an improper fraction.

$3\frac{1}{3} = \dfrac{10}{3}$

Multiply the numerators together and the denominators together.

$\dfrac{7}{8}\left(\dfrac{10}{3}\right) = \dfrac{7 \times 10}{8 \times 3} = \dfrac{70}{24}$

Reduce the fraction.

$= \dfrac{35}{12} = \mathbf{2\frac{11}{12}}$

15. $4\frac{1}{2} \div \frac{2}{3}$

Change the mixed number to an improper fraction.

$4\frac{1}{2} = \dfrac{9}{2}$

Multiply the first fraction by the reciprocal of the second fraction.

$$\frac{9}{2} \div \frac{2}{3} = \frac{9}{2} \times \frac{3}{2} = \frac{27}{4}$$

Simplify.

$$= 6\frac{3}{4}$$

16. Divide the denominator into the numerator using long division.

```
   0.875
8)7000
 -64↓
   60
  -56↓
    40
```

17. Dividing using long division yields a repeating decimal.

```
    0.4545
11)50000
  -44↓ ↓
    60  ↓
   -55↓ ↓
     50 ↓
    -44↓
      60
```

18. Create a fraction with 0.125 as the numerator and 1 as the denominator.

$$= \frac{0.125}{1}$$

Multiple by $\frac{10}{10}$ three times (one for each numeral after the decimal).

$$\frac{0.125}{1} \times \frac{10}{10} \times \frac{10}{10} \times \frac{10}{10} = \frac{125}{1000}$$

Simplify.

$$= \frac{1}{8}$$

Alternatively, recognize that 0.125 is read "one hundred twenty-five thousandths" and can therefore be written in fraction form as $\frac{125}{1000}$.

19. [A] The percent is written as a fraction over 100 and reduced:

$$\frac{18}{100} = \frac{9}{50}$$

[B] Dividing 5 by 3 gives the value 0.6, which is then multiplied by 100: **60%**.

[C] The decimal point is moved two places to the right:
$1.125 \times 100 = \textbf{112.5\%}$.

[D] The decimal point is moved two places to the left: $84 \div 100 = \textbf{0.84}$.

20. Identify the variables.

Percent of students who are girls = 100% − 54% = 46%

percent = 46% = 0.46

whole = 650 students

part = ?

Plug the variables into the appropriate equation.

part = whole × percent

= 0.46 × 650 = 299

There are 299 girls.

21. Identify the variables.

original amount =$1,500

percent change = 45% = 0.45

amount of change = ?

Plug the variables into the appropriate equation.

amount of change = original amount × percent change

= 1500 × 0.45 = 675

To find the new price, subtract the amount of change from the original price.

1500 − 675 = 825

The final price is $825.

22. Identify the variables.

original amount = $100,000

amount of change = 120,000 − 100,000 = 20,000

percent change = ?

Plug the variables into the appropriate equation.

$$\text{percent change} = \frac{\text{amount of change}}{\text{original amount}}$$

$$= \frac{20,000}{100,000} = 0.20$$

To find the percent growth, multiply by 100.

0.20 × 100 = **20%**

23. The 8 is in the thousands place, and the number to its right is 4. Because 4 is less than 5, the 8 remains and all numbers to the right become 0.

138,472 ≈ **138,000**

24. Round each value to the thousands place.

12,341 ≈ 12,000

8975 ≈ 9000

9431 ≈ 9000

10,521 ≈ 11,000

11,427 ≈ 11,000

Add.

12,000 + 9000 + 9000 + 11,000 + 11,000 = **52,000**

26. Change each fraction to a decimal.

$-\frac{2}{3} = -0.\overline{66}$

$\frac{5}{4} = 1.25$

$\frac{1}{8} = 0.125$

Place the decimals in order from greatest to least.

1.25, 1.2, 0.125, 0, $-0.\overline{66}$, −1, −2.1

Convert back to fractions if the problem requires it.

$\frac{5}{4}$, **1.2**, $\frac{1}{8}$, **0**, $-\frac{2}{3}$, **−1, −2.1**

26. Convert each value using the least common denominator of 24.

$\frac{1}{3} = \frac{8}{24}$

$-\frac{5}{6} = -\frac{20}{24}$

$1\frac{1}{8} = \frac{9}{8} = \frac{27}{24}$

$\frac{7}{12} = \frac{14}{24}$

$-\frac{3}{4} = -\frac{18}{24}$

$-\frac{3}{2} = -\frac{36}{24}$

Arrange the fractions in order from least to greatest by comparing the numerators.

$-\frac{36}{24}, -\frac{20}{24}, -\frac{18}{24}, \frac{8}{24}, \frac{14}{24}, \frac{27}{24}$

Put the fractions back in their original form if the problem requires it.

$-\frac{3}{2}, -\frac{5}{6}, -\frac{3}{4}, \frac{1}{3}, \frac{7}{12}, 1\frac{1}{8}$

CHAPTER TWO
Quantitative Reasoning, Algebra, and Statistics

Units of Measurement

The standard units for the metric and American systems are shown below, along with the prefixes used to express metric units.

Table 2.1. Units and Conversion Factors		
DIMENSION	**AMERICAN**	**SI**
length	inch/foot/yard/mile	meter
mass	ounce/pound/ton	gram
volume	cup/pint/quart/gallon	liter
force	pound-force	newton
pressure	pound-force per square inch	pascal
work and energy	cal/British thermal unit	joule
temperature	Fahrenheit	kelvin
charge	faraday	coulomb

Table 2.2. Metric Prefixes		
PREFIX	**SYMBOL**	**MULTIPLICATION FACTOR**
tera	T	1,000,000,000,000
giga	G	1,000,000,000
mega	M	1,000,000
kilo	k	1,000

Table 2.2. Metric Prefixes (continued)		
Prefix	**Symbol**	**Multiplication Factor**
hecto	h	100
deca	da	10
base unit	--	--
deci	d	0.1
centi	c	0.01
milli	m	0.001
micro	μ	0.000001
nano	n	0.000000001
pico	p	0.000000000001

Units can be converted within a single system or between systems. When converting from one unit to another unit, a conversion factor (a numeric multiplier used to convert a value with a unit to another unit) is used. The process of converting between units using a conversion factor is sometimes known as dimensional analysis.

Table 2.3. Conversion Factors	
1 in. = 2.54 cm	1 lb. = 0.454 kg
1 yd. = 0.914 m	1 cal = 4.19 J
1 mi. = 1.61 km	$1^\circ F = \frac{9}{5}{}^\circ C + 32^\circ C$
1 gal. = 3.785 L	$1 \text{ cm}^3 = 1 \text{ mL}$
1 oz. = 28.35 g	1 hr = 3600 s

EXAMPLES

1. Convert the following measurements in the metric system.

    [A] 4.25 kilometers to meters

    [B] 8 m^2 to mm^2

2. Convert the following measurements in the American system.

    [A] 12 feet to inches

    [B] 7 yd^2 to ft^2

3. Convert the following measurements in the metric system to the American system.

    [A] 23 meters to feet

    [B] 10 m^2 to yd^2

4. Convert the following measurements in the American system to the metric system.

   [A] 8 in^3 to milliliters

   [B] 16 kilograms to pounds

Ratios

A **RATIO** is a comparison of two numbers and can be represented as $\frac{a}{b}$, $a:b$, or a to b. The two numbers represent a constant relationship, not a specific value: for every a number of items in the first group, there will be b number of items in the second. For example, if the ratio of blue to red candies in a bag is 3:5, the bag will contain 3 blue candies for every 5 red candies. So, the bag might contain 3 blue candies and 5 red candies, or it might contain 30 blue candies and 50 red candies, or 36 blue candies and 60 red candies. All of these values are representative of the ratio 3:5 (which is the ratio in its lowest, or simplest, terms).

To find the "whole" when working with ratios, simply add the values in the ratio. For example, if the ratio of boys to girls in a class is 2:3, the "whole" is five: 2 out of every 5 students are boys, and 3 out of every 5 students are girls.

EXAMPLES

5. There are 10 boys and 12 girls in a first-grade class. What is the ratio of boys to the total number of students? What is the ratio of girls to boys?

6. A family spends $600 a month on rent, $400 on utilities, $750 on groceries, and $550 on miscellaneous expenses. What is the ratio of the family's rent to their total expenses?

Proportions

A **PROPORTION** is an equation which states that two ratios are equal. A proportion is given in the form $\frac{a}{b} = \frac{c}{d}$, where the a and d terms are the extremes and the b and c terms are the means. A proportion is solved using cross-multiplication ($ad = bc$) to create an equation with no fractional components. A proportion must have the same units in both numerators and both denominators.

EXAMPLES

7. Solve the proportion for x: $\frac{3x-5}{2} = \frac{x-8}{3}$.

8. A map is drawn such that 2.5 inches on the map equates to an actual distance of 40 miles. If the distance measured on the map between two cities is 17.25 inches, what is the actual distance between them in miles?

9. A factory knows that 4 out of 1000 parts made will be defective. If in a month there are 125,000 parts made, how many of these parts will be defective?

Exponents and Radicals
EXPONENTS

An expression in the form b^n is in an exponential notation where b is the **BASE** and n is an **EXPONENT**. To perform the operation, multiply the base by itself the number of times indicated by the exponent. For example, 2^3 is equal to $2 \times 2 \times 2$ or 8.

Table 2.4. Operations with Exponents

RULE	EXAMPLE	EXPLANATION
$a^0 = 1$	$5^0 = 1$	Any base (except 0) to the 0 power is 1.
$a^{-n} = \frac{1}{a^n}$	$5^{-3} = \frac{1}{5^3}$	A negative exponent becomes positive when moved from numerator to denominator (or vice versa).
$a^m a^n = a^{m+n}$	$5^3 5^4 = 5^{3+4} = 5^7$	Add the exponents to multiply two powers with the same base.
$(a^m)^n = a^{m \times n}$	$(5^3)^4 = 5^{3(4)} = 5^{12}$	Multiply the exponents to raise a power to a power.
$\frac{a^m}{a^n} = a^{m-n}$	$\frac{5^4}{5^3} = 5^{4-3} = 5^1$	Subtract the exponents to divide two powers with the same base.
$(ab)^n = a^n b^n$	$(5 \times 6)^3 = 5^3 6^3$	Apply the exponent to each base to raise a product to a power.
$\left(\frac{a}{b}\right)^n = \frac{a^n}{b^n}$	$\left(\frac{5}{6}\right)^3 = \frac{5^3}{6^3}$	Apply the exponent to each base to raise a quotient to a power.
$\left(\frac{a}{b}\right)^{-n} = \left(\frac{b}{a}\right)^n$	$\left(\frac{5}{6}\right)^{-3} = \left(\frac{6}{5}\right)^3$	Invert the fraction and change the sign of the exponent to raise a fraction to a negative power.
$\frac{a^m}{b^n} = \frac{b^{-n}}{a^{-m}}$	$\frac{5^3}{6^4} = \frac{6^{-4}}{5^{-3}}$	Change the sign of the exponent when moving a number from the numerator to denominator (or vice versa).

Remember !!

EXAMPLES

10. Simplify: $\frac{(10^2)^3}{(10^2)^2}$

11. Simplify: $\frac{(x^{-2}y^2)^2}{x^3 y}$

RADICALS

RADICALS are expressed as $\sqrt[b]{a}$, where b is called the **INDEX** and a is the **RADICAND**. A radical is used to indicate the inverse operation of an exponent: finding the base which can be raised to b to yield a. For example, $\sqrt[3]{125}$ is equal to 5 because $5 \times 5 \times 5$ equals 125. The same operation can be expressed using a fraction exponent, so $\sqrt[b]{a} = a^{\frac{1}{b}}$. Note that when no value is indicated for b, it is assumed to be 2 (square root).

When b is even and a is positive, $\sqrt[b]{a}$ is defined to be the positive real value n such that $nb = a$ (example: $\sqrt{16} = 4$ only, and not -4, even though $(-4)(-4) = 16$). If b is even and a is negative, $\sqrt[b]{a}$ will be a complex number (example: $\sqrt{-9} = 3i$). Finally if b is odd, $\sqrt[b]{a}$ will always be a real number regardless of the sign of a. If a is negative, $\sqrt[b]{a}$ will be negative since a number to an odd power is negative (example: $\sqrt[5]{-32} = -2$ since $(-2)^5 = -32$).

$\sqrt[n]{x}$ is referred to as the nth root of x.

▶ $n = 2$ is the square root

▶ $n = 3$ is the cube root

▶ $n = 4$ is the fourth root

▶ $n = 5$ is the fifth root

The following table of operations with radicals holds for all cases EXCEPT the case where b is even and a is negative (the complex case).

Table 2.5 Operations with Radicals		
RULE	EXAMPLE	EXPLANATION
$\sqrt[b]{ac} = \sqrt[b]{a}\,\sqrt[b]{c}$	$\sqrt[3]{81} = \sqrt[3]{27}\sqrt[3]{3} = 3\sqrt[3]{3}$	The values under the radical sign can be separated into values that multiply to the original value.
$\sqrt[b]{\dfrac{a}{c}} = \dfrac{\sqrt[b]{a}}{\sqrt[b]{c}}$	$\sqrt{\dfrac{4}{81}} = \dfrac{\sqrt{4}}{\sqrt{81}} = \dfrac{2}{9}$	The b-root of the numerator and denominator can be calculated when there is a fraction under a radical sign.
$\sqrt[b]{a^c} = (\sqrt[b]{a})^c = a^{\frac{c}{b}}$	$\sqrt[3]{6^2} = (\sqrt[3]{6})^2 = 6^{\frac{2}{3}}$	The b-root can be written as a fractional exponent. If there is a power under the radical sign, it will be the numerator of the fraction.
$\dfrac{c}{\sqrt[b]{a}} \times \dfrac{\sqrt[b]{a}}{\sqrt[b]{a}} = \dfrac{c\sqrt[b]{a}}{a}$	$\dfrac{5}{\sqrt{2}}\dfrac{\sqrt{2}}{\sqrt{2}} = \dfrac{5\sqrt{2}}{2}$	To rationalize the denominator, multiply the numerator and denominator by the radical in the denominator until the radical has been canceled out.
$\dfrac{c}{b - \sqrt{a}} \times \dfrac{b + \sqrt{a}}{b + \sqrt{a}}$ $= \dfrac{c(b + \sqrt{a})}{b^2 - a}$	$\dfrac{4}{3 - \sqrt{2}}\dfrac{3 + \sqrt{2}}{3 + \sqrt{2}}$ $= \dfrac{4(3 + \sqrt{2})}{9 - 2} = \dfrac{12 + 4\sqrt{2}}{7}$	To rationalize the denominator, the numerator and denominator are multiplied by the conjugate of the denominator.

12. Simplify: $\sqrt{48}$

13. Simplify: $\frac{6}{\sqrt{8}}$

Algebraic Expressions

The foundation of algebra is the **VARIABLE**, an unknown number represented by a symbol (usually a letter such as x or a). Variables can be preceded by a **COEFFICIENT**, which is a constant (i.e., a real number) in front of the variable, such as $4x$ or $-2a$. An **ALGEBRAIC EXPRESSION** is any sum, difference, product, or quotient of variables and numbers (for example $3x^2$, $2x + 7y - 1$, and $\frac{5}{x}$ are algebraic expressions). **TERMS** are any quantities that are added or subtracted (for example, the terms of the expression $x^2 - 3x + 5$ are x^2, $3x$, and 5). A **POLYNOMIAL EXPRESSION** is an algebraic expression where all the exponents on the variables are whole numbers. A polynomial with only two terms is known as a **BINOMIAL**, and one with three terms is a **TRINOMIAL**. A **MONOMIAL** has only one term.

DID YOU KNOW?

Simplified expressions are ordered by variable terms alphabetically with highest exponent first then down to constants.

EVALUATING EXPRESSIONS is another way of saying "find the numeric value of an expression if the variable is equal to a certain number." To evaluate the expression, simply plug the given value(s) for the variable(s) into the equation and simplify. Remember to use the order of operations when simplifying:

1. **P**arentheses
2. **E**xponents
3. **M**ultiplication
4. **D**ivision
5. **A**ddition
6. **S**ubtraction

14. If $m = 4$, find the value of the following expression: $5(m - 2)^3 + 3m^2 - \frac{m}{4} - 1$

Operations with Expressions
ADDING and SUBTRACTING

Expressions can be added or subtracted by simply adding and subtracting **LIKE TERMS**, which are terms with the same variable part (the variables must be the same, with the same exponents on each variable). For example, in the expressions $2x + 3xy − 2z$ and $6y + 2xy$, the like terms are $3xy$ and $2xy$. Adding the two expressions yields the new expression $2x + 6xy − 2z + 6y$. Note that the other terms did not change; they cannot be combined because they have different variables.

EXAMPLE

15. If $a = 12x + 7xy − 9y$ and $b = 8x − 9xz + 7z$, what is $a + b$?

DISTRIBUTING and FACTORING

Distributing and factoring can be seen as two sides of the same coin. **DISTRIBUTION** multiplies each term in the first factor by each term in the second factor to get rid of parentheses. **FACTORING** reverses this process, taking a polynomial in standard form and writing it as a product of two or more factors.

When distributing a monomial through a polynomial, the expression outside the parentheses is multiplied by each term inside the parentheses. Using the rules of exponents, coefficients are multiplied and exponents are added.

DID YOU KNOW?
Operations with polynomials can always be checked by evaluating equivalent expressions for the same value.

When simplifying two polynomials, each term in the first polynomial must multiply each term in the second polynomial. A binomial (two terms) multiplied by a binomial, will require 2×2 or 4 multiplications. For the binomial × binomial case, this process is sometimes called **FOIL**, which stands for first, outside, inside, and last. These terms refer to the placement of each term of the expression: multiply the first term in each expression, then the outside terms, then the inside terms, and finally the last terms. A binomial (two terms) multiplied by a trinomial (three terms), will require 2×3 or 6 products to simplify. The first term in the first polynomial multiplies each of the three terms in the second polynomial, then the second term in the first polynomial multiplies each of the three terms in the second polynomial. A trinomial (three terms) by a trinomial will require 3×3 or 9 products, and so on.

Figure 2.1. Distribution and Factoring

Factoring is the reverse of distributing: the first step is always to remove ("undistribute") the GCF of all the terms, if there is a GCF (besides 1). The GCF is the product of any constants and/or variables that <u>every</u> term shares. (For example, the GCF of $12x^3$, $15x^2$ and $6xy^2$ is $3x$ because $3x$ evenly divides all three terms.) This shared factor can be taken out of each term and moved to the outside of the parentheses, leaving behind a polynomial where each term is the original term divided by the GCF.

(The remaining terms for the terms in the example would be $4x^2$, $5x$, and $2xy$.) It may be possible to factor the polynomial in the parentheses further, depending on the problem.

EXAMPLES

16. Expand the following expression: $5x(x^2 - 2c + 10)$

17. Expand the following expression: $(x^2 - 5)(2x - x^3)$

18. Factor the expression $16z^2 + 48z$

19. Factor the expression $6m^3 + 12m^3n - 9m^2$

FACTORING TRINOMIALS

If the leading coefficient is $a = 1$, the trinomial is in the form $x^2 + bx + c$ and can often be rewritten in the factored form, as a product of two binomials: $(x + m)(x + n)$. Recall that the product of two binomials can be written in expanded form $x^2 + mx + nx + mn$. Equating this expression with $x^2 + bx + c$, the constant term c would have to equal the product mn. Thus, to work backward from the trinomial to the factored form, consider all the numbers m and n that multiply to make c. For example, to factor $x^2 + 8x + 12$, consider all the pairs that multiply to be 12 ($12 = 1 \times 12$ or 2×6 or 3×4). Choose the pair that will make the coefficient of the middle term (8) when added. In this example 2 and 6 add to 8, so making $m = 2$ and $n = 6$ in the expanded form gives:

$$x^2 + 8x + 12 = x^2 + 2x + 6x + 12$$

$= (x^2 + 2x) + (6x + 12)$	Group the first two terms and the last two terms.
$= x(x + 6) + 2(x + 6)$	Factor the GCF out of each set of parentheses.
$= (x + 6)(x + 2)$	The two terms now have the common factor $(x + 6)$, which can be removed, leaving $(x + 2)$ and the original polynomial is factored.

In general:

$$x^2 + bx + c = x^2 + mx + nx + mn, \text{ where } c = mn \text{ and } b = m + n$$

$= (x^2 + mx) + (nx + mn)$	Group.
$= x(x + m) + n(x + m)$	Factor each group.
$= (x + m)(x + n)$	Factor out the common binomial.

Note that if none of the factors of c add to the value b, then the trinomial cannot be factored, and is called PRIME.

If the leading coefficient is not 1 ($a \neq 1$), first make sure that any common factors among the three terms are factored out. If the a-value is negative, factor out –1 first as well. If the a-value of the new polynomial in the parentheses is still not 1, follow this rule: Identify two values r and s that multiply to be ac and add to be b. Then write the polynomial in this form: $ax^2 + bx + c = ax^2 + rx + sx + c$, and proceed by grouping, factoring, and removing the common binomial as above.

There are a few special factoring cases worth memorizing: difference of squares, binomial squared, and the sum and difference of cubes.

- ▶ **DIFFERENCE OF SQUARES** (each term is a square and they are subtracted):
    - ▷ $a^2 - b^2 = (a + b)(a - b)$
    - ▷ Note that a SUM of squares is never factorable.
- ▶ **BINOMIAL SQUARED:** $a^2 + 2ab + b^2 = (a + b)(a + b) = (a + b)^2$
- ▶ **SUM AND DIFFERENCE OF CUBES:**
    - ▷ $a^3 + b^3 = (a + b)(a^2 - ab + b^2)$
    - ▷ $a^3 - b^3 = (a - b)(a^2 + ab + b^2)$
    - ▷ Note that the second factor in these factorizations will never be able to be factored further.

EXAMPLES

20. Factor: $16x^2 + 52x + 30$

21. Factor: $-21x^2 - x + 10$

Linear Equations

An **EQUATION** states that two expressions are equal to each other. Polynomial equations are categorized by the highest power of the variables they contain: the highest power of any exponent of a linear equation is 1, a quadratic equation has a variable raised to the second power, a cubic equation has a variable raised to the third power, and so on.

SOLVING LINEAR EQUATIONS

Solving an equation means finding the value or values of the variable that make the equation true. To solve a linear equation, it is necessary to manipulate the terms so that the variable being solved for appears alone on one side of the equal sign while everything else in the equation is on the other side.

The way to solve linear equations is to "undo" all the operations that connect numbers to the variable of interest. Follow these steps:

1. Eliminate fractions by multiplying each side by the least common multiple of any denominators.

2. Distribute to eliminate parentheses, braces, and brackets.

3. Combine like terms.

4. Use addition or subtraction to collect all terms containing the variable of interest to one side, and all terms not containing the variable to the other side.

5. Use multiplication or division to remove coefficients from the variable of interest.

Sometimes there are no numeric values in the equation or there are a mix of numerous variables and constants. The goal is to solve the equation for one of the variables in terms of the other variables. In this case, the answer will be an expression involving numbers and letters instead of a numeric value.

EXAMPLES

22. Solve for x: $\frac{100(x + 5)}{20} = 1$

23. Solve for x: $2(x + 2)^2 - 2x^2 + 10 = 42$

24. Solve the equation for D: $\frac{A(3B + 2D)}{2N} = 5M - 6$

GRAPHS of LINEAR EQUATIONS

The most common way to write a linear equation is **SLOPE-INTERCEPT FORM**, $y = mx + b$. In this equation, m is the slope, which describes how steep the line is, and b is the y-intercept. Slope is often described as "rise over run" because it is calculated as the difference in y-values (rise) over the difference in x-values (run). The slope of the line is also the rate of change of the dependent variable y with respect to the independent variable x. The y-intercept is the point where the line crosses the y-axis, or where x equals zero.

To graph a linear equation, identify the y-intercept and place that point on the y-axis. If the slope is not written as a fraction, make it a fraction by writing it over 1 $\left(\frac{m}{1}\right)$. Then use the slope to count up (or down, if negative) the "rise" part of the slope and over the "run" part of the slope to find a second point. These points can then be connected to draw the line.

To find the equation of a line, identify the y-intercept, if possible, on the graph and use two easily identifiable points to find the slope. If the y-intercept is not easily identified, identify the slope by choosing easily identifiable points; then choose one point on the graph, plug the point and the slope values into the equation, and solve for the missing value *b*.

▶ standard form: $Ax + By = C$

▶ $m = -\dfrac{A}{B}$

▶ x-intercept = $\dfrac{C}{A}$

▶ y-intercept = $\dfrac{C}{B}$

Another way to express a linear equation is standard form: $Ax + By = C$. In order to graph equations in this form, it is often easiest to convert them to point-slope form. Alternately, it is easy to find the x- or y-intercept from this form, and once these two points are known, a line can be drawn through them. To find the x-intercept, simply make $y = 0$ and solve for x. Similarly, to find the y-intercept, make $x = 0$ and solve for y.

EXAMPLES

25. What is the equation of the following line?

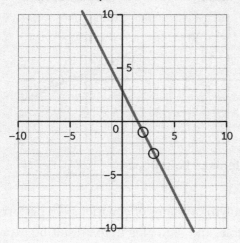

26. What is the equation of the following graph?

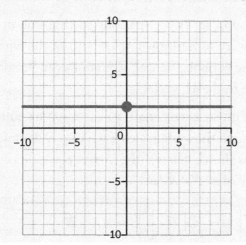

27. What is the slope of the line whose equation is 6x – 2y – 8 = 0?

28. Write the equation of the line which passes through the points (–2,5) and (–5,3).

SYSTEMS of LINEAR EQUATIONS

Systems of equations are sets of equations that include two or more variables. These systems can only be solved when there are at least as many equations as there are variables. Systems involve working with more than one equation to solve for more than one variable. For a system of linear equations, the solution to the system is the set of values for the variables that satisfies every equation in the system. Graphically, this will be the point where every line meets. If the lines are parallel (and hence do not intersect), the system will have no solution. If the lines are multiples of each other, meaning they share all coordinates, then the system has infinitely many solutions (because every point on the line is a solution).

DID YOU KNOW?
Plug answers back into both equations to ensure the system has been solved properly.

one solution   no solution   infinite solutions

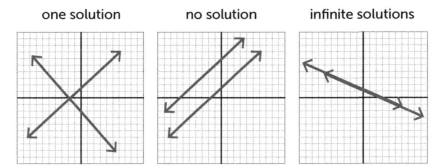

Figure 2.2. Systems of Equations

There are three common methods for solving systems of equations. To perform **SUB-STITUTION**, solve one equation for one variable, and then plug in the resulting expression for that variable in the second equation. This process works best for systems of two equations with two variables where the coefficient of one or more of the variables is 1.

To solve using **ELIMINATION**, add or subtract two equations so that one or more variables are eliminated. It's often necessary to multiply one or both of the equations by a scalar (constant) in order to make the variables cancel. Equations can be added or subtracted as many times as necessary to find each variable.

Yet another way to solve a system of linear equations is to use a **MATRIX EQUATION**. In the matrix equation $AX = B$, A contains the system's coefficients, X contains the variables, and B contains the constants (as shown below). The matrix equation can then be solved by multiplying B by the inverse of A: $X = A^{-1}B$

$$\begin{matrix} ax + by = e \\ cx + dy = f \end{matrix} \rightarrow A = \begin{bmatrix} a & b \\ c & d \end{bmatrix} \quad X = \begin{bmatrix} x \\ y \end{bmatrix} \quad B = \begin{bmatrix} e \\ f \end{bmatrix} \rightarrow AX = B$$

This method can be extended to equations with three or more variables. Technology (such as a graphing calculator) is often employed when solving using this method if more than two variables are involved.

EXAMPLES

29. Solve for x and y:

$2x - 4y = 28$

$4x - 12y = 36$

30. Solve for the system for x and y:

$3 = -4x + y$

$16x = 4y + 2$

31. Solve the system of equations:

$6x + 10y = 18$

$4x + 15y = 37$

32. Solve the following systems of equations using matrix arithmetic:

$2x - 3y = -5$

$3x - 4y = -8$

BUILDING EQUATIONS

In word problems, it is often necessary to translate a verbal description of a relationship into a mathematical equation. No matter the problem, this process can be done using the same steps:

1. Read the problem carefully and identify what value needs to be solved for.

2. Identify the known and unknown quantities in the problem, and assign the unknown quantities a variable.

3. Create equations using the variables and known quantities.

4. Solve the equations.

5. Check the solution: Does it answer the question asked in the problem? Does it make sense?

EXAMPLES

33. Kelly is selling shirts for her school swim team. There are two prices: a student price and a nonstudent price. During the first week of the sale, Kelly raised $84 by selling 10 shirts to students and 4 shirts to nonstudents. She earned $185 in the second week by selling 20 shirts to students and 10 shirts to nonstudents. What is the student price for a shirt?

34. A school is holding a raffle to raise money. There is a $3 entry fee, and each ticket costs $5. If a student paid $28, how many tickets did he buy?

Linear Inequalities
SOLVING LINEAR INEQUALITIES

An inequality shows the relationship between two expressions, much like an equation. However, the equal sign is replaced with an inequality symbol that expresses the following relationships:

▶   < less than

▶   > greater than

▶   ≤ less than or equal to

▶   ≥ greater than or equal to

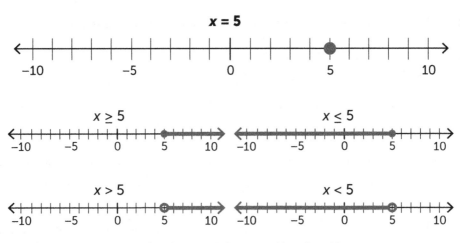

Figure 2.3. Inequalities on a Number Line

Inequalities are read from left to right. For example, the inequality $x \leq 8$ would be read as "x is less than or equal to 8," meaning x has a value smaller than or equal to 8. The set of solutions of an inequality can be expressed using a number line. The shaded region on the number line represents the set of all the numbers that make an inequality true. One major difference between equations and inequalities is that equations generally have a finite number of solutions, while inequalities generally have infinitely many solutions (an entire interval on the number line containing infinitely many values).

Linear inequalities can be solved in the same way as linear equations, with one exception. When multiplying or dividing both sides of an inequality by a negative number, the direction of the inequality sign must reverse—"greater than" becomes "less than" and "less than" becomes "greater than."

35. Solve for z: $3z + 10 < -z$

36. Solve for x: $2x - 3 > 5(x - 4) - (x - 4)$

COMPOUND INEQUALITIES

Compound inequalities have more than one inequality expression. Solutions of compound inequalities are the sets of all numbers that make *all* the inequalities true. Some compound inequalities may not have any solutions, some will have solutions that contain some part of the number line, and some will have solutions that include the entire number line.

	Table 2.6. Unions and Intersections	
INEQUALITY	MEANING IN WORDS	NUMBER LINE
$a < x < b$	All values x that are greater than a and less than b	
$a \leq x \leq b$	All values x that are greater than or equal to a and less than or equal to b	
$x < a$ or $x > b$	All values of x that are less than a or greater than b	
$x \leq a$ or $x \geq b$	All values of x that are less than or equal to a or greater than or equal to b	

Compound inequalities can be written, solved, and graphed as two separate inequalities. For compound inequalities in which the word *and* is used, the solution to the compound inequality will be the set of numbers on the number line where both inequalities have solutions (where both are shaded). For compound inequalities where *or* is used, the solution to the compound inequality will be *all* the shaded regions for *either* inequality.

EXAMPLES

37. Solve the compound inequalities: $2x + 4 < -18$ *or* $4(x + 2) > 18$

38. Solve the inequality: $-1 \leq 3(x + 2) - 1 \leq x + 3$

GRAPHING LINEAR INEQUALITIES
in TWO VARIABLES

Linear inequalities in two variables can be graphed in much the same way as linear equations. Start by graphing the corresponding equation of a line (temporarily replace the inequality with an equal sign, and then graph). This line creates a boundary line of two half-planes. If the inequality is a "greater/less than," the boundary should not be included and a dotted line is used. A solid line is used to indicate that the boundary should be included in the solution when the inequality is "greater/less than or equal to."

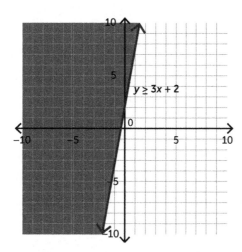

Figure 2.4. Graphing Inequalities

One side of the boundary is the set of all points (x, y) that make the inequality true. This side is shaded to indicate that all these values are solutions. If y is greater than the expression containing x, shade above the line; if it is less than, shade below. A point can also be used to check which side of the line to shade.

A set of two or more linear inequalities is a **SYSTEM OF INEQUALITIES**. Solutions to the system are all the values of the variables that make every inequality in the system true. Systems of inequalities are solved graphically by graphing all the inequalities in the same plane. The region where all the shaded solutions overlap is the solution to the system.

EXAMPLES

39. Graph the following inequality: $3x + 6y \leq 12$.

40. Graph the system of inequalities: $-x + y \leq 1, x \geq -1, y > 2x - 4$

41. What is the inequality represented on the graph below?

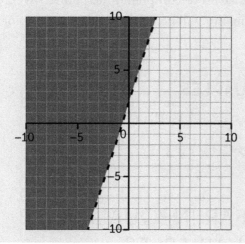

Properties of Shapes
BASIC DEFINITIONS

The basic figures from which many other geometric shapes are built are points, lines, and planes. A POINT is a location in a plane. It has no size or shape, but is represented by a dot. It is labeled using a capital letter.

A LINE is a one-dimensional collection of points that extends infinitely in both directions. At least two points are needed to define a line, and any points that lie on the same line are COLINEAR. Lines are represented by two points, such as A and B, and the line symbol: ($\overleftrightarrow{AB}$). Two lines on the same plane will intersect unless they are PARALLEL, meaning they have the same slope. Lines that intersect at a 90 degree angle are PERPENDICULAR.

A LINE SEGMENT has two endpoints and a finite length. The length of a segment, called the measure of the segment, is the distance from A to B. A line segment is a subset of a line, and is also denoted with two points, but with a segment symbol: ($\overline{AB}$). The MIDPOINT of a line segment is the point at which the segment is divided into two equal parts. A line, segment, or plane that passes through the midpoint of a segment is called a BISECTOR of the segment, since it cuts the segment into two equal segments.

A RAY has one endpoint and extends indefinitely in one direction. It is defined by its endpoint, followed by any other point on the ray: $\overrightarrow{AB}$. It is important that the first letter represents the endpoint. A ray is sometimes called a half line.

A PLANE is a flat sheet that extends indefinitely in two directions (like an infinite sheet of paper). A plane is a two-dimensional (2D) figure. A plane can always be defined through any three noncollinear points in three-dimensional (3D) space. A plane is named using any three points that are in the plane (for example, plane ABC). Any points lying in the same plane are said to be COPLANAR. When two planes intersect, the intersection is a line.

Table 2.7. Basic Geometric Figures			
TERM	DIMENSIONS	GRAPHIC	SYMBOL
point	zero	●	$\cdot A$
line segment	one	$A \longrightarrow B$	$\overline{AB}$
ray	one	$A \longrightarrow B$	$\overrightarrow{AB}$
line	one		$\overleftrightarrow{AB}$
plane	two		Plane M

EXAMPLE

42. Which points and lines are not contained in plane *M* in the diagram below?

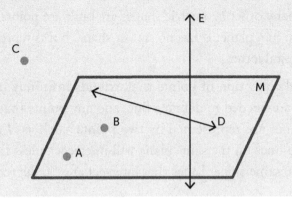

ANGLES

ANGLES are formed when two rays share a common endpoint. They are named using three letters, with the vertex point in the middle (for example $\angle ABC$, where *B* is the vertex). They can also be labeled with a number or named by their vertex alone (if it is clear to do so). Angles are also classified based on their angle measure. A **RIGHT ANGLE** has a measure of exactly 90°. **ACUTE ANGLES** have measures that are less than 90°, and **OBTUSE ANGLES** have measures that are greater than 90°.

DID YOU KNOW?

Angles can be measured in degrees or radian. Use the conversion factor 1 rad = 57.3 degrees to convert between them.

Any two angles that add to make 90° are called **COMPLEMENTARY ANGLES**. A 30° angle would be complementary to a 60° angle. **SUPPLEMENTARY ANGLES** add up to 180°. A supplementary angle to a 60° angle would be a 120° angle; likewise, 60° is the **SUPPLEMENT** of 120°. The complement and supplement of any angle must always be positive. For example, a 140 degree has no complement. Angles that are next to each other and share a common ray are called **ADJACENT ANGLES**. Angles that are adjacent and supplementary are called a **LINEAR PAIR** of angles. Their nonshared rays form a line (thus the *linear* pair). Note that angles that are supplementary do not need to be adjacent; their measures simply need to add to 180°.

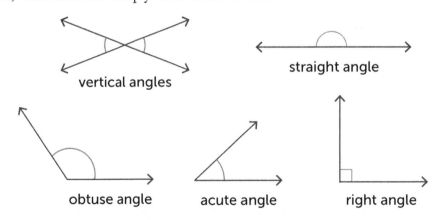

Figure 2.5. Types of Angles

Vᴇʀᴛɪᴄᴀʟ ᴀɴɢʟᴇs are formed when two lines intersect. Four angles will be formed; the vertex of each angle is at the intersection point of the lines. The vertical angles across from each other will be equal in measure. The angles adjacent to each other will be linear pairs and therefore supplementary.

A ray, line, or segment that divides an angle into two equal angles is called an Aɴɢʟᴇ ʙɪsᴇᴄᴛᴏʀ.

EXAMPLES

43. How many linear pairs of angles are there in the following figure?

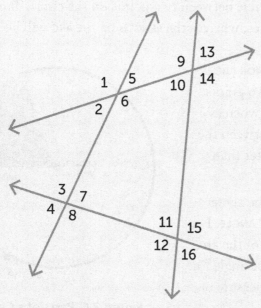

44. If angles *M* and *N* are supplementary and ∠*M* is 30° less than twice ∠*N*, what is the degree measurement of each angle?

CIRCLES

A ᴄɪʀᴄʟᴇ is the set of all the points in a plane that are the same distance from a fixed point called the ᴄᴇɴᴛᴇʀ. The distance from the center to any point on the circle is the ʀᴀᴅɪᴜs of the circle. The distance around the circle (the perimeter) is called the ᴄɪʀᴄᴜᴍғᴇʀᴇɴᴄᴇ.

The ratio of a circle's circumference to its diameter is a constant value called pi (π), an irrational number which is commonly rounded to 3.14. The formula to find a circle's circumference is $C = 2\pi r$. The formula to find the enclosed area of a circle is $A = \pi r^2$.

Circles have a number of unique parts and properties:

▶ The ᴅɪᴀᴍᴇᴛᴇʀ is the largest measurement across a circle. It passes through the circle's center, extending from one side of the circle to the other. The measure of the diameter is twice the measure of the radius.

▶ A line that cuts across a circle and touches it twice is called a SECANT line. The part of a secant line that lies within a circle is called a CHORD. Two chords within a circle are of equal length if they are are the same distance from the center.

▶ A line that touches a circle or any curve at one point is TANGENT to the circle or the curve. These lines are always exterior to the circle. A line tangent to a circle and a radius drawn to the point of tangency meet at a right angle (90°).

▶ An ARC is any portion of a circle between two points on the circle. The MEASURE of an arc is in degrees, whereas the LENGTH OF THE ARC will be in linear measurement (such as centimeters or inches). A MINOR ARC is the small arc between the two points (it measures less than 180°), whereas a MAJOR ARC is the large arc between the two points (it measures greater than 180°).

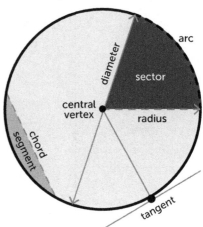

▶ An angle with its vertex at the center of a circle is called a CENTRAL ANGLE. For a central angle, the measure of the arc intercepted by the sides of the angle (in degrees) is the same as the measure of the angle.

Figure 2.6. Parts of a Circle

▶ A SECTOR is the part of a circle *and* its interior that is inside the rays of a central angle (its shape is like a slice of pie).

	Area of Sector	Length of an Arc
Degrees	$A = \frac{\theta}{360°} \times \pi r^2$	$s = \frac{\theta}{360°} \times 2\pi r$
Radians	$A = \frac{1}{2}\pi^2\theta$	$s = r\theta$

▶ An INSCRIBED ANGLE has a vertex on the circle and is formed by two chords that share that vertex point. The angle measure of an inscribed angle is one-half the angle measure of the central angle with the same endpoints on the circle.

▶ A CIRCUMSCRIBED ANGLE has rays tangent to the circle. The angle lies outside of the circle.

▶ Any angle outside the circle, whether formed by two tangent lines, two secant lines, or a tangent line and a secant line, is equal to half the difference of the intercepted arcs.

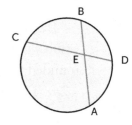

$m\angle E = \frac{1}{2}(\overset{\frown}{AC} + \overset{\frown}{BD})$

**Figure 2.7.
Intersecting Chords**

▶ Angles are formed within a circle when two chords intersect in the circle. The measure of the smaller angle formed is half the sum of the two smaller arc measures (in degrees). Likewise, the larger angle is half the sum of the two larger arc measures.

▶ If a chord intersects a line tangent to the circle, the angle formed by this intersection measures one half the measurement of the intercepted arc (in degrees).

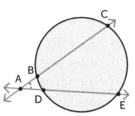

$m\angle A = \frac{1}{2}(\overset{\frown}{CE} \overset{\frown}{BD})$

Figure 2.8. Angles Outside a Circle

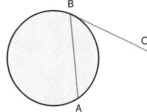

$m\angle ABC = \frac{1}{2}m\overset{\frown}{AB}$

Figure 2.9. Intersecting Chord and Tangent

EXAMPLES

45. Find the area of the sector *NHS* of the circle below with center at *H*:

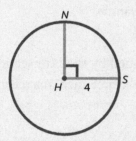

46. In the circle below with center *O*, the minor arc *ACB* measures 5 feet. What is the measurement of *m∠AOB*?

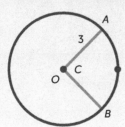

TRIANGLES

Much of geometry is concerned with triangles as they are commonly used shapes. A good understanding of triangles allows decomposition of other shapes (specifically polygons) into triangles for study.

Triangles have three sides, and the three interior angles always sum to 180°. The formula for the area of a triangle is $A = \frac{1}{2} bh$ or one-half the product of the base and height (or altitude) of the triangle.

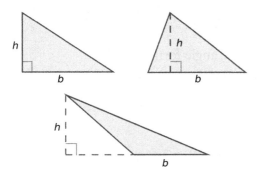

Figure 2.10. Finding the Base and Height of Triangles

Some important segments in a triangle include the angle bisector, the altitude, and the median. The **ANGLE BISECTOR** extends from the side opposite an angle to bisect that angle. The **ALTITUDE** is the shortest distance from a vertex of the triangle to the line containing the base side opposite that vertex. It is perpendicular to that line and can occur on the outside of the triangle. The **MEDIAN** extends from an angle to bisect the opposite side.

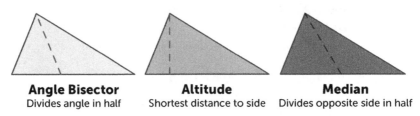

Angle Bisector
Divides angle in half

Altitude
Shortest distance to side

Median
Divides opposite side in half

Figure 2.11. Critical Segments in a Triangle

Triangles have two "centers." The **ORTHOCENTER** is formed by the intersection of a triangle's three altitudes. The **CENTROID** is where a triangle's three medians meet.

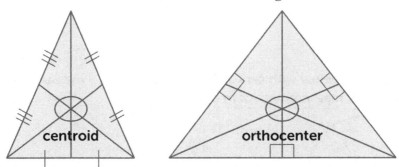

Figure 2.12. Centroid and Orthocenter of a Triangle

Triangles can be classified in two ways: by sides and by angles.

A **SCALENE TRIANGLE** has no equal sides or angles. An **ISOSCELES TRIANGLE** has two equal sides and two equal angles, often called **BASE ANGLES**. In an **EQUILATERAL TRIANGLE**, all three sides are equal as are all three angles. Moreover, because the sum of the angles of a triangle is always 180°, each angle of an equilateral triangle must be 60°.

A **RIGHT TRIANGLE** has one right angle (90°) and two acute angles. An **ACUTE TRIANGLE** has three acute angles (all angles are less than 90°). An **OBTUSE TRIANGLE** has one obtuse angle (more than 90°) and two acute angles.

Triangles Based on Sides

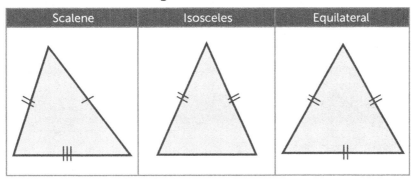

Triangles Based on Angles

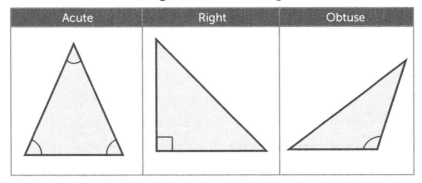

Figure 2.13. Types of Triangles

For any triangle, the side opposite the largest angle will have the longest length, while the side opposite the smallest angle will have the shortest length. The **TRIANGLE INEQUALITY THEOREM** states that the sum of any two sides of a triangle must be greater than the third side. If this inequality does not hold, then a triangle cannot be formed. A consequence of this theorem is the **THIRD-SIDE RULE**: if b and c are two sides of a triangle, then the measure of the third side a must be between the sum of the other two sides and the difference of the other two sides: $c - b < a < c + b$.

DID YOU KNOW?
Trigonometric functions can be employed to find missing sides and angles of a triangle.

Solving for missing angles or sides of a triangle is a common type of triangle problem. Often a right triangle will come up on its own or within another triangle. The relationship among a right triangle's sides is known as the **PYTHAGOREAN THEOREM**: $a^2 + b^2 = c^2$, where c is the hypotenuse and is across from the 90° angle. Right triangles with angle measurements of 90° – 45° – 45° and 90° – 60° – 30° are known as "special" right triangles and have specific relationships between their sides and angles.

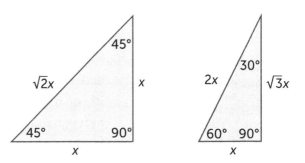

Figure 2.14. Special Right Triangles

47. What are the minimum and maximum values of x to the nearest hundredth?

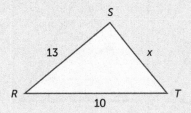

48. Given the diagram, if $XZ = 100$, $WZ = 80$, and $XU = 70$, then $WY = ?$

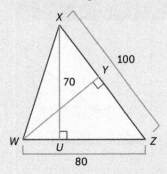

49. Examine and classify each of the following triangles:

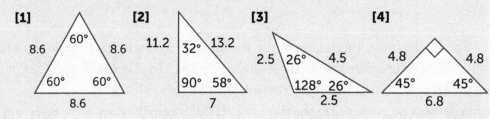

QUADRILATERALS

All closed, four-sided shapes are **QUADRILATERALS**. The sum of all internal angles in a quadrilateral is always 360°. (Think of drawing a diagonal to create two triangles. Since each triangle contains 180°, two triangles, and therefore the quadrilateral, must contain 360°.) The **AREA OF ANY QUADRILATERAL** is $A = bh$, where b is the base and h is the height (or altitude).

DID YOU KNOW?

All squares are rectangles and all rectangles are parallelograms; however, not all parallelograms are rectangles and not all rectangles are squares.

A **PARALLELOGRAM** is a quadrilateral with two pairs of parallel sides. A rectangle is a parallelogram with two pairs of equal sides and four right angles. A **KITE** also has two pairs of equal sides, but its equal sides are consecutive. Both a **SQUARE** and a **RHOMBUS** have four equal sides. A square has four right angles, while a rhombus has a pair of acute opposite angles and a pair of obtuse opposite angles. A **TRAPEZOID** has exactly one pair of parallel sides.

Table 2.8. Properties of Parallelograms

Term	Shape	Properties
Parallelogram		Opposite sides are parallel. Consecutive angles are supplementary. Opposite angles are equal. Opposite sides are equal. Diagonals bisect each other.
Rectangle		All parallelogram properties hold. Diagonals are congruent *and* bisect each other. All angles are right angles.
Square		All rectangle properties hold. All four sides are equal. Diagonals bisect angles. Diagonals intersect at right angles and bisect each other.
Kite		One pair of opposite angles is equal. Two pairs of consecutive sides are equal. Diagonals meet at right angles.
Rhombus		All four sides are equal. Diagonals bisect angles. Diagonals intersect at right angles and bisect each other.
Trapezoid		One pair of sides is parallel. Bases have different lengths. Isosceles trapezoids have a pair of equal sides (and base angles).

EXAMPLES

50. In parallelogram *ABCD*, the measure of angle *m* is is $m° = 260°$. What is the measure of $n°$?

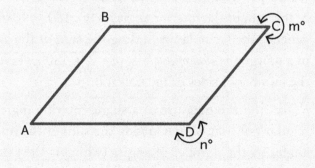

51. A rectangular section of a football field has dimensions of *x* and *y* and an area of 1000 square feet. Three additional lines drawn vertically divide the section into four smaller rectangular areas as seen in the diagram below. If all the lines shown need to be painted, calculate the total number of linear feet, in terms of *x*, to be painted.

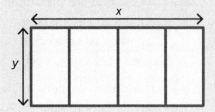

POLYGONS

Any closed shape made up of three or more line segments is a polygon. In addition to triangles and quadrilaterals, **HEXAGONS** and **OCTAGONS** are two common polygons.

The two polygons depicted in Figure 6.11 are **REGULAR POLYGONS**, meaning that they are equilateral (all sides having equal lengths) and equiangular (all angles having equal measurements). Angles inside a polygon are **INTERIOR ANGLES**, whereas those formed by one side of the polygon and a line extending outside the polygon are **EXTERIOR ANGLES**:

The sum of the all the exterior angles of a polygon is always 360°. Dividing 360° by the number of a polygon's sides finds the measure of the polygon's exterior angles.

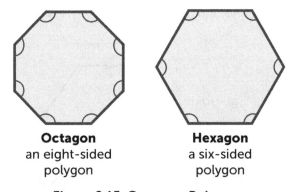

Octagon
an eight-sided polygon

Hexagon
a six-sided polygon

Figure 2.15. Common Polygons

To determine the sum of a polygon's interior angles, choose one vertex and draw diagonals from that vertex to each of the other vertices, decomposing the polygon into multiple triangles. For example, an octagon has six triangles within it, and therefore the sum of the interior angles is 6 × 180° = 1080°. In general, the formula for finding the sum of the angles in a polygon is *sum of angles* = (*n* − 2) × 180°, where *n* is the number of sides of the polygon.

To find the measure of a single interior angle in a regular polygon, simply divide the sum of the interior angles by the number of angles (which is the same as the number of sides). So, in the octagon example, each angle is $\frac{1080}{8}$ = 135°.

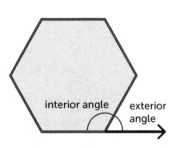

interior angle exterior angle

Figure 2.16. Interior and Exterior Angles

In general, the formula to find the measure of a regular polygon's interior angles is: *interior angle* = $\frac{(n-2)}{n} \times 180°$ where *n* is the number of sides of the polygon.

To find the area of a polygon, it is helpful to know the perimeter of the polygon (*p*), and the **APOTHEM** (*a*). The apothem is the shortest (perpendicular) distance from the polygon's center to one of the sides of the polygon. The formula for the area is: *area* = $\frac{ap}{2}$.

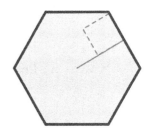

**Figure 2.17.
Apothem in a Hexagon**

Finally, there is no universal way to find the perimeter of a polygon (when the side length is not given). Often, breaking the polygon down into triangles and adding the base of each triangle all the way around the polygon is the easiest way to calculate the perimeter.

EXAMPLES

52. What is the measure of an exterior angle and an interior angle of a regular 400-gon?

53. The circle and hexagon below both share center point *T*. The hexagon is entirely inscribed in the circle. The circle's radius is 5. What is the area of the shaded area?

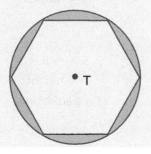

Three-Dimensional Shapes

THREE-DIMENSIONAL SHAPES have depth in addition to width and length. **VOLUME** is expressed as the number of cubic units any solid can hold—that is, what it takes to fill it up. **SURFACE AREA** is the sum of the areas of the two-dimensional figures that are found on its surface. Some three-dimensional shapes also have a unique property called a slant height (ℓ), which is the distance from the base to the apex along a lateral face.

Finding the surface area of a three-dimensional solid can be made easier by using a **NET**. This two-dimensional "flattened" version of a three-dimensional shape shows the component parts that comprise the surface of the solid.

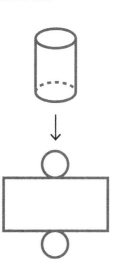

**Figure 2.18. Net
of a Cylinder**

Table 2.9. Three-Dimensional Shapes and Formulas

Term	Shape	Formula	
Prism		$V = Bh$ $SA = 2lw + 2wh + 2lh$ $d^2 = a^2 + b^2 + c^2$	B = area of base h = height l = length w = width d = longest diagonal
Cube		$V = s^3$ $SA = 6s^2$	s = cube edge
Sphere		$V = \frac{4}{3}\pi r^3$ $SA = 4\pi r^2$	r = radius
Cylinder		$V = Bh = \pi r^2 h$ $SA = 2\pi r^2 + 2\pi rh$	B = area of base h = height r = radius
Cone		$V = \frac{1}{3}\pi r^2 h$ $SA = \pi r^2 + \pi rl$	r = radius h = height l = slant height
Pyramid		$V = \frac{1}{3}Bh$ $SA = B + \frac{1}{2}(p)l$	B = area of base h = height p = perimeter l = slant height

EXAMPLES

54. A sphere has a radius z. If that radius is increased by t, by how much is the surface area increased? Write the answer in terms of z and t.

55. A cube with volume 27 cubic meters is inscribed within a sphere such that all of the cube's vertices touch the sphere. What is the length of the sphere's radius?

Describing Sets of Data
MEASURES of CENTRAL TENDENCY

Measures of central tendency help identify the center, or most typical, value within a data set. There are three such central tendencies that describe the "center" of the data in different ways. The **MEAN** is the arithmetic average and is found by dividing the sum of all measurements by the number of measurements. The mean of a population is written as μ and the mean of a sample is written as $\bar{x}$.

$$\text{population mean} = \mu = \frac{x_1 + x_2 + ...xN}{N} = \frac{\Sigma x}{N}$$

$$\text{sample mean} = \bar{x} = \frac{x_1 + x_2 + ...xn}{n} = \frac{\Sigma x}{n}$$

The data points are represented by x's with subscripts; the sum is denoted using the Greek letter sigma (Σ); N is the number of data points in the entire population; and n is the number of data points in a sample set.

The **MEDIAN** divides the measurements into two equal halves. The median is the measurement right in the middle of an odd set of measurements or the average of the two middle numbers in an even data set. When calculating the median, it is important to order the data values from least to greatest before attempting to locate the middle value. The **MODE** is simply the measurement that occurs most often. There can be many modes in a data set, or no mode. Since measures of central tendency describe a *center* of the data, all three of these measures will be between the lowest and highest data values (inclusive).

Unusually large or small values, called **OUTLIERS**, will affect the mean of a sample more than the mode. If there is a high outlier, the mean will be greater than the median; if there is a low outlier, the mean will be lower than the median. When outliers are present, the median is a better measure of the data's center than the mean because the median will be closer to the terms in the data set.

DID YOU KNOW?
When the same value is added to each term in a set, the mean increases by that value and the standard deviation is unchanged.
When each term in a set is multiplied by the same value, both the mean and standard deviation will also be multiplied by that value.

EXAMPLES

56. What is the mean of the following data set? {1000, 0.1, 10, 1}

57. What is the median of the following data set? {1000, 10, 1, 0.1}

58. Josey has an average of 81 on four equally weighted tests she has taken in her statistics class. She wants to determine what grade she must receive on her fifth test so that her mean is 83, which will give her a B in the course, but she does not remember her other scores. What grade must she receive on her fifth test?

MEASURES of VARIATION

The values in a data set can be very close together (close to the mean), or very spread out. This is called the SPREAD or DISPERSION of the data. There are a few MEASURES OF VARIATION (or MEASURES OF DISPERSION) that quantify the spread within a data set. RANGE is the difference between the largest and smallest data points in a set:

> *R = largest data point – smallest data point*

Notice range depends on only two data points (the two extremes). Sometimes these data points are outliers; regardless, for a large data set, relying on only two data points is not an exact tool.

The understanding of the data set can be improved by calculating QUARTILES. To calculate quartiles, first arrange the data in ascending order and find the set's median (also called quartile 2 or Q2). Then find the median of the lower half of the data, called quartile 1 (Q1), and the median of the upper half of the data, called quartile 3 (Q3). These three points divide the data into four equal groups of data (thus the word *quartile*). Each quartile contains 25% of the data.

INTERQUARTILE RANGE (IQR) provides a more reliable range that is not as affected by extremes. IQR is the difference between the third quartile data point and the first quartile data point and gives the spread of the middle 50% of the data:

$$IQR = Q_3 - Q_1$$

The VARIANCE of a data set is simply the square of the standard variation:

$$V = \sigma^2 = \frac{1}{N} \sum_{i=1}^{N} (x_i - \mu)^2$$

Variance measures how narrowly or widely the data points are distributed. A variance of zero means every data point is the same; a large variance means the data is widely spread out.

EXAMPLE

59. What are the range and interquartile range of the following set? {3, 9, 49, 64, 81, 100, 121, 144, 169}

BOX PLOTS

A box plot depicts the median and quartiles along a scaled number line. It is meant to summarize the data in a visual manner and emphasize central trends while decreasing the pull of outlier data. To construct a box plot:

1. Create a number line that begins at the lowest data point and terminates at the highest data point.

2. Find the quartiles of the data. Create a horizontal rectangle (the "box") whose left border is Q_1 and right border is Q_3.

3. Draw a vertical line within the box to mark the median.

4. Draw a horizontal line going from the left edge of the box to the smallest data value.

5. Draw a horizontal line going from the right edge of the box to the largest data value.

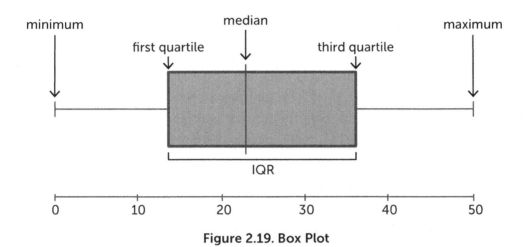

Figure 2.19. Box Plot

When reading a box plot, the following stands out:

▶ Reading from left to right: the horizontal line (whisker) shows the spread of the first quarter; the box's left compartment shows the spread of the second quarter; the box's right compartment shows the spread of the third quarter; and the right horizontal line shows the spread of the fourth quarter.

▶ The length of the box is the IQR, or the middle 50% of the data.

▶ Each of the four pieces (the whiskers and two pieces in the box) represent 25% of the data.

▶ The horizontal lines show by their length whether the data higher or lower than the middle 50% is prominent.

DID YOU KNOW?
Box plots are also known as box-and-whisker plots, because if they are drawn correctly the two horizontal lines look like whiskers.

EXAMPLE

60. A recent survey asked 8 people how many pairs of shoes they wear per week. Their answers are in the following data set: {1, 3, 5, 5, 7, 8, 12}. Construct a box plot from this data.

Probability

Probability describes how likely something is to happen. In probability, an **EVENT** is the single result of a trial, and an **OUTCOME** is a possible event that results from a trial. The collection of all possible outcomes for a particular trial is called the **SAMPLE SPACE**. For example, when rolling a die, the sample space is the numbers 1 – 6. Rolling a single number, such as 4, would be a single event.

SET THEORY

A **SET** is any collection of items. In mathematics, a set is represented by a capital letter and described inside curly brackets. For example, if S is the set of all integers less than 10, then $S = \{x|x$ is an integer and $x < 10\}$. The vertical bar | is read *such that*. The set that contains no elements is called the **EMPTY SET** or the **NULL SET** and is denoted by empty brackets { } or the symbol ∅.

Usually there is a larger set that any specific problem is based in, called the **UNIVERSAL SET** or **U**. For example, in the set S described above, the universal set might be the set of all real numbers. The **COMPLEMENT** of set A, denoted by $\bar{A}$ or A', is the set of all items in the universal set, but NOT in A. It can be helpful when working with sets to represent them with a **VENN DIAGRAM**.

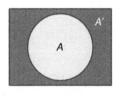

**Figure 2.20.
Venn Diagram**

Oftentimes, the task will be working with multiple sets: A, B, C, etc. A **UNION** between two sets means that the data in both sets is combined into a single, larger set. The union of two sets, denoted $A \cup B$ contains all the data that is in either set A or set B or both (called an **INCLUSIVE OR**). If $A = \{1, 4, 7\}$ and $B = \{2, 4, 5, 8\}$, then $A \cup B = \{1, 2, 4, 5, 7, 8\}$ (notice 4 is included only once). The **INTERSECTION** of two sets, denoted $A \cap B$ includes only elements that are in both A and B. Thus, $A \cap B = \{4\}$ for the sets given above.

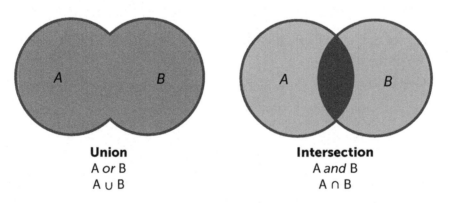

Union
A *or* B
A ∪ B

Intersection
A *and* B
A ∩ B

Figure 2.21. Unions and Intersections

If there is no common data in the sets in question, then the intersection is the null set. Two sets that have no elements in common (and thus have a null in the intersection

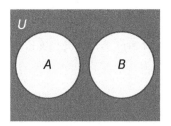

**Figure 2.22.
Disjoint Sets**

set) are said to be DISJOINT. The DIFFERENCE $B - A$ or RELATIVE COMPLEMENT between two sets is the set of all the values that are in B, but not in A. For the sets defined above, $B - A = \{2, 5, 8\}$ and $A - B = \{1, 7\}$. The relative complement is sometimes denoted as $B \backslash A$.

Mathematical tasks often involve working with multiple sets. Just like numbers, sets and set operations have identities and properties.

Set Identities

$A \cup \varnothing = A$	$A \cup U = U$	$A \cup \overline{A} = U$
$A \cap \varnothing = A$	$A \cap U = A$	$A \cap \overline{A} = \varnothing$

Set Properties

Commutative Property	$A \cup B = B \cup A$	$A \cap B = B \cap A$
Associative Property	$A \cup (B \cup C) = (A \cup B) \cup C$	$A \cap (B \cap C) = (A \cap B) \cap C$
Distributive Property	$A \cup (B \cap C) = (A \cup B) \cap (A \cup C)$	$A \cap (B \cup C) = (A \cap B) \cup (A \cap C)$

De Morgan's Laws

$$\overline{(A \cup B)} = \overline{A} \cap \overline{B} \qquad \overline{(A \cap B)} = \overline{A} \cup \overline{B}$$

The number of elements in a set A is denoted $n(A)$. For the set A above, $n(A) = 3$, since there are three elements in that set. The number of elements in the union of two sets is $n(A \cup B) = n(A) + n(B) - n(A \cap B)$. Note that the number of elements in the intersection of the two sets must be subtracted because they are being counted twice, since they are both in set A and in set B. The number of elements in the complement of A is the number of elements in the universal set minus the number in set A: $n(\overline{A}) = n(U) - n(A)$.

It is helpful to note here how similar set theory is to the logic operators of the previous section: negation corresponds to complements, the "and" ($\wedge$) operator to intersection ($\cap$), and the "or" ($\vee$) operator to unions ($\cup$); notice even the symbols are similar.

61. Construct a Venn diagram depicting the intersection, if any, of $Y = \{x \mid x$ is an integer and $0 < x < 9\}$ and $Z = \{-4, 0, 4, 8, 12, 16\}$.

62. Suppose the universal set U is the set of all integers between -10 and 10 inclusive. If $A = \{x \in U \mid x$ is a multiple of $5\}$ and $B = \{x \in U \mid x$ is a multiple of $2\}$ are subsets within the universal set, find $\overline{A}$, $A \cup B$ and $A \cap B$, and $\overline{A} \cap B$.

    [A] $\overline{A}$

    [B] $A \cup B$

    [C] $A \cap B$

    [D] $\overline{A} \cap \overline{B}$

COUNTING PRINCIPLES

Counting principles are methods used to find the number of possible outcomes for a given situation. The **FUNDAMENTAL COUNTING PRINCIPLE** states that, for a series of independent events, the number of outcomes can be found by multiplying the number of possible outcomes for each event. For example, if a die is rolled (6 possible outcomes) and a coin is tossed (2 possible outcomes), there are $6 \times 2 = 12$ total possible outcomes.

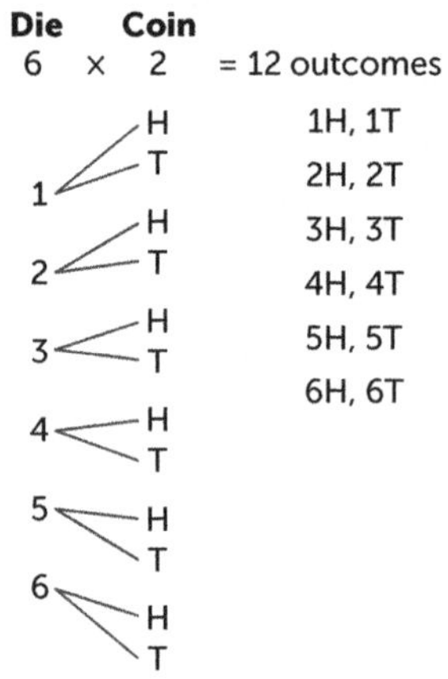

Figure 2.23. Fundamental Counting Principle

Combinations and permutations describe how many ways a number of objects taken from a group can be arranged. The number of objects in the group is written n, and the number of objects to be arranged is represented by r (or k). In a **COMBINATION**, the order of the selections does not matter because every available slot to be filled is the same. Examples of combinations include:

▶ picking 3 people from a group of 12 to form a committee (220 possible committees)

▶ picking 3 pizza toppings from 10 options (120 possible pizzas)

In a **PERMUTATION**, the order of the selection matters, meaning each available slot is different. Examples of permutations include:

▶ handing out gold, silver, and bronze medals in a race with 100 participants (970,200 possible combinations)

▶ selecting a president, vice-president, secretary, and treasurer from among a committee of 12 people (11,880 possible combinations)

The formulas for the both calculations are similar. The only difference—the $r!$ in the denominator of a combination—accounts for redundant outcomes. Note that both permutations and combinations can be written in several different shortened notations.

$$\text{Permutation: } P(n, r) = nPr = \frac{n!}{(n-r)!}$$

$$\text{Combination: } C(n, r) = nCr = \frac{n!}{(n-r)!r!}$$

EXAMPLES

63. A personal assistant is struggling to pick a shirt, tie, and cufflink set that go together. If his client has 70 shirts, 2 ties, and 5 cufflinks, how many possible combinations does he have to consider?

64. If there are 20 applicants for 3 open positions, in how many different ways can a team of 3 be hired?

65. Calculate the number of unique permutations that can be made with five of the letters in the word *pickle*.

66. Find the number of permutations that can be made out of all the letters in the word *cheese*.

PROBABILITY of a SINGLE EVENT

The probability of a single event occurring is the number of outcomes in which that event occurs (called **FAVORABLE EVENTS**) divided by the number of items in the sample space (total possible outcomes):

$$P \text{ (an event)} = \frac{number\ of\ favorable\ outcomes}{total\ number\ of\ possible\ outcomes}$$

The probability of any event occurring will always be a fraction or decimal between 0 and 1. It may also be expressed as a percent. An event with 0 probability will never occur and an event with a probability of 1 is certain to occur. The probability of an event not occurring is referred to as that event's **COMPLEMENT**. The sum of an event's probability and the probability of that event's complement will always be 1.

EXAMPLES

67. What is the probability that an even number results when a six-sided die is rolled? What is the probability the die lands on 5?

68. Only 20 tickets were issued in a raffle. If someone were to buy 6 tickets, what is the probability that person would not win the raffle?

69. A bag contains 26 tiles representing the 26 letters of the English alphabet. If 3 tiles are drawn from the bag without replacement, what is the probability that all 3 will be consonants?

PROBABILITY of MULTIPLE EVENTS

If events are **INDEPENDENT**, the probability of one occurring does not affect the probability of the other event occurring. Rolling a die and getting one number does not change the probability of getting any particular number on the next roll. The number of faces has not changed, so these are independent events.

DID YOU KNOW?
When drawing objects, the phrase *with replacement* describes independent events, and *without replacement* describes dependent events.

If events are **DEPENDENT**, the probability of one occurring changes the probability of the other event occurring. Drawing a card from a deck without replacing it will affect the probability of the next card drawn because the number of available cards has changed.

To find the probability that two or more independent events will occur (A and B), simply multiply the probabilities of each individual event together. To find the probability that one, the other, or both will occur (A or B), it's necessary to add their probabilities and then subtract their overlap (which prevents the same values from being counted twice).

CONDITIONAL PROBABILITY is the probability of an event occurring given that another event has occurred. The notation $P(B|A)$ represents the probability that event B occurs, given that event A has already occurred (it is read "probability of B, given A").

Table 2.10. Probability Formulas		
INDEPENDENT EVENTS		**DEPENDENT EVENTS**
Intersection *and*	Union *or*	Conditional
$P(A \cap B) = P(A) \times P(B)$	$P(A \cup B) = P(A) + P(B) - P(A \cap B)$	$P(B|A) = \dfrac{P(A \cap B)}{P(A)}$

Two events that are **MUTUALLY EXCLUSIVE** CANNOT happen at the same time. This is similar to disjoint sets in set theory. The probability that two mutually exclusive events will occur is zero. **MUTUALLY INCLUSIVE** events share common outcomes.

EXAMPLES

70. A card is drawn from a standard 52 card deck. What is the probability that it is either a queen or a heart?

71. A group of ten individuals is drawing straws from a group of 28 long straws and 2 short straws. If the straws are not replaced, what is the probability, as a percentage, that neither of the first two individuals will draw a short straw?

Answer Key

1. [A] 4.25 km $\left(\frac{1000 \text{ m}}{1 \text{ km}}\right)$ = **4250 m**

    [B] $\frac{8 \text{ m}^2}{1} \times \frac{1000 \text{ mm}}{1 \text{ m}} \times \frac{1000 \text{ mm}}{1 \text{ m}}$ =
    8,000,000 mm²

    Since the units are square units (m²), multiply by the conversion factor twice, so that both meters cancel.

2. [A] 12 ft $\left(\frac{12 \text{ in}}{1 \text{ ft}}\right)$ = **144 in**

    [B] 7 yd² $\left(\frac{3 \text{ ft}^2}{1 \text{ yd}^2}\right)\left(\frac{3 \text{ ft}^2}{1 \text{ yd}^2}\right)$ = **63 ft²**

    Since the units are square units (ft²), multiply by the conversion factor twice.

3. [A] 23 m $\left(\frac{3.28 \text{ ft}}{1 \text{ m}}\right)$ = **75.44 ft**

    [B] $\frac{10 \text{ m}^2}{1} \times \frac{1.094 \text{ yd}}{1 \text{ m}} \times \frac{1.094 \text{ yd}}{1 \text{ m}}$ =
    11.97 yd²

4. [A] 8 in³ $\left(\frac{16.39 \text{ ml}}{1 \text{ in}^3}\right)$ = **131.12 mL**

    [B] 16 kg $\left(\frac{2.2 \text{ lb}}{1 \text{ kg}}\right)$ = **35.2 lb**

5. Identify the variables.

    number of boys: 10

    number of girls: 12

    number of students: 22

    Write out and simplify the ratio of boys to total students.

    number of boys : number of students

    = 10 : 22 = $\frac{10}{22}$ = $\frac{5}{11}$

    Write out and simplify the ratio of girls to boys.

    number of girls : number of boys

    = 12 : 10 = $\frac{12}{10}$ = $\frac{6}{5}$

6. Identify the variables.

    rent = 600

    utilities = 400

    groceries = 750

    miscellaneous = 550

    total expenses =

    600 + 400 + 750 + 550 = 2300

    Write out and simplify the ratio of rent to total expenses.

    rent : total expenses

    = 600 : 2300 = $\frac{60}{2300}$ = $\frac{6}{23}$

7. $\frac{(3x - 5)}{2}$ = $\frac{(x - 8)}{3}$

    Cross-multiply.

    3(3x − 5) = 2(x − 8)

    Solve the equation for x.

    9x − 15 = 2x − 16

    7x − 15 = −16

    7x = −1

    $x = -\frac{1}{7}$

8. Write a proportion where x equals the actual distance and each ratio is written as inches : miles.

    $\frac{2.5}{40}$ = $\frac{17.25}{x}$

    Cross-multiply and divide to solve for x.

    2.5x = 690

    x = 276

    The two cities are **276 miles apart**.

9. Write a proportion where x is the number of defective parts made and both ratios are written as defective : total.

    $\frac{4}{1000}$ = $\frac{x}{125,000}$

    Cross-multiply and divide to solve for x.

    1000x = 500,000

    x = 500

    There are **500 defective parts** for the month.

10. $\frac{(10^2)^3}{(10^2)^2}$

Multiply the exponents raised to a power.

$= \frac{10^6}{10^{-4}}$

Subtract the exponent in the denominator from the one in the numerator.

$= 10^{6-(-4)}$

Simplify.

$= 10^{10} = \mathbf{10{,}000{,}000{,}000}$

11. $\frac{(x^{-2}y^2)^2}{x^3y}$

Multiply the exponents raised to a power.

$= \frac{x^{-4}y^4}{x^3y}$

Subtract the exponent in the denominator from the one in the numerator.

$= x^{-4-3}y^{4-1} = x^{-7}y^3$

Move negative exponents to the denominator.

$= \boldsymbol{\frac{y^3}{x^7}}$

12. $\sqrt{48}$

Determine the largest square number that is a factor of the radicand (48) and write the radicand as a product using that square number as a factor.

$= \sqrt{16 \times 3}$

Apply the rules of radicals to simplify.

$= \sqrt{16}\sqrt{3} = \sqrt[4]{\mathbf{3}}$

13. $\frac{6}{\sqrt{8}}$

Apply the rules of radicals to simplify.

$= \frac{6}{\sqrt{4}\sqrt{2}} = \frac{6}{2\sqrt{2}}$

Multiply by $\frac{\sqrt{2}}{\sqrt{2}}$ to rationalize the denominator.

$= \frac{6}{2\sqrt{2}}\left(\frac{\sqrt{2}}{\sqrt{2}}\right) = \boldsymbol{\frac{3\sqrt{2}}{2}}$

14. $5(m-2)^3 + 3m^2 - \frac{m}{4} - 1$

Plug the value 4 in for m in the expression.

$= 5(4-2)^3 + 3(4)^2 - \frac{4}{4} - 1$

Calculate all the expressions inside the parentheses.

$= 5(2)^3 + 3(4)^2 - \frac{4}{4} - 1$

Simplify all exponents.

$= 5(8) + 3(16) - \frac{4}{4} - 1$

Perform multiplication and division from left to right.

$= 40 + 48 - 1 - 1$

Perform addition and subtraction from left to right.

$= \mathbf{86}$

15. The only like terms in both expressions are $12x$ and $8x$, so these two terms will be added, and all other terms will remain the same.

$a + b = (12x + 8x) + 7xy - 9y - 9xz + 7z = \mathbf{20x + 7xy - 9y - 9xz + 7z}$

16. $5x(x^2 - 2c + 10)$

Distribute and multiply the term outside the parentheses to all three terms inside the parentheses.

$(5x)(x^2) = 5x^3$

$(5x)(-2c) = -10xc$

$(5x)(10) = 50x$

$= \mathbf{5x^3 - 10xc + 50x}$

17. $(x^2 - 5)(2x - x^3)$

Apply FOIL: first, outside, inside, and last.

$(x^2)(2x) = 2x^3$

$(x^2)(-x^3) = -x^5$

$(-5)(2x) = -10x$

$(-5)(-x^3) = 5x^3$

Combine like terms and put them in order.

$= 2x^3 - x^5 - 10x + 5x^3$

$= -x^5 + 7x^3 - 10x$

18. $16z^2 + 48z$

Both terms have a z, and 16 is a common factor of both 16 and 48. So the greatest common factor is $16z$. Factor out the GCF.

$16z^2 + 48z$

$= 16z(z + 3)$

19. $6m^3 + 12m^3n - 9m^2$

All the terms share the factor m^2, and 3 is the greatest common factor of 6, 12, and 9. So, the GCF is $3m^2$.

$= 3m^2(2m + 4mn - 3)$

20. $16x^2 + 52x + 30$

Remove the GCF of 2.

$= 2(8x^2 + 26x + 15)$

To factor the polynomial in the parentheses, calculate $ac = (8)(15) = 120$, and consider all the pairs of numbers that multiply to be 120: 1×120, 2×60, 3×40, 4×30, 5×24, 6×20, 8×15, and 10×12. Of these pairs, choose the pair that adds to be the b-value 26 (6 and 20).

$= 2(8x^2 + 6x + 20x + 15)$

Group.

$= 2[(8x^2 + 6x) + (20x + 15)]$

Factor out the GCF of each group.

$= 2[(2x(4x + 3) + 5(4x + 3)]$

Factor out the common binomial.

$= 2[(4x + 3)(2x + 5)]$

$= 2(4x + 3)(2x + 5)$

If there are no values r and s that multiply to be ac and add to be b, then the polynomial is prime and cannot be factored.

21. $-21x^2 - x + 10$

Factor out the negative.

$= -(21x^2 + x - 10)$

Factor the polynomial in the parentheses.

$ac = 210$ and $b = 1$

The numbers 15 and -14 can be multiplied to get 210 and subtracted to get 1.

$= -(21x^2 - 14x + 15x - 10)$

Group.

$= -[(21x^2 - 14x) + (15x - 10)]$

Factor out the GCF of each group.

$= -[7x(3x - 2) + 5(3x - 2)]$

Factor out the common binomial.

$= -(3x - 2)(7x + 5)$

22. $\dfrac{100(x + 5)}{20} = 1$

Multiply both sides by 20 to cancel out the denominator.

$(20)\left(\dfrac{100(x + 5)}{20}\right) = (1)(20)$

$100(x + 5) = 20$

Distribute 100 through the parentheses.

$100x + 500 = 20$

"Undo" the +500 by subtracting 500 on both sides of the equation to isolate the variable term.

$100x = -480$

"Undo" the multiplication by 100 by dividing by 100 on both sides to solve for x.

$x = \dfrac{-480}{100}$

$x = -4.8$

23. $2(x + 2)^2 - 2x^2 + 10 = 42$

Eliminate the exponents on the left side.

$2(x + 2)(x + 2) - 2x^2 + 10 = 42$

Apply FOIL.

$2(x^2 + 4x + 4) - 2x^2 + 10 = 42$

Distribute the 2.

$2x^2 + 8x + 8 - 2x^2 + 10 = 42$

Combine like terms on the left-hand side.

$8x + 18 = 42$

Isolate the variable. "Undo" +18 by subtracting 18 on both sides.

$8x = 24$

"Undo" multiplication by 8 by dividing both sides by 8.

$x = 3$

24. $\frac{A(3B + 2D)}{2N} = 5M - 6$

Multiply both sides by $2N$ to clear the fraction, and distribute the A through the parentheses.

$3AB + 2AD = 10MN - 12N$

Isolate the term with the D in it by moving $3AB$ to the other side of the equation.

$2AD = 10MN - 12N - 3AB$

Divide both sides by $2A$ to get D alone on the right-hand side.

$D = \frac{(10MN - 12N - 3AB)}{2A}$

25. The y-intercept can be identified on the graph as $(0,3)$.

$b = 3$

To find the slope, choose any two points and plug the values into the slope equation. The two points chosen here are $(2,-1)$ and $(3,-3)$.

$m = \frac{(-3) - (-1)}{3 - 2} = \frac{-2}{1} = -2$

Replace m with -2 and b with 3 in $y = mx + b$.

$y = -2x + 3$

26. The line has a rise of 0 and a run of 1, so the slope is $\frac{0}{1} = 0$. There is no x-intercept. The y-intercept is $(0,2)$, meaning that the b-value in the slope-intercept form is 2.

$y = 0x + 2$, or $y = 2$

27. $6x - 2y - 8 = 0$

Rearrange the equation into slope-intercept form by solving the equation for y.

$-2y = -6x + 8$

$y = \frac{-6x + 8}{-2}$

$y = 3x - 4$

The slope is 3, the value attached to x.

$m = 3$

28. $(-2,5)$ and $(-5,3)$

Calculate the slope.

$m = \frac{3 - 5}{(-5) - (-2)} = \frac{-2}{-3} = \frac{2}{3}$

To find b, plug into the equation $y = mx + b$ the slope for m and a set of points for x and y.

$5 = \frac{2}{3}(-2) + b$

$5 = \frac{-4}{3} + b$

$b = \frac{19}{3}$

Replace m and b to find the equation of the line.

$y = \frac{2}{3}x + \frac{19}{3}$

29. Solve the system with substitution. Solve one equation for one variable.

$2x - 4y = 28$

$x = 2y + 14$

Plug in the resulting expression for x in the second equation and simplify.

$4x - 12y = 36$

$4(2y + 14) - 12y = 36$

$8y + 56 - 12y = 36$

$-4y = -20$

$y = 5$

Plug the solved variable into either equation to find the second variable.

$2x - 4y = 28$

$2x - 4(5) = 28$

$2x - 20 = 28$

$2x = 48$

$x = 24$

The answer is $y = 5$ and $x = 24$ or **(24,5)**.

30. Isolate the variable in one equation.

$3 = -4x + y$

$y = 4x + 3$

Plug the expression into the second equation.

Both equations have slope 4. This means the graphs of the equations are parallel lines, so no intersection (solution) exists.

$16x = 4y + 2$

$16x = 4(4x + 3) + 2$

$16x = 16x + 12 + 2$

$0 = 14$

No solution exists.

31. Because solving for x or y in either equation will result in messy fractions, this problem is best solved using elimination. The goal is to eliminate one of the variables by making the coefficients in front of one set of variables the same, but with different signs, and then adding both equations.

To eliminate the x's in this problem, find the least common multiple of coefficients 6 and 4. The smallest number that both 6 and 4 divide into evenly is 12. Multiply the top equation by -2, and the bottom equation by 3.

$6x + 10y = 18 \xrightarrow{(-2)} {}^{-12}x - {}^{20}y = {}^{-36}$

$4x + 15y = 37 \xrightarrow{(3)} {}^{12}x + {}^{45}y = {}^{1}\underline{11}$

Add the two equations to eliminate the x's.

$25y = 75$

Solve for y.

$y = 3$

Replace y with 3 in either of the original equations.

$6x + 10(3) = 18$

$6x + 30 = 18$

$x = -2$

The solution is **(−2,3)**.

32. Write the system in matrix form, $AX = B$.

$$\begin{bmatrix} 2 & -3 \\ 3 & -4 \end{bmatrix} \begin{bmatrix} x \\ y \end{bmatrix} = \begin{bmatrix} -5 \\ -8 \end{bmatrix}$$

Calculate the inverse of Matrix **A**.

$$\begin{bmatrix} 2 & -3 \\ 3 & -4 \end{bmatrix}^{-1} = \frac{1}{(2)(-4) - (-3)(3)} \begin{bmatrix} -4 & 3 \\ -3 & 2 \end{bmatrix}$$

$$= \begin{bmatrix} -4 & 3 \\ -3 & 2 \end{bmatrix}$$

Multiply **B** by the inverse of **A**.

$$\begin{bmatrix} x \\ y \end{bmatrix} = \begin{bmatrix} -4 & 3 \\ -3 & 2 \end{bmatrix} \begin{bmatrix} -5 \\ -8 \end{bmatrix} = \begin{bmatrix} -4 \\ -1 \end{bmatrix}$$

Match up the 2×1 matrices to identify x and y.

$x = -4$

$y = -1$

33. Assign variables.

Student price $= s$

Nonstudent price $= n$

Create two equations using the number of shirts Kelly sold and the money she earned.

$10s + 4n = 84$

$20s + 10n = 185$

Solve the system of equations using substitution.

$10s + 4n = 84$

$10n = -20s + 185$

$n = -2s + 18.5$

$10s + 4(-2s + 18.5) = 84$

$10s - 8s + 74 = 84$

$2s + 74 = 84$

$2s = 10$

$s = 5$

The student cost for shirts is **$5**.

34. Identify the quantities.

Number of tickets = x

Cost per ticket = 5

Cost for x tickets = $5x$

Total cost = 28

Entry fee = 3

Set up equations. The total cost for x tickets will be equal to the cost for x tickets plus the $3 flat fee.

$5x + 3 = 28$

Solve the equation for x.

$5x + 3 = 28$

$5x = 25$

$x = 5$

The student bought **5 tickets**.

35. $3z + 10 < -z$

Collect nonvariable terms to one side.

$3z < -z - 10$

Collect variable terms to the other side.

$4z < -10$

Isolate the variable.

$z < -2.5$

36. $2x - 3 > 5(x - 4) - (x - 4)$

Distribute 5 through the parentheses and -1 through the parentheses.

$2x - 3 > 5x - 20 - x + 4$

Combine like terms.

$2x - 3 > 4x - 16$

Collect x-terms to one side, and constant terms to the other side.

$-2x > -13$

Divide both sides by -2; since dividing by a negative, reverse the direction of the inequality.

$x < 6.5$

37. $2x + 4 < -18$ *or* $4(x + 2) > 18$

Solve each inequality independently.

$2x < -14$ $4x + 8 > 18$

$x < -7$ $4x > 10$

                   $x > 2.5$

The solution to the original compound inequality is **the set of all x for which $x < -7$ or $x > 2.5$.**

38. $-1 \leq 3(x + 2) - 1 \leq x + 3$

Break up the compound inequality into two inequalities.

$-1 \leq 3(x + 2) - 1$ *and* $3(x + 2) - 1 \leq x + 3$

Solve separately.

$-1 \leq 3x + 6 - 1$ $3x + 6 - 1 \leq x + 3$

$-6 \leq 3x$ $2x \leq -2$

$-2 \leq x$ and $x \leq -1$

The only values of x that satisfy *both* inequalities are the values between -2 and -1 (inclusive).

$-2 \leq x \leq -1$

39. Find the x- and y-intercepts.

$3x + 6y \leq 12$

$3(0) + 6y = 12$

$y = 2$

y-intercept: $(0, 2)$

$3x + 6(0) \leq 12$

$x = 4$

x-intercept: (4,0)

Graph the line using the intercepts, and shade below the line.

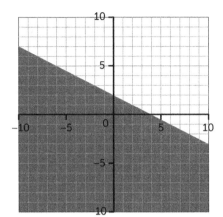

40. To solve the system, graph all three inequalities in the same plane; then identify the area where the three solutions overlap. All points (x,y) in this area will be solutions to the system since they satisfy all three inequalities.

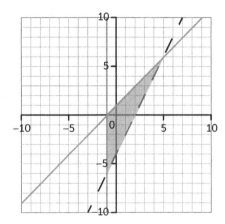

41. Determine the equation of the boundary line.

y-intercept: (0,2)

slope: 3

$y = 3x + 2$

Replace the equal sign with the appropriate inequality: the line is dotted and the shading is above the line, indicating that the symbol

should be "greater than." Check a point: for example (1,5) is a solution since $5 > 3(-1) + 2$.

$y > 3x + 2$

42. Points A and B and line D are all on plane M. Point C is above the plane, and line E cuts through the plane and thus does not lie on plane M. The point at which line E intersects plane M is on plane M but the line as a whole is not.

43. Any two adjacent angles that are supplementary are linear pairs, so there are 16 linear pairs in the figure ($\angle 1$ and $\angle 5$, $\angle 2$ and $\angle 6$, $\angle 5$ and $\angle 6$, $\angle 2$ and $\angle 1$, and so on).

44. Set up a system of equations.

$\angle M + \angle N = 180°$

$\angle M = 2\angle N - 30°$

Use substitution to solve for $\angle N$.

$\angle M + \angle N = 180°$

$(2\angle N - 30°) + \angle N = 180°$

$3\angle N - 30° = 180°$

$3\angle N = 210°$

$\angle N = $ **70°**

Solve for $\angle M$ using the original equation.

$\angle M + \angle N = 180°$

$\angle M + 70° = 180°$

$\angle M = $ **110°**

45. Identify the important parts of the circle.

$r = 4$

$\angle NHS = 90°$

Plug these values into the formula for the area of a sector.

$A = \frac{\theta}{360°} \times \pi r^2$

$= \frac{90}{360} \times \pi(4)^2 = \frac{1}{4} \times 16\pi$

$= $ **4π**

46. Identify the important parts of the circle.

$r = 3$

length of $\overline{ACB} = 5$

Plug these values into the formula for the length of an arc and solve for θ.

$s = \dfrac{\theta}{360°} \times 2\pi r$

$5 = \dfrac{\theta}{360°} \times 2\pi(3)$

$\dfrac{5}{6\pi} = \dfrac{\theta}{360°}$

$\theta = 95.5°$

$m\angle AOB = 95.5°$

47. The sum of two sides is 23 and their difference is 3. To connect the two other sides and enclose a space, x must be less than the sum and greater than the difference (that is, $3 < x < 23$). Therefore, **x's minimum value to the nearest hundredth is 3.01 and its maximum value is 22.99.**

48. $WZ = b_1 = 80$

$XU = h_1 = 70$

$XZ = b_2 = 100$

$WY = h_2 = ?$

The given values can be used to write two equation for the area of $\triangle WXZ$ with two sets of bases and heights.

$A = \dfrac{1}{2} bh$

$A_1 = \dfrac{1}{2}(80)(70) = 2800$

$A_2 = \dfrac{1}{2}(100)(h_2)$

Set the two equations equal to each other and solve for WY.

$2800 = \dfrac{1}{2}(100)(h_2)$

$h_2 = 56$

$WY = 56$

49. Triangle 1 is an equilateral triangle (all 3 sides are equal, and all 3 angles are equal)

Triangle 2 is a scalene, right triangle (all 3 sides are different, and there is a 90° angle)

Triangle 3 is an obtuse, isosceles triangle (there are 2 equal sides and, consequently, 2 equal angles)

Triangle 4 is a right, isosceles triangle (there are 2 equal sides and a 90° angle)

50. Find $\angle C$ using the fact that the sum of $\angle C$ and m is 360°.

$260° + m\angle C = 360°$

$m\angle C = 100°$

Solve for $\angle D$ using the fact that consecutive interior angles in a quadrilateral are supplementary.

$m\angle C + m\angle D = 180°$

$100° + m\angle D = 180°$

$m\angle D = 80°$

Solve for n by subtracting $m\angle D$ from 360°.

$m\angle D + n = 360°$

$n = 280°$

51. Find equations for the area of the field and length of the lines to be painted (L) in terms of x and y.

$A = 1000 = xy$

$L = 2x + 5y$

Substitute to find L in terms of x.

$y = \dfrac{1000}{x}$

$L = 2x + 5y$

$L = 2x + 5\left(\dfrac{1000}{x}\right)$

$L = 2x + \dfrac{5000}{x}$

52. The sum of the exterior angles is 360°. Dividing this sum by 400 gives $\dfrac{360°}{400} = \mathbf{0.9°}$. Since an interior angle is supplementary to an exterior angle, all the interior angles have measure $180 - 0.9$ = **179.1°**. Alternately, using the formula for calculating the interior angle gives the same result:

$interior\ angle = \frac{400 - 2}{400} \times 180°$

$= 179.1°$

53. The area of the shaded region will be the area of the circle minus the area of the hexagon. Use the radius to find the area of the circle.

$A_C = \pi r^2 = \pi(5)^2 = 25\pi$

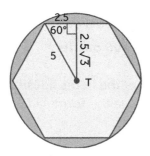

To find the area of the hexagon, draw a right triangle from the vertex, and use special right triangles to find the hexagon's apothem. Then, use the apothem to calculate the area.

$a = 2.5\sqrt{3}$

$A_H = \frac{ap}{2} = \frac{(2.5\sqrt{3})(30)}{2} = 64.95$

Subtract the area of the hexagon from the circle to find the area of the shaded region.

$= A_C - A_H$

$= 25\pi - 2.5\sqrt{3} \approx$ **13.59**

54. Write the equation for the area of the original sphere.

$SA_1 = 4\pi z^2$

Write the equation for the area of the new sphere.

$SA_2 = 4\pi(z + t)^2$

$= 4\pi(z^2 + 2zt + t^2)$

$= 4\pi z^2 + 8\pi zt + 4\pi t^2$

To find the difference between the two, subtract the original from the increased surface area:

$A_2 - A_1 = 4\pi z^2 + 8\pi zt + 4\pi t^2 - 4\pi z^2$

$= \mathbf{4\pi t^2 + 8\pi zt}$

55. Since the cube's volume is 27, each side length is equal to $\sqrt[3]{27}$ = 3. The long diagonal distance from one of the cube's vertices to its opposite vertex will provide the sphere's diameter:

$d = \sqrt{3^2 + 3^2 + 3^2} = \sqrt{27} = 5.2$

Half of this length is the radius, which is **2.6 meters**.

56. Use the equation to find the mean of a sample:

$\frac{1000 + 0.1 + 10 + 1}{4} = \mathbf{252.78}$

57. Since there are an even number of data points in the set, the median will be the mean of the two middle numbers. Order the numbers from least to greatest: 0.1, 1, 10, and 1000. The two middle numbers are 1 and 10, and their mean is:

$\frac{1 + 10}{2} = \mathbf{5.5}$

58. Even though Josey does not know her test scores, she knows her average. Therefore it can be assumed that each test score was 81, since four scores of 81 would average to 81. To find the score, x, that she needs use the equation for the mean of a sample:

$\frac{4(81) + x}{5} = 83$

$324 + x = 415$

$\mathbf{x = 91}$

59. Use the equation for range.

$R =$ largest point − smallest point = $169 - 3 = \mathbf{166}$

Place the terms in numerical order and identify Q1, Q2, and Q3.

3

9

→ Q1 = $\frac{49 + 9}{2}$ = 29

49

64

81 → Q2

100

121

→ Q3 = $\frac{121 + 144}{2}$ = 132.5

144

169

Find the IQR by subtracting Q1 from Q3.

IQR = Q3 − Q1 = 132.5 − 29 = **103.5**

60. Create a number line that begins at 1 and ends at 12. Q_1 is 3, the median (Q_2) is 5, and Q_3 is 8. A rectangle must be drawn whose length is 5 and that borders on Q_1 and Q_3. Mark the median of 5 within the rectangle. Draw a horizontal line going left to 1.

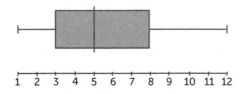

Draw a horizontal line going right to 12.

61.

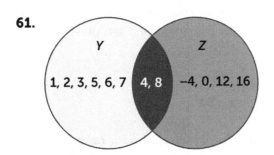

62. [A] $\overline{A}$ includes all elements of the universal set that are not in set A: $\overline{A}$ = {**−9, −8, −7, −6, −4, −3, −2, −1, 1, 2, 3, 4, 6, 7, 8, 9**}.

[B] $A \cup B$ is all elements in either A or B: $A \cup B$ = {**−10, −5, 0, 5, 10, −8, −6, −4, −2, 2, 4, 6, 8**}

[C] $A \cap B$ is all elements in both A and B: $A \cap B$ = {**−10, 0, 10**}

[D] $\overline{A} \cap \overline{B}$ is all the elements of the universal set that are not in either A or B: $\overline{A} \cap \overline{B}$ = {**−9, −7, −3, −1, 1, 3, 7, 9**}

63. Multiply the number of outcomes for each individual event:

(70)(2)(5) = **700 outfits**

64. The order of the items doesn't matter, so use the formula for combinations:

$C(n,r) = \frac{n!}{(n-r)!r!}$

$C(20,3) = \frac{20!}{(20-3)!3!}$

$= \frac{20!}{(17!\ 3!)} = \frac{(20)(19)(18)}{3!} = $ **1140 possible teams**

65. To find the number of unique permutations of 5 letters in pickle, use the permutation formula:

$P(n,r) = \frac{n!}{(n-r)!}$

$P(6,5) = \frac{6!}{(6-5)!}$

$= \frac{720}{1} = $ **720**

66. The letter *e* repeats 3 times in the word *cheese*, meaning some permutations of the 6 letters will be indistinguishable from others. The number of permutations must be divided by the number of ways the three *e*'s can be arranged to account for these redundant outcomes:

total number of permutations

$= \dfrac{\text{number of ways of arranging 6 letters}}{\text{number of ways of arranging 3 letters}}$

$= \dfrac{6!}{3!} = 6 \times 5 \times 4 = \textbf{120}$

67. P(rolling even) =

$\dfrac{\text{number of favorable outcomes}}{\text{total number of possible outcomes}} =$

$\dfrac{3}{2} = \dfrac{\textbf{1}}{\textbf{2}}$

P(*rolling 5*) = number of favorable outcomes/total number of possible outcomes = $\dfrac{\textbf{1}}{\textbf{6}}$

68. P(not winning) =

$\dfrac{\text{number of favorable outcomes}}{\text{total number of possible outcomes}} =$

$\dfrac{14}{20} = \dfrac{\textbf{7}}{\textbf{10}}$

or

P(not winning) = 1 − P(winning)

$= 1 - \dfrac{6}{20} = \dfrac{14}{20} = \dfrac{\textbf{7}}{\textbf{10}}$

69. P $= \dfrac{\text{number of favorable outcomes}}{\text{total number of possible outcomes}}$

$= \dfrac{\text{number of 3 consonant combinations}}{\text{number of 3-tile combinations}}$

$= \dfrac{_{21}C_3}{_{26}C_3}$

$= \dfrac{1330}{2600} = 0.511 = \textbf{51\%}$

70. This is a union (*or*) problem.

P(A) = the probability of drawing a queen = $\dfrac{1}{13}$

P(B) = the probability of drawing a heart = $\dfrac{1}{4}$

P(A ∩ B) = the probability of drawing a heart and a queen = $\dfrac{1}{52}$

P(A ∩ B) = P(A) + P(B) − P(A ∩ B)

$= \dfrac{1}{13} + \dfrac{1}{4} - \dfrac{1}{52} = \textbf{0.31}$

71. This scenario includes two events, *A* and *B*.

The probability of the first person drawing a long straw is an independent event:

$P(A) = \dfrac{28}{30}$

The probability the second person draws a long straw changes because one long straw has already been drawn. In other words, it is the probability of event *B* given that event *A* has already happened:

$P(B|A) = \dfrac{27}{29}$

The conditional probability formula can be used to determine the probability of both people drawing long straws:

P(A ∩ B) = P(A)P(B|A)

$= \left(\dfrac{28}{30}\right)\left(\dfrac{27}{29}\right) = 0.87$

There is an **87% chance** that neither of the first two individuals will draw short straws.

CHAPTER THREE
Advanced Algebra and Functions

Quadratic Equations

Quadratic equations are degree 2 polynomials; the highest power on the dependent variable is two. While linear functions are represented graphically as lines, the graph of a quadratic function is a **PARABOLA**. The graph of a parabola has three important components. The **VERTEX** is where the graph changes direction. In the parent graph $y = x^2$, the origin $(0, 0)$ is the vertex. The **AXIS OF SYMMETRY** is the vertical line that cuts the graph into two equal halves. The line of symmetry always passes through the vertex. On the parent graph, the y-axis is the axis of symmetry. The **ZEROS** or **ROOTS** of the quadratic are the x-intercepts of the graph.

FORMS of QUADRATIC EQUATIONS

Quadratic equations can be expressed in two forms:

- ► **STANDARD FORM:** $y = ax^2 + bx + c$
  - ▷ Axis of symmetry: $x = -\frac{b}{2a}$
  - ▷ Vertex: $(-\frac{b}{2a}, f(-\frac{b}{2a}))$
- ► **VERTEX FORM:** $y\ a(x - h)^2 + k$
  - ▷ Vertex: (h, k)
  - ▷ Axis of symmetry: $x = h$

In both equations, the sign of a determines which direction the parabola opens: if a is positive, then it opens upward; if a is negative, then it opens downward. The wideness or narrowness is also determined by a. If the absolute value of a is less than one (a proper fraction), then the parabola will get wider the closer

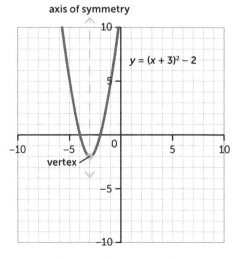

Figure 3.1. Parabola

$|a|$ is to zero. If the absolute value of a is greater than one, then the larger $|a|$ becomes, the narrower the parabola will be.

Equations in vertex form can be converted to standard form by squaring out the $(x - h)^2$ part (using FOIL), distributing the a, adding k, and simplifying the result.

Equations can be converted from standard form to vertex form by **COMPLETING THE SQUARE**. Take an equation in standard form, $y = ax^2 + bc + c$.

1. Move c to the left side of the equation.

2. Divide the entire equation through by a (to make the coefficient of x^2 be 1).

3. Take half of the coefficient of x, square that number, and then add the result to both sides of the equation.

4. Convert the right side of the equation to a perfect binomial squared, $(x + m)^2$.

5. Isolate y to put the equation in proper vertex form.

EXAMPLES

1. What is the line of symmetry for $y = -2(x + 3)^2 + 2$?

2. What is the vertex of the parabola $y = -3x^2 + 24x -27$?

3. Write $y = -3x^2 + 24x - 27$ in vertex form by completing the square.

SOLVING QUADRATIC EQUATIONS

Solving the quadratic equation $ax^2 + bx + c = 0$ finds x-intercepts of the parabola (by making $y = 0$). These are also called the **ROOTS** or **ZEROS** of the quadratic function. A quadratic equation may have zero, one, or two real solutions. There are several ways of finding the zeros. One way is to factor the quadratic into a product of two binomials, and then use the zero product property. (If $m \times n = 0$, then either $m = 0$ or $n = 0$.)

Another way is to complete the square and square root both sides. One way that works every time is to memorize and use the **QUADRATIC FORMULA**:

$$x = \frac{-b \pm \sqrt{b^2 - 4ac}}{2a}$$

The a, b, and c come from the standard form of quadratic equations above. (Note that to use the quadratic equation, the right-hand side of the equation must be equal to zero.)

The part of the formula under the square root radical $(b^2 - 4ac)$ is known as the **DISCRIMINANT**. The discriminant tells how many and what type of roots will result without actually calculating the roots.

Table 3.1. Discriminants

IF $B^2 - 4AC$ IS	THERE WILL BE	AND THE PARABOLA
zero	only 1 real root	has its vertex on the x-axis
positive	2 real roots	has two x-intercepts
negative	0 real roots 2 complex roots	has no x-intercepts

EXAMPLES

4. Find the zeros of the quadratic equation: $y = -(x + 3)^2 + 1$.

5. Find the root(s) for: $z^2 - 4z + 4 = 0$

6. Write a quadratic function that has zeros at $x = -3$ and $x = 2$ that passes through the point $(-2,8)$.

GRAPHING QUADRATIC EQUATIONS

The final expected quadratic skills are graphing a quadratic function given its equation and determining the equation of a quadratic function from its graph. The equation's form determines which quantities are easiest to obtain:

Table 3.2. Obtaining Quantities from Quadratic Functions

NAME OF FORM	EQUATION OF QUADRATIC	EASIEST QUANTITY TO FIND	HOW TO FIND OTHER QUANTITIES
vertex form	$y = a(x - h)^2 + k$	vertex at (h,k) and axis of symmetry $x = h$	Find zeros by making $y = 0$ and solving for x.
factored form	$y = a(x - m)(x - n)$	x – intercepts at $x = m$ and $x = n$	Find axis of symmetry by averaging m and n: $x = \frac{m + n}{2}$. This is also the x-value of the vertex.
standard form	$y = ax^2 + bx + c$	y–intercept at $(0,c)$	Find axis of symmetry and x-value of the vertex using $x = \frac{-b}{2a}$. Find zeros using quadratic formula.

To graph a quadratic function, first determine if the graph opens up or down by examining the *a*-value. Then determine the quantity that is easiest to find based on the form given, and find the vertex. Then other values can be found, if necessary, by choosing *x*-values and finding the corresponding *y*-values. Using symmetry instantly doubles the number of points that are known.

Given the graph of a parabola, the easiest way to write a quadratic equation is to identify the vertex and insert the *h*- and *k*-values into the vertex form of the equation. The *a*-value can be determined by finding another point the graph goes through, plugging these values in for *x* and *y*, and solving for *a*.

EXAMPLES

7. Graph the quadratic $y = 2(x - 3)^2 + 4$.

8. What is the vertex form of the equation shown on the following graph?

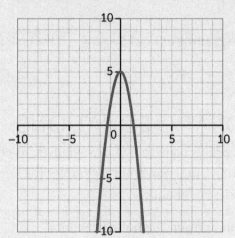

QUADRATIC INEQUALITIES

Quadratic inequalities with two variables, such as $y < (x + 3)^2 - 2$ can be graphed much like linear inequalities: graph the equation by treating the inequality symbol as an equal sign, then shade the graph. Shade above the graph when *y* is greater is than, and below the graph when *y* is less than.

Quadratic inequalities with only one variable, such as $x^2 - 4x > 12$, can be solved by first manipulating the inequality so that one side is zero. The zeros can then be found and used to determine where the inequality is greater than zero (positive) or less than zero (negative). Often it helps to set up intervals on a number line and test a value within each range created by the zeros to identify the values that create positive or negative values.

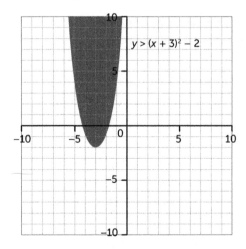

Figure 3.2. Quadratic Inequality

9. Find the values of x such that $x^2 - 4x > 12$.

Absolute Value Equations and Inequalities

The **ABSOLUTE VALUE** of a number means the distance between that number and zero. The absolute value of any number is positive since distance is always positive. The notation for absolute value of a number is two vertical bars:

$|-27| = 27$	The distance from –27 to 0 is 27.
$|27| = 27$	The distance from 27 to 0 is 27.

Solving equations and simplifying inequalities with absolute values usually requires writing two equations or inequalities, which are then solved separately using the usual methods of solving equations. To write the two equations, set one equation equal to the positive value of the expression inside the absolute value and the other equal to the negative value. Two inequalities can be written in the same manner. However, the inequality symbol should be flipped for the negative value. The formal definition of the absolute value is

$$|x| = \begin{cases} -x, & x < 0 \\ x, & x \geq 0 \end{cases}$$

This is true because whenever x is negative, the opposite of x is the answer (for example, $|-5| = -(-5) = 5$, but when x is positive, the answer is just x. This type of function is called a **PIECE-WISE FUNCTION**. It is defined in two (or more) distinct pieces. To graph the absolute value function, graph each piece separately. When $x < 0$ (that is, when it is negative), graph the line $y = -x$. When $x > 0$ (that is, when x is positive), graph the line $y = x$. This creates a V-shaped graph that is the parent function for absolute value functions.

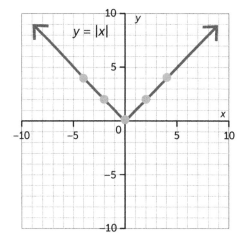

Figure 3.3. Absolute Value Parent Function

EXAMPLES

10. Solve for x: $|x - 3| = 27$

11. Solve for r: $\frac{|r - 7|}{5} = 27$

12. Find the solution set for the following inequality: $\left|\frac{3x}{7}\right| \geq 4 - x$.

Functions
WORKING with FUNCTIONS

Functions can be thought of as a process: when something is put in, an action (or operation) is performed, and something different comes out. A **FUNCTION** is a relationship between two quantities (for example x and y) in which, for every value of the independent variable (usually x), there is exactly one value of the dependent variable (usually y). Briefly, each input has *exactly one* output. Graphically this means the graph passes the **VERTICAL LINE TEST**: anywhere a vertical line is drawn on the graph, the line hits the curve at exactly one point.

The notation $f(x)$ or $g(t)$, etc., is often used when a function is being considered. This is **FUNCTION NOTATION**. The input value is x and the output value y is written as $y = f(x)$. Thus, $f(2)$ represents the output value (or y value) when $x = 2$, and $f(2) = 5$ means that when $x = 2$ is plugged into the $f(x)$ function, the output (y value) is 5. In other words, $f(2) = 5$ represents the point $(2, 5)$ on the graph of $f(x)$.

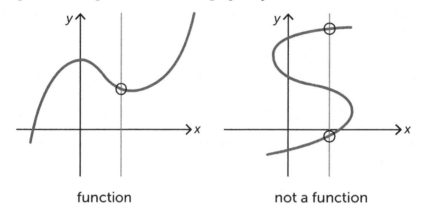

function   not a function

Figure 3.4. Vertical Line Test

Every function has an **INPUT DOMAIN** and **OUTPUT RANGE**. The domain is the set of all the possible x values that can be used as input values (these are found along the horizontal axis on the graph), and the range includes all the y values or output values that result from applying $f(x)$ (these are found along the vertical axis on the graph). Domain and range are usually intervals of numbers and are often expressed as inequalities, such as $x < 2$ (the domain is all values less than 2) or $3 < x < 15$ (all values between 3 and 15).

A function $f(x)$ is **EVEN** if $f(-x) = f(x)$. Even functions have symmetry across the y-axis. An example of an even function is the parent quadratic $y = x^2$, because any value of x (for example, 3) and its opposite $-x$ (for example, -3) have the same y value (for example, $3^2 = 9$ and $(-3)^2 = 9$). A function is **ODD** if $f(-x) = -f(x)$. Odd functions have symmetry about the origin. For example, $f(x) = x^3$ is an odd function because $f(3) = 27$, and $f(-3) = -27$. A function may be even, odd, or neither.

even

odd

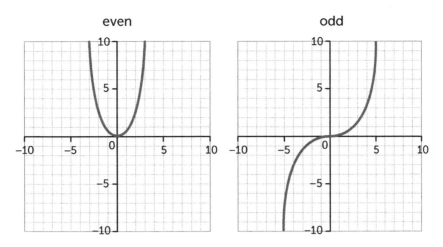

Figure 3.5. Even and Odd Functions

EXAMPLES

13. Evaluate: $f(4)$ if $f(x) = x^3 - 2x + \sqrt{x}$

14. What are the domain and range of the following function?

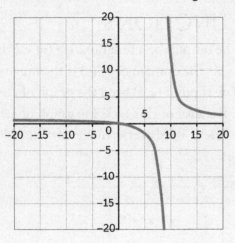

15. What is the domain and the range of the following graph?

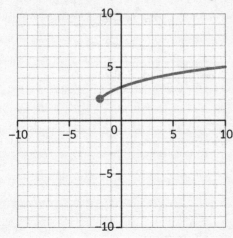

16. Which of the following represents a function?

A)

x	g(x)
0	0
1	1
2	2
1	3

B)

x	f(x)
0	1
0	2
0	3
0	4

C)

t	f(t)
1	1
2	2
3	3
4	4

D)

x	f(x)
0	0
5	1
0	2
5	3

INVERSE FUNCTIONS

INVERSE FUNCTIONS switch the inputs and the outputs of a function. If $f(x) = k$ then the inverse of that function would read $f^{-1}(k) = x$. The domain of $f^{-1}(x)$ is the range of $f(x)$, and the range of $f^{-1}(x)$ is the domain of $f(x)$. If point (a, b) is on the graph of $f(x)$, then point (b, a) will be on the graph of $f^{-1}(x)$. Because of this fact, the graph of $f^{-1}(x)$ is a reflection of the graph of $f(x)$ across the line $y = x$. Inverse functions "undo" all the operations of the original function.

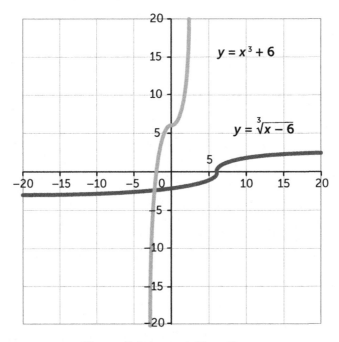

Figure 3.6. Inverse Functions

The steps for finding an inverse function are:

1. Replace $f(x)$ with y to make it easier manipulate the equation.

2. Switch the x and y.

3. Solve for y.

4. Label the inverse function as $f^{-1}(x) =$.

EXAMPLES

17. What is the inverse of function of $f(x) = 5x + 5$?

18. Find the inverse of the graph of $f(x) = -1 - \frac{1}{5}x$.

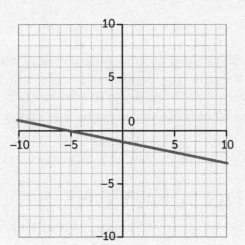

COMPOUND FUNCTIONS

COMPOUND FUNCTIONS take two or more functions and combine them using operations or composition. Functions can be combined using addition, subtraction, multiplication, or division:

▶ addition: $(f + g)(x) = f(x) + g(x)$

▶ subtraction: $(f - g)(x) = f(x) - g(x)$

▶ multiplication: $(fg)(x) = f(x)g(x)$

▶ division: $\left(\frac{f}{g}\right)(x) = \frac{f(x)}{g(x)}$ (note that $g(x) \neq 0$)

Functions can also be combined using **COMPOSITION**. Composition of functions is indicated by the notation $(f \circ g)(x)$. Note that the $\circ$ symbol does NOT mean multiply. It means take the output of $g(x)$ and make it the input of $f(x)$:

$$(f \circ g)(x) = f(g(x))$$

This equation is read f of g of x, and will be a new function of x. Note that order is important. In general, $f(g(x)) \neq g(f(x))$. They *will* be equal when $f(x)$ and $g(x)$ are inverses of each other, however, as both will simplify to the original input x. This is because performing a function on a value and then using that output as the input to the inverse function should bring you back to the original value.

The domain of a composition function is the set of x values that are in the domain of the "inside" function $g(x)$ such that $g(x)$ is in the domain of the outside function $f(x)$. For example, if $f(x) = \frac{1}{x}$ and $g(x) = \sqrt{x}$, $f(g(x))$ has a domain of $x > 0$ because $g(x)$ has a domain of $x \geq 0$. But when $f(x)$ is applied to the $\sqrt{x}$ function, the composition function becomes $\frac{1}{\sqrt{x}}$ and the value $x = 0$ is no longer allowed because it would result in 0 in the denominator, so the domain must be further restricted.

EXAMPLES

19. If $z(x) = 3x - 3$ and $y(x) = 2x - 1$, find $(y \circ z)(-4)$.

20. Find $(k \circ t)(x)$ if $k(x) = \frac{1}{2}x - 3$ and $t(x) = \frac{1}{2}x - 2$.

21. The wait (W) (in minutes) to get on a ride at an amusement park depends on the number of people (N) in the park. The number of people in the park depends on the number of hours, t, that the park has been open. Suppose $N(t) = 400t$ and $W(N) = 5(1.2)\frac{N}{100}$. What is the value and the meaning in context of $N(4)$ and $W(N(4))$?

TRANSFORMING FUNCTIONS

Many functions can be graphed using simple transformation of parent functions. Transformations include reflections across axes, vertical and horizontal translations (or shifts), and vertical or horizontal stretches or compressions. The table gives the effect of each transformation to the graph of any function $y = f(x)$.

Table 3.3. Effects of Transformations

EQUATION	EFFECT ON GRAPH
$y = -f(x)$	reflection across the x-axis (vertical reflection)
$y = f(x) + k$	vertical shift up k units ($k > 0$) or down k units ($k < 0$)
$y = kf(x)$	vertical stretch (if $k > 1$) or compression (if $k < 1$)
$y = f(-x)$	reflection across the y-axis (horizontal reflection)
$y = f(x + k)$	horizontal shift right k units ($k < 0$) or left k units ($k > 0$)
$y = f(kx)$	horizontal stretch ($k < 1$) or compression ($k > 1$)

Note that the first three equations have an operation applied to the *outside* of the function $f(x)$ and these all cause *vertical changes* to the graph of the function that are **INTUITIVE** (for example, adding a value moves it up). The last three equations have an operation applied to the *inside* of the function $f(x)$ and these all cause **HORIZONTAL CHANGES** to the graph of the function that are **COUNTERINTUITIVE** (for example, multiplying the x's by a fraction results in stretch, not compression, which would seem more intuitive). It is helpful to group these patterns together to remember how each transformation affects the graph.

EXAMPLES

22. Graph: $y = |x + 1| + 4$

23. Graph: $y = -3|x - 2| + 2$

Polynomial Functions

A polynomial is any equation or expression with two or more terms with whole number exponents. All polynomials with only one variable are functions. The zeros, or roots, of a polynomial function are where the function equals zero and crosses the x-axis.

A linear function is a degree 1 polynomial and always has one zero. A quadratic function is a degree 2 polynomial and always has exactly two roots (including complex roots and counting repeated roots separately). This pattern is extended in the **FUNDAMENTAL THEOREM OF ALGEBRA:**

DID YOU KNOW?

All polynomials where n is an odd number will have at least one real zero or root. Complex zeros always come in pairs (specifically, complex conjugate pairs).

A polynomial function with degree $n > 0$ such as $f(x) = ax^n + bx^{n-1} + cx^{n-2} + \ldots + k$, has exactly n (real or complex) roots (some roots may be repeated). Simply stated, whatever the degree of the polynomial is, that is how many roots it will have.

Table 3.4. Zeros of Polynomial Functions

POLYNOMIAL DEGREE, N	NUMBER AND POSSIBLE TYPES OF ZEROS
1	1 real zero (guaranteed)
2	0, 1, or 2 real zeros possible 2 real *or* complex zeros (guaranteed)
3	1, 2, or 3 real zeros possible (there must be at least one real zero) Or 1 real zero (guaranteed) and 2 complex zeros (guaranteed)
4	0, 1, 2, 3, or 4 real zeros (possible) Or 2 real zeros and 2 complex zeros or 4 complex zeros
...	...

All the zeros of a polynomial satisfy the equation $f(x) = 0$. That is, if k is a zero of a polynomial, then plugging in $x = k$ into the polynomial results in 0. This also means that the polynomial is evenly divisible by the factor $(x - k)$.

EXAMPLE

24. Find the roots of the polynomial: $y = 3t^4 - 48$

Rational Functions

WORKING with RATIONAL FUNCTIONS

Rational functions are ratios of polynomial functions in the form $f(x) = \frac{g(x)}{h(x)}$. Just like rational numbers, rational functions form a closed system under addition, subtraction, multiplication, and division by a nonzero rational expression. This means adding two rational functions, for example, results in another rational function.

To add or subtract rational expressions, the least common denominator of the factors in the denominator must be found. Then, numerators are added, just like adding rational numbers. To multiply rational expressions, factors can be multiplied straight across, canceling factors that appear in the numerator and denominator. To divide rational functions, use the "invert and multiply" rule.

Rational equations are solved by multiplying through the equation by the least common denominator of factors in the denominator. Just like with radical equations, this process can result in extraneous solutions, so all answers need to be checked by plugging them into the original equation.

EXAMPLES

25. If $f(x) = \frac{2}{3x^2y}$ and $g(x) = \frac{5}{21y}$, find the difference between the functions, $f(x) - g(x)$.

26. If $f(x) = \frac{(x-1)(x+2)^2}{5x^2 + 10x}$ and $g(x) = \frac{x^2 + x - 2}{x + 5}$, find the quotient $\frac{f(x)}{g(x)}$.

27. Solve the rational equation $\frac{x}{x+2} + \frac{2}{x^2 + 5x + 6} = \frac{5}{x+3}$.

GRAPHING RATIONAL FUNCTIONS

Rational functions are graphed by examining the function to find key features of the graph, including asymptotes, intercepts, and holes.

A **vertical asymptote** exists at any value that makes the denominator of a (simplified) rational function equal zero. A vertical asymptote is a vertical line through an x value that is not in the domain of the rational function (the function is undefined at this value because division by 0 is not allowed). The function approaches, but never crosses, this line, and the y values increase (or decrease) without bound (or "go to infinity") as this x value is approached.

To find x-intercepts and vertical asymptotes, factor the numerator and denominator of the function. Cancel any terms that appear in the numerator and denominator (if there are any). These values will appear as **holes** on the final graph. Since a fraction only equals 0 when its numerator is 0, set the simplified numerator equal to 0 and solve to find the x-intercepts. Next, set the denominator equal to 0 and solve to find the vertical asymptotes.

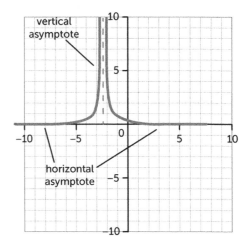

Figure 3.7. Graphing Rational Functions

Horizontal asymptotes are horizontal lines that describe the "end behavior" of a rational function. In other words, the horizontal asymptote describes what happens to the y-values of the function as the x-values get very large ($x \rightarrow \infty$) or very small ($x \rightarrow -\infty$). A horizontal asymptote occurs if the degree of the numerator of a rational function is less than or equal to the degree in the denominator. The table summarizes the conditions for horizontal asymptotes:

Table 3.5. Conditions for Horizontal Asymptotes		
For polynomials with first terms $\frac{ax^n}{bx^d}$ ...		
$n < d$	as $x \rightarrow \infty, y \rightarrow 0$ as $x \rightarrow -\infty, y \rightarrow 0$	The x-axis ($y = 0$) is a horizontal asymptote.
$n = d$	as $x \rightarrow \pm\infty, y \rightarrow \frac{a}{b}$	There is a horizontal asymptote at $y = \frac{a}{b}$.
$n > d$	as $x \rightarrow \infty, y \rightarrow \infty$ or $-\infty$ as $x \rightarrow -\infty, y \rightarrow \infty$ or $-\infty$	There is no horizontal asymptote.

EXAMPLES

28. Create a function that has an x-intercept at (5, 0) and vertical asymptotes at $x = 1$ and $x = -1$.

29. Graph the function: $f(x) = \frac{3x^2 - 12x}{x^2 - 2x - 3}$.

Radical Functions

RADICAL FUNCTIONS have rational (fractional) exponents, or include the radical symbol. For example, $f(x) = 2(x - 5)^{\frac{1}{3}}$ and $g(t) = \sqrt[4]{5 - x}$ are radical functions. The domain of even root parent functions is $0 \leq x \leq \infty$ and the range is $y \geq 0$. For odd root parent functions, the domain is all real numbers (because you can take cube roots, etc., of negative numbers). The range is also all real numbers.

To solve equations involving radical functions, first isolate the radical part of the expression. Then "undo" the fractional exponent by raising both sides to the reciprocal of the fractional exponent (for example, undo square roots by squaring both sides). Then solve the equation using inverse operations, as always. All answers should be checked by plugging them back into the original equation, as EXTRANEOUS SOLUTIONS result when an equation is raised to powers on both sides. This means there may be some answers that are not actually solutions, and should be eliminated.

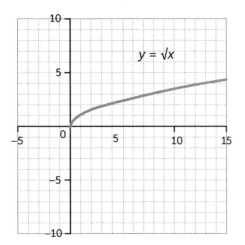

Figure 3.8. Radical Parent Function

EXAMPLES

30. Solve the equation: $\sqrt{2x - 5} + 4 = x$

31. Solve the equation: $2(x^2 - 7x)^{\frac{2}{3}} = 8$

Exponential and Logarithmic Functions

EXPONENTIAL FUNCTIONS

An EXPONENTIAL FUNCTION has a constant base and a variable in the exponent: $f(x) = b^x$ is an exponential function with base b and exponent x. The value b is the quantity that the y value is multiplied by each time the x value is increased by 1. When looking at a table of values, an exponential function can be identified because the $f(x)$ values are being multiplied. (In contrast, linear $f(x)$ values are being added to.)

The graph of the exponential parent function does not cross the x-axis, which is the function's horizontal asymptote. The y-intercept of the function is at $(0, 1)$.

DID YOU KNOW?

To solve an exponential equation, start by looking for a common base:
$$4^{(x - 2)} = \sqrt{8}$$
can be rewritten as
$$(2^2)^{(x - 2)} = (2^3)^{\frac{1}{2}}$$
If no common base can be found, logarithms can be used to move the variable out of the exponent position.

The general formula for an exponential function, $f(x) = ab^{(x-h)} + k$, allows for transformations to be made to the function. The value h moves the function left or right (moving the y-intercept) while the value k moves the function up or down (moving both the y-intercept and the horizontal asymptote). The value a stretches or compresses the function (moving the y-intercept).

Exponential equations have at least one variable in an exponent position. One way to solve these equations is to make the bases on both side of the equation equivalent, and then equate the exponents. Many exponential equations do not have a solution. Negative numbers often lead to no solutions: for example, $2^x = -8$. The domain of exponential functions is only positive numbers, as seen above, so there is no x value that will result in a negative output.

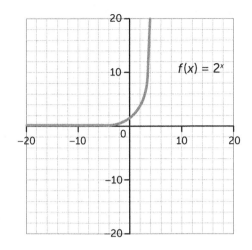

Figure 3.9. Exponential Parent Function

EXAMPLES

32. Graph the exponential function $f(x) = 5^x - 2$.

33. If the height of grass in a yard in a humid summer week grows by 5% every day, how much taller would the grass be after six days?

34. Solve for x: $4^{x+1} = \frac{1}{256}$

LOGARITHMIC FUNCTIONS

The **LOGARITHMIC FUNCTION (LOG)** is the inverse of the exponential function.

A log is used to find out to what power an input is raised to get a desired output. In the table, the base is 3. The log function determines to what power 3 must be raised so that $\frac{1}{9}$ is the result in the table (the answer is –2). As with all inverse functions, these exponential and logarithmic functions are reflections of each other across the line $y = x$.

A **NATURAL LOGARITHM (LN)** has the number e as its base. Like π, e is an irrational number that is a nonterminating decimal. It is usually shortened to 2.71 when doing calculations. Although the proof of e is beyond the scope of this book, e is to be understood as the upper limit of the range of this rational function: $\left(1 + \frac{1}{n}\right)^n$.

$$y = \log_3 x \Rightarrow 3^y = x$$

x	y
$\frac{1}{9}$	–2
$\frac{1}{3}$	–1
1	0
3	1
9	2
27	3

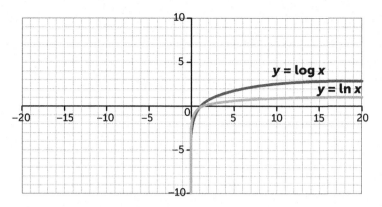

Figure 3.10. Logarithmic Parent Functions

In order to make use of and solve logarithmic functions, log rules are often employed that allow simplification:

Table 3.6. Properties of Logarithms	
Change of base	$\log_b(m) = \dfrac{\log(m)}{\log(b)}$
Logs of products	$\log_b(mn) = \log_b(m) + \log_b(n)$
Logs of quotients	$\log_b\left(\dfrac{m}{n}\right) = \log_b(m) - \log_b(n)$
Log of a power	$\log_b(m^n) = n \times \log_b(m)$
Equal logs/equal arguments	$\log_b M = \log_b N \Leftrightarrow M = N$

Note that when the base is not written out, such as in $\log(m)$, it is understood that the base is 10. Just like a 1 is not put in front of a variable because its presence is implicitly understood, 10 is the implicit base whenever a base is not written out.

EXAMPLES

35. Expand $\log_5\left(\dfrac{25}{x}\right)$

36. Solve for x: $\ln x + \ln 4 = 2\ln 4 - \ln 2$

37. Solve for x: $2^x = 40$

SPECIAL EQUATIONS

There are three exponential function formulas that frequently show up in word problems:

> **THE GROWTH FORMULA:** $y = a(1 + r)^t$
> Initial amount a increases at a rate of r per time period

> **THE DECAY FORMULA:** $y = a(1 - r)^t$
> Initial amount a decreases at a rate of r per time period

In these formulas, a is the initial amount (at time $t = 0$), r is the rate of growth or decay (written as a decimal in the formula), and t is the number of growth or decay cycles that have passed.

A special case of the growth function is known as:

> **THE COMPOUND-INTEREST FORMULA:** $A = P\left(1 + \frac{r}{n}\right)^{nt}$

In this formula, A is the future value of an investment, P is the initial deposit (or principal), r is the interest rate as a percentage, n is the number of times interest is compounded within a time period, or how often interest is applied to the account in a year (once per year, $n = 1$; monthly, $n = 12$; etc.), and t is the number of compounding cycles (usually years).

EXAMPLES

38. In the year 2000, the number of text messages sent in a small town was 120. If the number of text messages grew every year afterward by 124%, how many years would it take for the number of text messages to surpass 36,000?

39. The half-life of a certain isotope is 5.5 years. If there were 20 grams of one such isotope left after 22 years, what was its original weight?

40. If there were a glitch at a bank and a savings account accrued 5% interest five times per week, what would be the amount earned on a $50 deposit after twelve weeks?

Trigonometry

Trigonometry comes from the Greek words for *triangle* and *measuring*. Appropriately enough, trigonometry is used to find missing angles or side lengths in a triangle. Trigonometric questions often require use of algebraic skills with geometric concepts.

THE SIX TRIGONOMETRIC FUNCTIONS

There are six different trigonometric functions that are the foundations of trigonometry. They can be thought of as three pairs, as

DID YOU KNOW?
SOHCAHTOA, or Some Old Horse Caught Another Horse Taking Oats Away, is a way to remember that Sine is Opposite over Hypotenuse, Cosine is Adjacent over Hypotenuse, and Tangent is Opposite over Adjacent.

they are reciprocals of one another. All of these functions are ratios of the side lengths of a right triangle. The longest side of a right triangle (opposite the 90-degree angle) is called the **HYPOTENUSE**. The side directly opposite the angle being used is the **OPPOSITE**, and the side next to the angle is called the **ADJACENT** side.

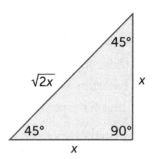

There are a couple of special triangles that are used frequently and whose properties are worth memorizing. They are the 30° – 60° – 90° and the 45° – 45° – 90° triangles.

For the 30° – 60° – 90° triangle, the side opposite the 30° angle (the shortest side) is always half the hypotenuse length, and the medium side (opposite the 60° angle) is $\sqrt{3}$ times the shortest side.

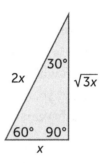

For the 45° – 45° – 90° triangle, two legs have the same length since two angles are equal (the triangle is isosceles), and the hypotenuse is always $\sqrt{2}$ times the length of a leg.

Figure 3.11. Special Right Triangles

Table 3.7. The Six Trigonometric Functions		
Sine Function $\sin\theta = \dfrac{\text{opposite}}{\text{hypotenuse}}$	Cosine Function $\cos\theta = \dfrac{\text{adjacent}}{\text{hypotenuse}}$	Tangent Function $\tan\theta = \dfrac{\text{opposite}}{\text{adjacent}}$
Cosecant Function $\csc\theta = \dfrac{\text{hypotenuse}}{\text{opposite}}$	Secant Function $\sec\theta = \dfrac{\text{hypotenuse}}{\text{adjacent}}$	Cotangent Function $\cot\theta = \dfrac{\text{adjacent}}{\text{opposite}}$

EXAMPLES

41. Find all six trigonometric ratios for θ in the following triangle:

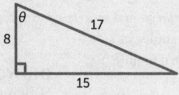

42. Find the missing length:

43. Find the angle θ in degrees:

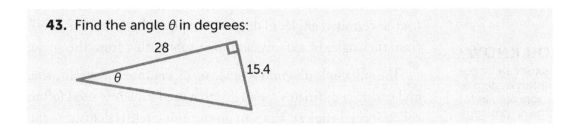

THE UNIT CIRCLE

The **UNIT CIRCLE** is on the coordinate plane, with its center at the origin $(0, 0)$ and a radius of 1. By using triangles within the unit circle (which will all have a hypotenuse of 1), the trigonometric ratios can be extended so that trigonometric functions of *any* angle may be evaluated. In fact, each point (x, y) on the unit circle can be expressed as trig functions of the angle θ: $(x, y) = (\cos\theta, \sin\theta)$.

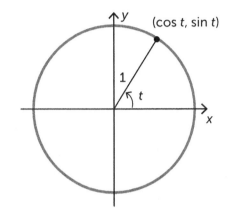

An angle in **STANDARD POSITION** in the plane has an initial (beginning) ray on the x-axis and a terminal (end) ray on the radius of the circle. Positive angles are measured in the counterclockwise direction, and negative angles are measured clockwise from the x-axis. One complete circle contains $360°$.

Another way to measure angles is with radians, which involves finding the length of the arc on the circle intercepted by the terminal ray of the angle. Since the circumference of the circle is $C = 2\pi r = 2\pi(1) = 2\pi$, the angle corresponding to one complete circle ($360°$) has a radian measure of 2π. Other angles can be expressed as fractions of 2π. For example, $90°$ is $\frac{1}{4}$ of a circle, so its radian measure is $\frac{1}{4}(2\pi) = \frac{\pi}{2}$. A $30°$ angle would be $\frac{30}{360}(2\pi)$ or $\frac{\pi}{6}$ radians. When the angle intersects the circle such that the arc length is 1, the corresponding angle is 1 radian. The angle in degrees at which this occurs is about $57.3°$, so 1 radian $\approx 57.3°$.

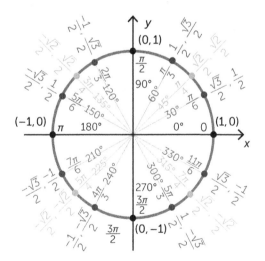

Figure 3.12. Unit Circle

Angles can be converted between degrees and radians using these conversion factors:

$$\text{degrees} = \text{radians} \times \frac{180}{\pi} \qquad \text{radians} = \text{degrees} \times \frac{\pi}{180}$$

Any angle has an infinite number of **COTERMINAL ANGLES** associated with it. These are angles that share the same terminal ray. For example, $390°$ is coterminal with $30°$, because $390°$ is one complete revolution around the circle plus $30°$ more, so it lands on the same terminal ray. Another co-terminal angle to this angle would be $-330°$. To find co-terminal angles in degrees, simply add to or subtract 360° from the angle. In radians, add to or subtract 2π from the angle.

DID YOU KNOW?

A calculator can be put in either radian or degree mode as appropriate for the given problem.

The unit circle diagram is made up of a number of specific sine and cosine coordinates for angles that are frequently used (often called special angles). Tangent on the unit circle is defined as the ratio of sine to cosine, $\tan\theta = \frac{\sin\theta}{\cos\theta}$.

Table 3.8. Special Angle Values in the First Quadrant

Degrees	**0**	**30**	**45**	**60**	**90**
Radians	**0**	$\frac{\pi}{6}$	$\frac{\pi}{4}$	$\frac{\pi}{3}$	$\frac{\pi}{2}$
$\sin\theta$	0	$\frac{1}{2}$	$\frac{\sqrt{2}}{2}$	$\frac{\sqrt{3}}{2}$	1
$\cos\theta$	1	$\frac{\sqrt{3}}{2}$	$\frac{\sqrt{2}}{2}$	$\frac{1}{2}$	0
$\tan\theta$	0	$\frac{\sqrt{3}}{3}$	1	$\sqrt{3}$	undefined

When calculating trig functions of angles in other quadrants, make a sketch of the angle and drop a perpendicular altitude down to the nearest x-axis. This forms a triangle. The angle between the x-axis and the terminal ray is called the **REFERENCE ANGLE.** It will always be an angle between 0 and $\frac{\pi}{2}$ (or 0 and 90°). If it is one of the special angles, either label the sides of the triangles using the special triangle rules, or use the table above to find the value. In either case, care must be given to the *sign* of the value. As the terminal ray travels into quadrants 2, 3, and 4, the signs of the x- and y-coordinates are sometimes negative, so the corresponding trig functions will also be negative. This diagram summarizes where each trig function is *positive* (where it is not positive, it is negative!).

DID YOU KNOW?

To remember in which quadrant each trig function is positive, starting in quad 1, remember **ASTC**, or **A**ll **S**tudents **T**hrow **C**halk: A = all, S = sine, T = tangent, and C = cosine.

Q 2 $\sin\theta$ and $\csc\theta$ +	Q 1 ALL trig functions +
Q 3 $\tan\theta$ and $\cot\theta$ +	Q 4 $\cos\theta$ and $\sec\theta$ +

Figure 3.13. Trigonometric Signs by Quadrant

EXAMPLES

44. Find $\sin\frac{\pi}{2}$.

45. Find $\csc(\frac{7\pi}{4})$.

GRAPHING TRIGONOMETRIC FUNCTIONS

Each trigonometric function can be graphed as a function of the angle θ. The graph of $\sin\theta$ can be understood by considering the height of the altitude of the right triangle (the y value) in the unit circle at different values of θ. Consider what happens to the y values as θ increases as it goes around the circle from 0 to 2π: $\sin\theta$ begins at 0, because there is no height when the angle is 0; then the height increases to a maximum value of 1 as θ increases to $\frac{\pi}{2}$. Then it decreases back to 0 at $\theta = \pi$, and so on. Similarly, the x-values associated with the triangle within the unit circle begin at 1 and vary between 1 and –1, which traces out the $\cos\theta$ curve. Both the sine and cosine functions trace out waves and are called **SINUSOIDAL** graphs/functions.

Except sine and cosine, what defines all these graphs are the many asymptotes. These occur when the ratios that make up the trigonometric functions have a zero in the denominator. For example, since $\csc\theta = \frac{1}{\sin\theta}$, whenever $\sin\theta$ is equal to zero, $\csc\theta$ has an asymptote at $\theta = 0$.

Note that all of the trigonometric functions are **PERIODIC**. This means they repeat at regular intervals called the **PERIOD**. The period of the functions $y = \sin\theta$, $\cos\theta$, $\csc\theta$, and $\sec\theta$ is 2π. (This is because each revolution around the unit circle traces out one complete cycle of the graph.) The functions $y = \tan\theta$ and $\cot\theta$ both have a period of π.

The transformations learned in this chapter can be applied to these new trigonometric parent functions. There is some specialized vocabulary associated with these functions, however. Consider the function $y = a\sin(b(x + c)) + d$ (sin could be replaced

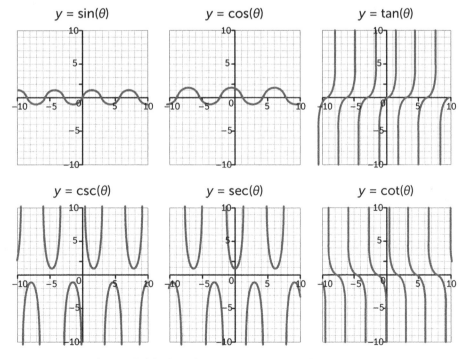

Figure 3.14. Graphs of Trigonometric Functions

with cos). For sine and cosine, the MIDLINE of the graph is the value of the vertical shift (*d*). It is the horizontal line through the middle of the wave. The AMPLITUDE of the wave is the vertical stretch or compression value ($|a|$). It gives the distance the graph reaches above and below the midline (amplitude is always positive). As always, if the *a* is negative, the graph will be reflected across the *x*-axis. The horizontal shift is sometimes called the PHASE SHIFT in sinusoidal functions (*c*).

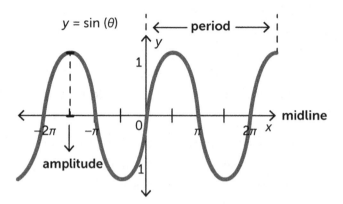

Figure 3.15. Parts of a Trigonometric Graph

Finally, the horizontal stretch or compression value (*b*) causes a period change in the function. For sine and cosine, the normal period of the function is 2π, so when there is a *b*-value other than 1, the new period is period = $\frac{2\pi}{b}$. The value *b* is also called the FREQUENCY since it gives the number of complete cycles that occur over the interval $[0, 2\pi]$. For tangent, the normal period is π, so the transformed period is $\frac{\pi}{b}$.

EXAMPLE

46. Graph: $f(x) = -3\cos(2x - 6\pi) + 1$

NON-RIGHT TRIANGLES

Trigonometry is usually associated with right triangles. However, trigonometric functions can be used to solve for a missing side or angle in an oblique triangle (a triangle without any 90° angles). To solve an oblique triangle, either two sides and one angle, two angles and any one side, or all three sides must be known.

THE LAW OF SINES is based on the proportionality between the sine of angles in a triangle and the sides of the triangle. It states, based on a triangle *ABC* with angles *A*, *B*, and *C* and corresponding sides *a*, *b*, *c* (*a* is the side opposite angle *A*, etc.):

$$\frac{a}{\sin A} = \frac{b}{\sin B} = \frac{c}{\sin C}$$

While all three proportionalities always hold, in practice only two of the three ratios are used at one time.

THE LAW OF COSINES can be used when three sides are known, or when two sides and the included angle between those two sides are known. The law of cosines is based on Pythagorean identities:

$$c^2 = a^2 + b^2 - 2ab\cos(C)$$
$$b^2 = a^2 + c^2 - 2ac\cos(B)$$
$$a^2 = b^2 + c^2 - 2bc\cos(A)$$

EXAMPLES

47. Find the degree measure of C in the following triangle, where $c = 12$, $b = 7$, and $a = 8$.

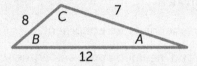

48. If there is a triangle where $a = 110$, $c = 40$, and the measure of angle $A = 110°$, what is the measure of angle C?

Equality, Congruence, and Similarity

When discussing shapes in geometry, the term **CONGRUENT** is used to mean that two shapes have the same shape and size (but not necessarily the same orientation or location). This concept is slightly different from equality, which is used in geometry to describe numerical values. For example, if the length of two lines are equal, the two lines themselves are called congruent. Congruence is written using the symbol $\cong$. On figures, congruent parts are denoted with hash marks.

Shapes which are **SIMILAR** have the same shape but the not the same size, meaning their corresponding angles are the same but their lengths are not. For two shapes to be similar, the ratio of their corresponding sides must be a constant (usually written as k). Similarity is described using the symbol ~.

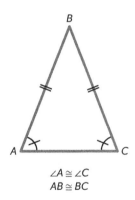

$\angle A \cong \angle C$
$AB \cong BC$

Figure 3.16. Congruent Parts of a Triangle

CONGRUENCE and SIMILARITY in TRIANGLES

Congruence and similarity in triangles is governed by a set of theorems that make it easy to determine the relationship

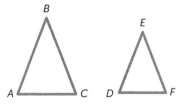

$ABC \sim DEF$
$\dfrac{AB}{DE} = \dfrac{BC}{EF} = \dfrac{AC}{DF}$

Figure 3.17. Similar Triangles

between two triangles. These theorems can be used by looking at the number and location of congruent sides and angles shared by the triangles.

Table 3.9. Triangle Congruence	
TRIANGLES ARE CONGRUENT IF...	
SSS	all three corresponding sides are congruent.
SAS	two sides and the included angle are congruent.
AAS	two angles and one side are congruent.
ASA	two angles and the included side are congruent.
TRIANGLES ARE SIMILAR IF...	
AA	two angles (and thus the third) are congruent.
SAS	two sides are proportional and included angle is congruent.
SSS	the ratio between all three corresponding sides is constant.

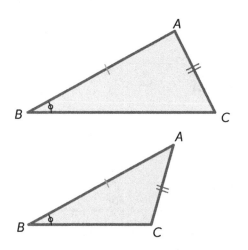

Figure 3.18. Two Possible Triangles Formed from Two Sides and One Non-Included Angle

A note of caution about the SSA case (also known as the ASS case): Two triangles that have congruent (or proportional) sides and one congruent (but not included) angle are NOT necessarily congruent (or similar). This is because, given two side lengths and a nonincluded angle, it is often possible to draw an acute triangle and an obtuse triangle. Thus, there is NOT an SSA congruence theorem.

Right triangles, in general, have a couple of simpler similarity and congruence theorems. Since any pair of right triangles already has one angle that is the same (the right angle), any two pairs of corresponding sides that are either congruent or proportional will guarantee congruence or similarity between the triangles, respectively.

Table 3.10. Right Triangle Congruence	
RIGHT TRIANGLES ARE CONGRUENT IF...	
HL	the hypotenuse and one leg are congruent.
LL	the two pairs of corresponding legs are congruent.
RIGHT TRIANGLES ARE SIMILAR IF...	
HL	the hypotenuse and one leg are proportional.
LL	two pairs of corresponding legs are similar.

49. Determine whether the following sets of triangles are congruent. If they are, state why.

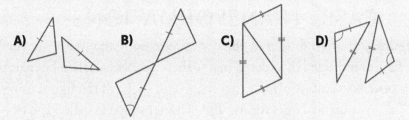

50. If △ABC ~ △DEF, what is the length of $\overline{DE}$?

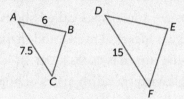

CONGRUENCE and SIMILARITY in THREE-DIMENSIONAL SHAPES

Three-dimensional shapes may also be congruent if they are the same size and shape, or similar if their corresponding parts are proportional. For example, a pair of cones is similar if the ratios of the cones' radii and heights are proportional. For rectangular prisms, all three dimensions must be proportional for the prisms to be similar. If two shapes are similar, their corresponding areas and volumes will also be proportional. If the constant of proportionality of the linear measurements of a 3D shape is k, the constant of proportionality between the areas will be k^2, and the constant of proportionality between the volumes will be k^3.

All spheres are similar as a dilation of the radius of a sphere will make it equivalent to any other sphere.

EXAMPLES

51. A square-based pyramid has a height of 10 cm. If the length of the side of the square is 6 cm, what is the surface area of the pyramid?

52. Given that two cones are similar and one cone's radius is three times longer than the other's radius, what is the volume of the smaller cone if the larger cone has a volume of 81π cubic inches and a height of 3 inches?

Transformations of Geometric Figures

BASIC TRANSFORMATIONS

Geometric figures are often drawn in the coordinate xy-plane, with the vertices or centers of the figures indicated by ordered pairs. These shapes can then be manipulated by performing **TRANSFORMATIONS**, which alter the size or shape of the figure using mathematical operations. The original shape is called the **PRE-IMAGE**, and the shape after a transformation is applied is called the **IMAGE**.

A **TRANSLATION** transforms a shape by moving it right or left, or up or down. Translations are sometimes called slides. After this transformation, the image is identical in size and shape to the pre-image. In other words, the image is **CONGRUENT**, or identical in size, to the pre-image. All corresponding pairs of angles are congruent, and all corresponding side lengths are congruent.

Translations are often in brackets: (x, y). The first number represents the change in the x direction (left/right), while the second number shows the change in the y direction (up/down).

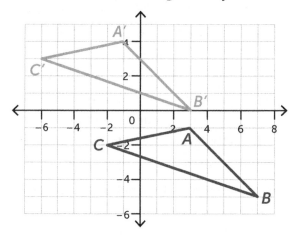

The translation moved triangle ABC left 4 units and up 6 units to produce triangle $A'B'C'$.

Figure 3.19. Translation

Similarly, rotations and reflections preserve the size and shape of the figure, so congruency is preserved. A **ROTATION** takes a pre-image and rotates it about a fixed point (often the origin) in the plane. Although the position or orientation of the shape changes, the angles and side lengths remain the same.

A **REFLECTION** takes each point in the pre-image and flips it over a point or line in the plane (often the x- or y-axis, but not necessarily). The image is congruent to the pre-image. When a figure is flipped across the y-axis, the signs of all x-coordinates will change. The y-coordinates change sign when a figure is reflected across the x-axis.

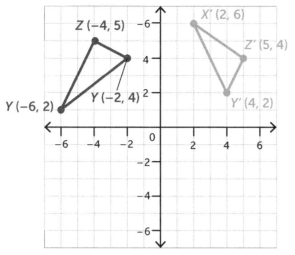

The triangle *XYZ* is rotated 90 in the clockwise direction about the origin (0, 0).

Figure 3.20. Rotation

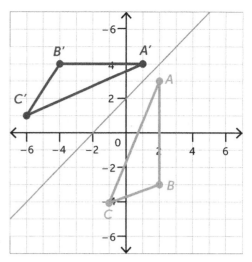

The triangle *ABC* is reflected over the line to produce the triangle *A'B'C'*.

Figure 3.21. Reflection

EXAMPLE

53. If quadrilateral *ABCD* has vertices *A* (−6, 4), *B* (−6, 8), *C* (2, 8), and *D* (4, −4), what are the new vertices if *ABCD* is translated 2 units down and 3 units right?

DILATIONS and SIMILARITY

A **DILATION** increases (or decreases) the size of a figure by some **SCALE FACTOR**. Each coordinate of the points that make up the figure is multiplied by the same factor. If the factor is greater than 1, multiplying all the factors enlarges the shape; if the factor is less than 1 (but greater than 0), the shape is reduced in size.

In addition to the scale factor, a dilation needs a **CENTER OF DILATION**, which is a fixed point in the plane about which the points are multiplied. Usually, but not always, the center of dilation is the origin (0, 0). For dilations about the origin, the image coordinates are calculated by multiplying each coordinate by the scale factor k. Thus, point $(x, y) \rightarrow (kx, ky)$. Although dilations do not result in congruent figures, the orientation of the figure is preserved; consequently, corresponding line segments will be parallel.

DID YOU KNOW?

If two shapes are similar, their angle measurements will be equal and the ratio of equivalent sides will be the value k.

Importantly, dilations do NOT create images that are congruent to the original because the size of each dimension is increased or decreased (the only exception being if the scale factor is exactly 1). However, the shape of the figure is maintained. The corresponding angle measures will be congruent, but the corresponding side lengths will be *proportional*. In other words, the image and pre-image will be **SIMILAR** shapes (described with the symbol ~).

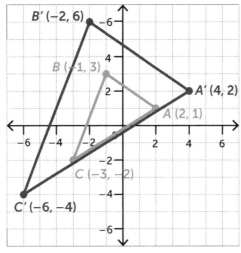

The triangle *ABC* is dilated by the scale factor 2 to produce triangle *A'B'C'*.

Figure 3.22. Dilation

EXAMPLE

54. If quadrilateral *ABCD* has vertices *A* (–6,4), *B* (–6,8), *C* (2,8), and *D* (4,–4), what are the new vertices if *ABCD* is increased by a factor of 5 about the origin?

TRANSFORMING COORDINATES

Transformations in a plane can actually be thought of as functions. An input pair of coordinates, when acted upon by a transformation, results in a pair of output coordinates. Each point is moved to a unique new point (a one-to-one correspondence).

Table 3.11. How Coordinates Change for Transformations in a Plane	
TYPE OF TRANSFORMATION	COORDINATE CHANGES
Translation right *m* units and up *n* units	$(x,y) \rightarrow (x + m, y + n)$
Rotations about the origin in positive (counterclockwise) direction	
Rotation 90°	$(x,y) \rightarrow (-y,x)$
Rotation 180°	$(x,y) \rightarrow (-x,-y)$
Rotation 270°	$(x,y) \rightarrow (y,-x)$
Reflections about the	
***x*-axis**	$(x,y) \rightarrow (x,-y)$
***y*-axis**	$(x,y) \rightarrow (-x,y)$
line ***y = x***	$(x,y) \rightarrow (y,x)$

Type of Transformation	Coordinate Changes
Dilations about the origin by a factor of k $0 < k < 1 \rightarrow$ **size reduced** $k > 1 \rightarrow$ **size enlarged**	$(x,y) \rightarrow (kx,ky)$

EXAMPLES

55. Triangle *ABC* with coordinates (2,8), (10,2), and (6,8) is transformed in the plane as shown in the diagram. What transformations result in the image triangle *A'B'C'*?

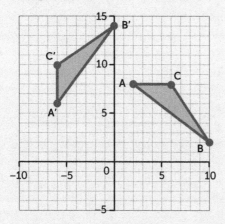

56. If quadrilateral *ABCD* has vertices *A* (−6,4), *B* (−6,8), *C* (2,8), and *D* (4,−4), what are the new vertices if *ABCD* is rotated 270° and then reflected across the *x*-axis?

Answer Key

1. This quadratic is given in vertex form, with $h = -3$ and $k = 2$. The vertex of this equation is $(-3, 2)$. The line of symmetry is the vertical line that passes through this point. Since the x-value of the point is -3, the line of symmetry is **$x = -3$**.

2. $y = -3x^2 + 24x - 27$

This quadratic equation is in standard form. Use the formula for finding the x-value of the vertex.

$x = -\dfrac{b}{2a}$ where $a = -3$, $b = 24$

$x = -\dfrac{24}{2(-3)} = 4$

Plug $x = 4$ into the original equation to find the corresponding y-value.

$y = -3(4)^2 + 24(4) - 27 = 21$

The vertex is at **$(4, 21)$**.

3. $y = -3x^2 + 24x - 27$

Move c to the other side of the equation.

$y + 27 = -3x^2 + 24x$

Divide through by a (-3 in this example).

$\dfrac{y}{-3} - 9 = x^2 - 8x$

Take half of the new b, square it, and add that quantity to both sides: $\frac{1}{2}(-8) = -4$. Squaring it gives $(-4)2 = 16$.

$\dfrac{y}{-3} - 9 + 16 = x^2 - 8x + 16$

Simplify the left side, and write the right side as a binomial squared.

$\dfrac{y}{-3} + 7 = (x - 4)^2$

Subtract 7, and then multiply through by -3 to isolate y.

$y = -3(x - 4)^2 + 21$

4. Method 1: Make $y = 0$; isolate x by square rooting both sides:

Make $y = 0$.

$0 = -(x + 3)^2 + 1$

Subtract 1 from both sides.

$-1 = -(x + 3)^2$

Divide by -1 on both sides.

$1 = (x + 3)^2$

Square root both sides. Don't forget to write plus OR minus 1.

$(x + 3) = \pm 1$

Write two equations using $+1$ and -1.

$(x + 3) = 1$ or $(x + 3) = -1$

Solve both equations. These are the zeros.

$x = -2$ or $x = -4$

Method 2: Convert vertex form to standard form, and then use the quadratic formula.

Put the equation in standard form by distributing and combining like terms.

$y = -(x + 3)^2 + 1$

$y = -(x^2 + 6x + 9) + 1$

$y = -x^2 - 6x - 8$

Find the zeros using the quadratic formula.

$x = \dfrac{-b \pm \sqrt{(b^2 - 4ac)}}{2a}$

$x = \dfrac{-(-6) \pm \sqrt{(-6)^2 - 4(-1)(-8)}}{2(-1)}$

$x = \dfrac{6 \pm \sqrt{36 - 32}}{-2}$

$x = \dfrac{6 \pm \sqrt{4}}{-2}$

$x = -4, -2$

5. This polynomial can be factored in the form $(z - 2)(z - 2) = 0$, so the only root is $z = 2$. There is only one *x*-intercept, and the vertex of the graph is *on* the *x*-axis.

6. If the quadratic has zeros at $x = -3$ and $x = 2$, then it has factors of $(x + 3)$ and $(x - 2)$. The quadratic function can be written in the factored form $y = a(x + 3)(x - 2)$. To find the *a*-value, plug in the point $(-2, 8)$ for *x* and *y*:

$$8 = a(-2 + 3)(-2 - 2)$$
$$8 = a(-4)$$
$$a = -2$$

The quadratic function is:

$$y = -2(x + 3)(x - 2).$$

7. Start by marking the vertex at $(3, 4)$ and recognizing this parabola opens upward. The line of symmetry is $x = 3$. Now, plug in an easy value for *x* to get one point on the curve; then use symmetry to find another point. In this case, choose $x = 2$ (one unit to the left of the line of symmetry) and solve for *y*:

$$y = 2(2 - 3)^2 + 4$$
$$y = 2(1) + 4$$
$$y = 6$$

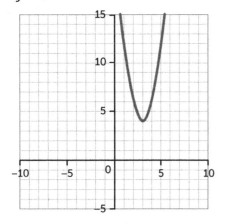

Thus the point $(2, 6)$ is on the curve. Then use symmetry to find the corresponding point one unit to the right of the line of symmetry, which must also have

a *y* value of 6. This point is $(4, 6)$. Draw a parabola through the points.

8. Locate the vertex and plug values for *h* and *k* into the vertex form of the quadratic equation.

$$(h, k) = (0, 5)$$
$$y = a(x - h)^2 + k$$
$$y = a(x - 0)^2 + 5$$
$$y = ax^2 + 5$$

Choose another point on the graph to plug into this equation to solve for *a*.

$$(x, y) = (1, 2)$$
$$y = ax^2 + 5$$
$$2 = a(1)^2 + 5$$
$$a = -3$$

Plug *a* into the vertex form of the equation.

$$y = -3x^2 + 5$$

9. Find the zeros of the inequality.

$$x^2 - 4x = 12$$
$$x^2 - 4x - 12 = 0$$
$$(x + 2)(x - 6) = 0$$
$$x = -2, 6$$

Create a table or number line with the intervals created by the zeros. Use a test value to determine whether the expression is positive or negative.

x	$(x + 2)(x - 6)$
$-\infty < x < -2$	$+$
$-2 < x < 6$	$-$
$6 < x < \infty$	$+$

Identify the values of *x* which make the expression positive.

$$x < -2 \text{ or } x > 6$$

10. Set the quantity inside the parentheses equal to 27 or –27, and solve:

$x - 3 = 27$	$x - 3 = -27$
$x = 30$	$x = -24$

11. The first step is to isolate the absolute value part of the equation. Multiplying both sides by 5 gives:

$|r - 7| = 135$

If the quantity in the absolute value bars is 135 or –135, then the absolute value would be 135:

$r - 7 = 135$	$r - 7 = -135$
$r = 142$	$r = -128$

12. $\left|\frac{3x}{7}\right| \geq 4 - x$

Simplify the equation.

$\left|\frac{3x}{7}\right| \geq 4 - x$

$\frac{|3x|}{7} \geq 4 - x$

$|3x| \geq 28 - 7x$

Create and solve two inequalities. When including the negative answer, flip the inequality.

$3x \geq 28 - 7x$

$10x \geq 28$

$x \geq \frac{28}{10}$

$-(3x) \leq 28 - 7x$

$-3x \leq 28 - 7x$

$4x \leq 28$

$x \leq 7$

Combine the two answers to find the solution set.

$\frac{28}{10} \leq x \leq 7$

13. $f(4)$ if $f(x) = x^3 - 2x + \sqrt{x}$

Plug in 4.

$f(4) = (4)^3 - 2(4) + \sqrt{(4)}$

Follow the PEMDAS order of operations.

$= 64 - 8 + 2 = 58$

14. This function has an asymptote at $x = 9$, so is not defined there. Otherwise, the function is defined for all other values of x.
D: $-\infty < x < 9$ *or* $9 < x < \infty$

Interval notation can also be used to show domain and range. Round brackets indicate that an end value is not included, and square brackets show that it is. The symbol ∪ means *or*, and the symbol ∩ means *and*. For example, the statement (–infinity,4) ∪ (4,infinity) describes the set of all real numbers except 4.

Since the function has a horizontal asymptote at $y = 1$ that it never crosses, the function never takes the value 1, so the range is all real numbers except 1:
R: $-\infty < y < 1$ *or* $1 < y < \infty$.

15. For the domain, this graph goes on to the right to positive infinity. Its leftmost point, however, is $x = -2$. Therefore, its domain is all real numbers equal to or greater than –2, **D**: $-2 \leq x < \infty$, or **[–2,∞)**.

The lowest range value is $y = 2$. Although it has a decreasing slope, this function continues to rise. Therefore, the domain is all real numbers greater than 2, **R**: $2 \leq y < \infty$ or **[2,∞)**.

16. For a set of numbers to represent a function, every input must generate a unique output. Therefore, if the same input (x) appears more than once in the table, determine if that input has two different outputs. If so, then the table does not represent a function.

A) This table is not a function because input value 1 has two different outputs (1 and 3).

B) Table B is not a function because 0 is the only input and results in four different values.

C) This table shows a function because each input has one output.

D) This table also has one input going to two different values, so it is not a function.

17. Replace $f(x)$ with y.

$y = 5x + 5$

Switch the places of y and x.

$x = 5y + 5$

Solve for y.

$x = 5y + 5$

$x - 5 = 5y$

$y = \frac{x}{5} - 1$

$\boldsymbol{f^{-1}(x) = \frac{x}{5} - 1}$

18. This is a linear graph with some clear coordinates: $(-5,0)$, $(0,-1)$, $(5,-2)$, and $(10,-3)$. This means the inverse function will have coordinate $(0,-5)$, $(-1,0)$, $(-2,5)$, and $(-3,10)$. The inverse function is reflected over the line $y = x$ and is the line $f^{-1}(x) = -5(x + 1)$ below.

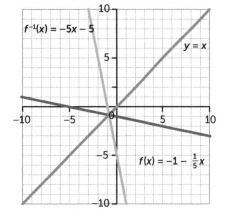

19. $(y \circ z)(-4) = y(z(-4))$

Starting on the inside, evaluate z.

$z(-4)$

$= 3(-4) - 3 = -12 - 3 = -15$

Replace $z(-4)$ with -15, and simplify.

$y(z(-4))$

$= y(-15) = 2(-15) - 1$

$= -30 - 1 = \boldsymbol{-31}$

20. Replace x in the $k(x)$ function with $\left(\frac{1}{2}x - 2\right)$

$(k \circ t)(x) = k(t(x))$

$= k\left(\frac{1}{2}x - 2\right) = \frac{1}{2}\left(\frac{1}{2}x - 2\right) - 3$

Simplify.

$= \frac{1}{4}x - 1 - 3 = \frac{1}{4}x - 4$

$\boldsymbol{(k \circ t)(x) = \frac{1}{4x} - 4}$

21. $N(4) = 400(4) = 1600$ and means that 4 hours after the park opens there are 1600 people in the park. $W(N(4)) = W(1600) = 96$ and means that 4 hours after the park opens the wait time is about **96 minutes** for the ride.

22. This function is the absolute value function with a vertical shift up of 4 units (since the 4 is outside the absolute value bars), and a horizontal shift left of 1 unit (since it is inside the bars). The vertex of the graph is at $(-1,4)$ and the line $x = -1$ is an axis of symmetry.

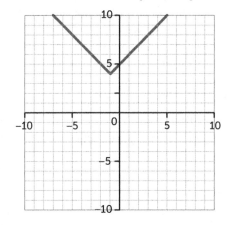

23. The negative sign in front of the absolute value means the graph will be reflected across the x-axis, so it will open down. The 3 causes a vertical stretch of the function, which results in a narrower graph. The basic curve is shifted 2 units right (since the -2 is an inside change) and 2 units up (since the $+2$ is an outside change), so the vertex is at $(2,2)$.

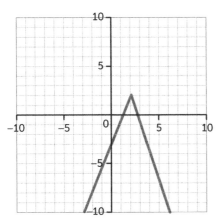

24. $y = 3t^4 - 48$

Factor the polynomial. Remove the common factor of 3 from each term and make $y = 0$.

$3(t^4 - 16) = 0$

Factor the difference of squares.

$t^2 - 4$ is also a difference of squares.

$3(t^2 - 4)(t^2 + 4) = 0$

$3(t + 2)(t - 2)(t^2 + 2) = 0$

Set each factor equal to zero. Solve each equation.

$t + 2 = 0$	$t - 2 = 0$	$t^2 + 2 = 0$
$t = -2$	$t = 2$	$t^2 = -2$
$t = \pm\sqrt{-2} = \pm 2i$		

This degree 4 polynomial has four roots, two real roots: **2 or -2**, and two complex roots: **2i or $-2i$**. The graph will have two x-intercepts at $(-2,0)$ and $(2,0)$.

25. Write the difference.

$f(x) - g(x) = \dfrac{2}{3x^2y} - \dfrac{5}{21y}$

Figure out the least common denominator. Every factor must be represented to the highest power it appears in either denominator. So, the LCD $= 3(7)x^2y$.

$= \dfrac{2}{3x^2y}\left(\dfrac{7}{7}\right) - \dfrac{5}{21y}\left(\dfrac{x^2}{x^2}\right)$

$= \dfrac{14}{21x^2y} - \dfrac{5x^2}{21x^2y}$

Subtract the numerators the find the answer.

$f(x) - g(x) = \dfrac{\mathbf{14 - 5x^2}}{\mathbf{21x^2y}}$

26. Write the quotient; then invert and multiply.

$\dfrac{f(x)}{g(x)} = \dfrac{\dfrac{(x - 1)(x + 2)^2}{5x^2 + 10x}}{\dfrac{x^2 + x - 2}{x + 5}}$

$= \dfrac{(x - 1)(x + 2)^2}{5x^2 + 10x} \times \dfrac{x + 5}{x^2 + x - 2}$

Factor all expressions, and then cancel any factors that appear in both the numerator and the denominator.

$= \dfrac{(x - 1)(x + 2)^2}{5x(x + 2)} \times \dfrac{x + 5}{(x + 2)(x - 1)}$

$= \dfrac{\mathbf{x + 5}}{\mathbf{5x}}$

27. $\dfrac{x}{x + 2} + \dfrac{2}{x^2 + 5x + 6} = \dfrac{5}{x + 3}$

Factor any denominators that need factoring.

$\dfrac{x}{x + 2} + \dfrac{2}{(x + 3)(x + 2)} = \dfrac{5}{x + 3}$

Multiply through by the LCM of the denominators, which is $(x + 2)(x + 3)$.

$x(x + 3) + 2 = 5(x + 2)$

Simplify the expression.

$x^2 + 3x + 2 - 5x - 10 = 0$

$x^2 - 2x - 8 = 0$

Factor the quadratic.

$(x - 4)(x + 2) = 0$

Plugging $x = -2$ into the original equation results in a 0 in the denominator. So this solution is an extraneous solution and must be thrown out.

Plugging in $x = 4$ gives:

$\frac{4}{6} + \frac{2}{16 + 20 + 6} = \frac{5}{7}$.

So **x = 4** is a solution to the equation.

28. The numerator will have a factor of $(x - 5)$ in order to have a zero at $x = 5$. The denominator will need factors of $(x - 1)$ and $(x + 1)$ in order for the denominator to be 0 when x is 1 or -1. Thus, one function that would have these features is

$$y = \frac{(x - 5)}{(x + 1)(x - 1)} = \frac{x - 5}{x^2 - 1}$$

29. $f(x) = \frac{3x^2 - 12x}{x^2 - 2x - 3}$.

Factor the equation.

$$y = \frac{3x^2 - 12x}{x^2 - 2x - 3} \quad \frac{3x(x - 4)}{(x - 3)(x + 1)}$$

Find the roots by setting the numerator equal to zero.

$3x(x - 4) = 0$

$x = 0, 4$

Find the vertical asymptotes by setting the denominator equal to zero.

$(x - 3)(x + 1) = 0$

$x = -1, 3$

Find the horizontal asymptote by looking at the degree of the numerator and the denominator.

The degree of the numerator and denominator are equal, so the asymptote is the ratio of the coefficients:

$y = \frac{3}{1} = 3$

Use the roots and asymptotes to graph the function.

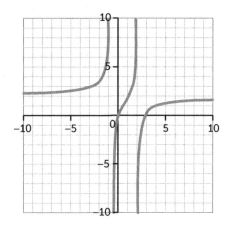

30. $\sqrt{2x - 5} + 4 = x$

Isolate the $\sqrt{2x - 5}$ by subtracting 4.

$\sqrt{2x - 5} = x - 4$

Square both sides to clear the $\sqrt{}$.

$2x - 5 = x^2 - 8x + 16$

Collect all variables to one side.

$x^2 - 10x + 21 = 0$

Factor and solve.

$(x - 7)(x - 3) = 0$

$x = 7$ or $x = 3$

Check solutions by plugging into the original, as squaring both sides can cause extraneous solutions.

True, $x = 7$ is a solution.

False, $x = 3$ is NOT a solution (extraneous solution).

$\sqrt{2(7) - 5} + 4 = 7$

$\sqrt{2(3) - 5} + 4 = 3$

$\sqrt{9} + 4 = 7$

$\sqrt{1} + 4 = 3$

x = 7

31. $2(x^2 - 7x)^{\frac{2}{3}} = 8$

Divide by 2 to isolate the radical.

$(x^2 - 7x)^{\frac{2}{3}} = 4$

Raise both sides to the $\frac{3}{2}$ power to clear the $\frac{2}{3}$ exponent.

$x^2 - 7x = 4^{\frac{3}{2}}$

$x^2 - 7x = 8$

This is a quadratic, so collect all terms to one side.

$x^2 - 7x - 8 = 0$

Factor and solve for x.

$(x - 8)(x + 1) = 0$

$x = 8$ or $x = -1$

Plugging both solutions into the original equation confirms that both are solutions.

32. One way to do this is to use a table:

x	$5^x - 2$
-2	$\frac{1}{25} - 2 = -\frac{49}{25}$
-1	$\frac{1}{5} - 2 = -\frac{9}{5}$
0	$1 - 2 = -1$
1	$5 - 2 = 3$
2	$25 - 2 = 23$

Another way to graph this is simply to see this function as the parent function $y = b^x$ (with $b = 5$), shifted down by a vertical shift of 2 units. Thus the new horizontal asymptote will be at $y = 2$, and the new y-intercept will be $y = -1$.

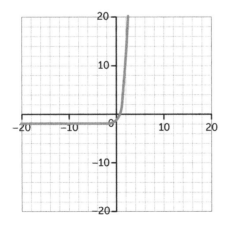

33. Any time a question concerns growth or decay, an exponential function must be created to solve it. In this case, create a table with initial value a, and a daily growth rate of $(1+0.05) = 1.05$ per day.

Days (x)	Height (h)
0	a
1	$1.05a$
2	$1.05(1.05a) = (1.05)^2a$
3	$(1.05)^2(1.05a) = (1.05)^3a$
x	$(1.05)^xa$

After six days the height of the grass is $(1.05)^6 = $ **1.34 times as tall**. The grass would grow 34% in one week.

34. $4^{x+1} = \frac{1}{256}$

Find a common base and rewrite the equation.

$4^{x+1} = 4^{-4}$

Set the exponents equal and solve for x.

$x + 1 = -4$

$x = -5$

35. Since division of a term can be written as a subtraction problem, this simplifies to:

$\log_5(25) - \log_5(x)$

The first term asks "what power of 5 gives 25?" The power is 2. Therefore, the most expanded form is:

$2 - \log_5(x)$

36. $\ln x + \ln 4 = 2\ln 4 - \ln 2$

Apply the log of product and log of exponent rules.

$\ln(4x) = \ln 4^2 - \ln 2$

$\ln(4x) = \ln 16 - \ln 2$

Follow log of quotient rule.

$\ln(4x) = \ln 8$

Set the arguments equal to each other.

$4x = 8$

$x = 2$

37. $2^x = 40$

Take the $\log_2$ of both sides.

$\log_2 2^x = \log_2 40$

Drop the x down using properties of logs.

$x\log_2 2 = \log_2 40$

$\log_2 2$ simplifies to 1.

$x = \log_2 40$

Use the change of base rule or a calculator to calculate the value of $\log_2(40)$.

≈ 5.32

38. Plug the given values into the growth equation.

$y = a(1 + r)^t$

$36{,}000 = 120(1 + 1.24)^t$

Use the properties of logarithms to solve the equation.

$300 = (2.24)^t$

$\log_{2.24} 300 = \log_{2.24}(2.24)^t$

$7.07 \approx t$

The number of text messages will pass 36,000 in **7.07 years**.

39. Identify the variables.

$t = \frac{22}{5.5} = 4$

$r = 0.5$

$a = ?$

Plug these values into the decay formula and solve.

$20 = a(1 - 0.50)^4$

$20 = a(0.5)^4$

$20 = a\left(\frac{1}{2}\right)^4$

$20 = a\left(\frac{1}{16}\right)$

$320 = a$

The original weight is **320 grams**.

40. Identify the variables.

$r = 0.05$

$n = 5$

$t = 12$

$P = 50$

Use the compound-interest formula, since this problem has many steps of growth within a time period.

$A = 50\left(1 + \frac{0.05}{5}\right)^{5(12)}$

$A = 50(1.01)^{60}$

$A = 50(1.82) = 90.83$

Subtract the original deposit to find the amount of interest earned.

$90.83 - 50 =$ **$40.83**

41. The side directly opposite of θ is 15. The hypotenuse is the longest side with a length of 17. This leaves the 8 as the adjacent.

Sine function	Cosine function	Tangent function
$\sin\theta = \frac{15}{17}$ $= 0.88$	$\cos\theta = \frac{8}{17}$ $= 0.47$	$\tan\theta = \frac{15}{8}$ $= 1.88$
Cosecant function	Secant function	Cotangent function
$\csc\theta = \frac{17}{15}$ $= 1.13$	$\sec\theta = \frac{17}{8}$ $= 2.13$	$\cot\theta = \frac{8}{15}$ $= 0.53$

42. Identify which side length is known, and which is being solved for in relation to the given angle. With respect to the 47-degree angle, the **h**ypotenuse is the unknown, and the known value is the **a**djacent. The trig function that uses adjacent and hypotenuse is cosine.

Identify the given parts of the triangle.

$\theta = 47$ degrees

$a = 3$

$h = x$

Plug these values into the equation for cosine and solve.

$\cos 47° = \frac{3}{x}$

$x(\cos 47°) = 3$

$x = \frac{3}{\cos 47°} = \textbf{4.40}$

43. Identify the given parts of the triangle.

$adjacent = 28$

$opposite = 15.4$

$\theta = ?$

Use the equation for the tangent function to find the angle.

$\tan\theta = \frac{opposite}{adjacent}$

$\tan\theta = \frac{15.4}{28}$

$\theta = \tan^{-1}\left(\frac{15.4}{28}\right)$

$\theta = \textbf{28.81°}$

44. To make use of a graphing calculator's trigonometric function, make sure it is in radian mode and type in: $\sin\frac{\pi}{2}$, which returns a value of 1. To understand *why* this is true, locate the angle $\frac{\pi}{2}$ on the unit circle. The $\sin\frac{\pi}{2}$ is the *y*-coordinate of the intersection of the terminal ray of angle $\frac{\pi}{2}$ with the unit circle, which is 1 because the ray intersects the circle at point (0,1).

45. Rewrite the expression using the reciprocal identity.

$\csc\frac{7\pi}{4} = \frac{1}{\sin\frac{7\pi}{4}}$

Find $\frac{7\pi}{4}$ on the unit circle.

$\sin\frac{7\pi}{4} = \frac{-1}{\sqrt{2}}$

Convert sine into cosecant.

$\csc\frac{7\pi}{4} = \frac{1}{\sin\frac{7\pi}{4}} = \frac{1}{\frac{-1}{\sqrt{2}}} = \textbf{-}\boldsymbol{\sqrt{2}}$

46. Begin by factoring out the 2 from the parentheses to get the function into the form $y = a\sin(b(x + c)) + d$:

$f(x) = -3\cos(2(x - 3\pi)) + 1$

The *a* value of −3 means the graph wil be reflected across the *x*-axis, and the amplitude of the graph is 3. The *b* value of 2 means the period is $\frac{2\pi}{2} = \pi$. The *c* value of −3π means the graph will be shifted to the right 3π units. The *d* value of 1 indicates a vertical translation up 1 unit.

$f(x) = -3\cos(2x - 6\pi) + 1$

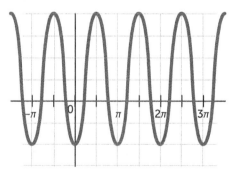

47. Since three sides are given, use the law of cosines:

Begin with "$12^2 =$ " because 12 is opposite the angle sought.

$12^2 = 8^2 + 7^2 - 2(8)(7)\cos C$

Simplify squares and products.

$144 = 64 + 49 - 112\cos C$

Subtract 64 and 49 from both sides.

$31 = -112\cos C$

Divide both sides by −112.

$\cos C = \frac{31}{-112}$

Use inverse cosine to find the angle.

$= \cos^{-1}\left(-\frac{31}{112}\right) = \textbf{106.1°}$

48. Because an angle and the side opposite is known, and the side opposite the unknown angle is known, use the law of sines for this triangle:

Identify the parts of the triangle given.

$a = 110$

$A = 110°$

$c = 40$

$C = ?$

Plug these values into the law of sines and solve for angle C.

$\frac{40}{\sin C} = \frac{110}{\sin 110}$

$40(\sin 110) = 110\sin C$

$\frac{37.6}{110} = \sin C$

$.34 = \sin C$

$C = \sin^{-1}(.34) = \mathbf{20°}$

49. A) Not enough information is provided to determine if the triangles are congruent.

B) Congruent (ASA). The vertical angle shared by the triangles provides the second angle.

C) Congruent (SSS). The shared side is the third congruent side.

D) Not enough information is provided: SSA cannot be used to prove congruence.

50. Set up a proportion among the sides:

$\frac{AB}{AC} = \frac{ED}{DF}$

$\frac{6}{7.5} = \frac{DE}{15}$

$\mathbf{DE = 12}$

51. The surface area will be the area of the square base plus the area of the four triangles.

Find the area of the square.

$A = s^2 = 6^2 = 36$

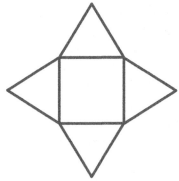

To find the area of the triangles, first find the pyramid's slant height.

$c^2 = a^2 + b^2$

$l^2 = 100 + 9$

$l = \sqrt{109}$

Find the area of the triangle face using the slant height as the height of the triangle face.

$A = \frac{1}{2}bh$

$A = \frac{1}{2}(6)(\sqrt{109})$

$A = 3\sqrt{109}$

Add the area of the square base and the four triangles to find the total surface area.

$SA = 36 + 4(3\sqrt{109}) \approx \mathbf{161.3 \ cm^2}$

52. Identify the given variables.

$V_1 = 81\pi$

$h_1 = 3$

Find the radius of the larger cone with the given information.

$V_1 = \frac{1}{3}\pi r_1^2 h_1$

$81\pi = \frac{1}{3}\pi(r_1)(3)$

$r_1 = 9$

Use the given scale factor to find the second cone's radius and height.

$r_2 = \frac{1}{3}r_1$

$r_2 = \frac{1}{3}(9)$

$r_2 = 3$

$h_2 = \frac{1}{3}h_1$

$h_2 = \frac{1}{3}(3)$

$h_2 = 1$

Find the area of the smaller cone.

$V_2 = \frac{1}{3}\pi r_2^2 h_2$

$V_2 = \frac{1}{3}\pi(3)^2(1)$

$\boldsymbol{V_2 = 3\pi}$

53. Translating two units down decreases each *y*-value by 2, and moving 3 units to the right increases the *x*-value by 3. The new vertices are *A* (−3,2), *B* (−3,6), *C* (5,6), and *D* (7,−6).

54. Multiply each point by the scale factor of 5 to find the new vertices: ***A* (−30,20), *B* (−30,40), *C* (10,40), and *D* (20,−20).**

55. Since the orientation of the triangle is different from the original, it must have been rotated. A counterclockwise rotation of 90° about the point *A* (2,8) results in a triangle with the same orientation. Then the triangle must be translated to move it to the image location. Pick one point, say *A*, and determine the translation necessary to move it to point *A'*. In this case, each point on the pre-image must be translated 8 units left and 2 units down, or (−8,−2). (Note that this is one of many possible answers.)

56. When a figure is rotated 270°, the coordinates change: (*a*,*b*) → (*b*,−*a*). After the rotation, the new coordinates are (4,6), (8,6), (8,−2), and (−4,−4). Reflecting across the *x*-axis requires that every *y*-value is multiplied by −1 to arrive at the completely transformed quadrilateral with vertices of (4,−6), (8,−6), (8,2), and (−4,4).

PART II
Reading

CHAPTER FOUR
Reading

The Main Idea

The main idea of a text describes the author's main topic and general concept; it also generalizes the author's point of view about a subject. It is contained within and throughout the text. The reader can find the main idea by considering how the main topic is addressed throughout a passage. On reading questions, you are expected not only to identify the main idea but also to be able to differentiate it from a text's theme and to summarize the main idea clearly and concisely. For instance, you might be asked to pick an answer choice that best summarizes the main idea of a passage.

The main idea is closely connected to topic sentences and how they are supported in a text. Questions may deal with finding topic sentences, summarizing a text's ideas, or locating supporting details. The sections and practice examples that follow detail the distinctions between these aspects of text.

DID YOU KNOW?
The author's perspective on the subject of the text and how he or she has framed the argument or story hints at the main idea. For example, if the author framed the story with a description, image, or short anecdote, he or she is hinting at a particular idea or point of view.

IDENTIFYING the MAIN IDEA

To identify the main idea, first identify the topic. The difference between these two things is simple: the **TOPIC** is the overall subject matter of a passage; the **MAIN IDEA** is what the author wants to say about that topic. The main idea covers the author's direct perspective about a topic, as distinct from the **THEME**, which is a generally true idea that the reader might derive from a text. Most of the time, fiction has a theme, whereas nonfiction has a main idea. This is the case because in a nonfiction text, the author speaks more directly to the audience about a topic—his or her perspective is more visible. For example, the following passage conveys the topic as well as what the author wants to communicate about that topic.

The "shark mania" of recent years can be largely pinned on the sensationalistic media surrounding the animals: from the release of *Jaws* in 1975 to the week of ultra-hyped shark feeding frenzies and "worst shark attacks" countdowns known as *Shark Week*, popular culture both demonizes and fetishizes sharks until the public cannot get enough. Swimmers and beachgoers may look nervously for the telltale fin skimming the surface, but the reality is that shark bites are extremely rare and they are almost never unprovoked. Sharks attack people at very predictable times and for very predictable reasons. Rough surf, poor visibility, or a swimmer sending visual and physical signals that mimic a shark's normal prey are just a few examples.

Of course, some places are just more dangerous to swim. Shark attack "hot spots," such as the coasts of Florida, South Africa, and New Zealand try a variety of solutions to protect tourists and surfers. Some beaches employ "shark nets," meant to keep sharks away from the beach, though these are controversial because they frequently trap other forms of marine life as well. Other beaches use spotters in helicopters and boats to alert beach officials when there are sharks in the area. In addition, there is an array of products that claim to offer personal protection from sharks, ranging from wetsuits in different colors to devices that broadcast electrical signals in an attempt to confuse the sharks' sensory organs. At the end of the day, though, beaches like these remain dangerous, and swimmers must assume the risk every time they paddle out from shore.

The author of this passage has a clear topic: sharks and their relationship with humans. In order to identify the main idea of the passage, the reader must ask, What does the author want to say about this topic? What is the reader meant to think or understand?

DID YOU KNOW?

Readers should identify the topic of a text and pay attention to how the details about it relate to one another. A passage may discuss, for example, topic similarities, characteristics, causes, and/ or effects.

The author makes sure to provide information about several different aspects of the relationship between sharks and humans, and points out that humans must respect sharks as dangerous marine animals, without sensationalizing the risk of attack. The reader can figure this out by looking at the various pieces of information the author includes as well as the similarities between them. The passage describes sensationalistic media, then talks about how officials and governments try to protect beaches, and ends with the observation that people must take personal responsibility. These details clarify what the author's main idea is: thanks to safety precautions and their natural behavior, sharks are not as dangerous as they are portrayed to be. Summarizing that main idea by focusing on the connection between the different details helps the reader draw a conclusion.

EXAMPLES

The art of the twentieth and twenty-first centuries demonstrates several aspects of modern social advancement. A primary example is the advent of technology: new technologies have developed new avenues for art making, and the globalization brought about by the internet has both diversified the art world and brought it together simultaneously. Even as artists are able to engage in a global conversation about the categories and characteristics of art, creating a more uniform understanding, they can now express themselves in a diversity of ways for a diversity of audiences. The result has been a rapid change in how art is made and consumed.

1. This passage is primarily concerned with
    A) the importance of art in the twenty-first century.
    B) the use of art to communicate overarching ideals to diverse communities.
    C) the importance of technology to art criticism.
    D) the change in understanding and creation of art in the modern period.

2. Which of the following best describes the main idea of the passage?
    A) Modern advances in technology have diversified art making and connected artists to distant places and ideas.
    B) Diversity in modern art is making it harder for art viewers to understand and talk about that art.
    C) The use of technology to discuss art allows us to create standards for what art should be.
    D) Art-making before the invention of technology such as the internet was disorganized and poorly understood.

TOPIC and SUMMARY SENTENCES

Identifying the main idea requires understanding the structure of a piece of writing. In a short passage of one or two paragraphs, the topic and summary sentences quickly relate what the paragraphs are about and what conclusions the author wants the reader to draw. These sentences function as bookends to a paragraph or passage, telling readers what to think and keeping the passage tied tightly together.

Generally, the **TOPIC SENTENCE** is the first, or very near the first, sentence in a paragraph. It is a general statement that introduces the topic, clearly and specifically directing the reader to access any previous experience with that topic.

The **SUMMARY SENTENCE**, on the other hand, frequently—but not always!—comes at the end of a paragraph or passage, because

DID YOU KNOW?

A summary is a very brief restatement of the most important parts of an argument or text. Building a summary begins with the most important idea in a text. A longer summary also includes supporting details. The text of a summary should be much shorter than the original.

it wraps up all the ideas presented. This sentence provides an understanding of what the author wants to say about the topic and what conclusions to draw about it. While a topic sentence acts as an introduction to a topic, allowing the reader to activate his or her own ideas and experiences, the summary statement asks the reader to accept the author's ideas about that topic. Because of this, a summary sentence helps the reader quickly identify a piece's main idea.

EXAMPLES

There is nowhere more beautiful and interesting than California. With glimmering azure seas, fertile green plains, endless deserts, and majestic mountains, California offers every landscape. Hikers can explore the wilderness in Yosemite National Park, where a variety of plants and animals make their home. Farmers grow almonds, apricots, cotton, tomatoes, and more in the Central Valley that winds through the middle of the state. Skiers enjoy the slopes and backcountry of the Sierra Nevada and Lake Tahoe area. In the desert of Death Valley, temperatures rise well over one hundred degrees Fahrenheit. And of course, California's famous beaches stretch from the Mexican border to Oregon. Furthermore, California features some of America's most important cities. In the south, Los Angeles is home to the movie industry and Hollywood. Farther north, the San Francisco Bay Area includes Silicon Valley, where the US tech industry is based. Both places are centers of commercial activity. In fact, California is the most populous state in the country. There is no shortage of things to do or sights to see!

3. Which of the following best explains the general idea and focus indicated by the topic sentence?
   A) The diversity of California's landscape allows agriculture to flourish, and the most important crops will be detailed.
   B) California is beautiful and diverse; the reader will read on to find out what makes it so interesting.
   C) California is a peaceful place; its people live with a sense of predictability and the state is prosperous.
   D) The incredible geography of California is the reason it is a rural state, and the reader can expect a discussion of the countryside.

4. Which of the following best states what the author wants the reader to understand after reading the summary sentence?
   A) Tourists should see everything in California when they visit.
   B) The cities of California are interesting, but the rural parts are better.
   C) The resources of California are nearly exhausted.
   D) California is an inspiring and exciting place.

Supporting Details

Between a topic sentence and a summary sentence, the rest of a paragraph is built with **SUPPORTING DETAILS.** Supporting details come in many forms; the purpose of the passage dictates the type of details that will support the main idea. A persuasive passage may use facts and data or detail specific reasons for the author's opinion. An informative passage will primarily use facts about the topic to support the main idea. Even a narrative passage will have supporting details—specific things the author says to develop the story and characters.

The most important aspect of supporting details is exactly what it sounds like: they support the main idea. Examining the various supporting details and how they work with one another will reveal how the author views a topic and what the main idea of the passage is. Supporting details are key to understanding a passage.

Supporting details can often be found in texts by looking for **SIGNAL WORDS**—transitions that explain to the reader how one sentence or idea is connected to another. Signal words can add information, provide counterarguments, create organization in a passage, or draw conclusions. Some common signal words and phrases include *in particular*, *in addition*, *besides*, *contrastingly*, *therefore*, and *because*.

EXAMPLE

Increasingly, companies are turning to subcontracting services rather than hiring full-time employees. This provides companies with advantages like greater flexibility, reduced legal responsibility to employees, and lower possibility of unionization within the company. However, this has led to increasing confusion and uncertainty over the legal definition of employment. Courts have grappled with questions about the hiring company's responsibility in maintaining fair labor practices. Companies argue that they delegate that authority to subcontractors, while unions and other worker advocate groups argue that companies still have a legal obligation to the workers who contribute to their business.

5. According to the passage, why do companies use subcontractors?
Hiring subcontractors

  A) costs less money than hiring full-time employees.

  B) increases the need for unionization of employees.

  C) reduces the company's legal responsibilities.

  D) gives the company greater control over worker's hours.

The Author's Purpose

The author of a passage sets out with a specific goal in mind: to communicate a particular idea to an audience. The **AUTHOR'S PURPOSE** is determined by asking why the author wants the reader to understand the passage's main idea. There are four basic purposes to which an author can write: narrative, expository, technical, and persuasive. Within each of these general purposes, the author may direct the audience to take a clear action or respond in a certain way.

The purpose for which an author writes a passage is also connected to the structure of that text. In a **NARRATIVE**, the author seeks to tell a story, often to illustrate a theme or idea the reader needs to consider. In a narrative, the author uses characteristics of storytelling, such as chronological order, characters, and a defined setting, and these characteristics communicate the author's theme or main idea.

In an **EXPOSITORY** passage, on the other hand, the author simply seeks to explain an idea or topic to the reader. The main idea will probably be a factual statement or a direct assertion of a broadly held opinion. Expository writing can come in many forms, but one essential feature is a fair and balanced representation of a topic. The author may explore one detailed aspect or a broad range of characteristics, but he or she mainly seeks to prompt a decision from the reader.

Similarly, in **TECHNICAL** writing, the author's purpose is to explain specific processes, techniques, or equipment in order for the reader to use that process or equipment to obtain a desired result. Writing like this employs chronological or spatial structures, specialized vocabulary, and imperative or directive language.

In **PERSUASIVE** writing, the author actively seeks to convince the reader to accept an opinion or belief. Much like expository writing, persuasive writing is presented in many organizational forms.

EXAMPLE

University of California, Berkeley, researchers decided to tackle an age-old problem: why shoelaces come untied. They recorded the shoelaces of a volunteer walking on a treadmill by attaching devices to record the acceleration, or g-force, experienced by the knot. The results were surprising. A shoelace knot experiences more g-force from a person walking than any rollercoaster can generate. However, if the person simply stomped or swung their feet—the two movements that make up a walker's stride—the g-force was not enough to undo the knots.

6. What is the purpose of this passage?

    A) to confirm if shoelaces always come undone

    B) to compare the force of treadmills and rollercoasters

    C) to persuade readers to tie their shoes tighter

    D) to describe the results of an experiment on shoelaces

Organization and Text Structures

It's important to analyze the organization and structure of informational texts, as these details can provide valuable insight into the author's purpose and the overall meaning of a text. Several common structures are used in informative texts, and understanding these structures will help readers quickly make sense of new texts. Texts may be organized in one of the following ways:

▶ CHRONOLOGICAL texts describe events in the order they occurred.

▶ PROBLEM-SOLUTION texts begin by describing a problem and then offer a possible solution to the issue.

▶ CAUSE-EFFECT is a text structure that shows a causal chain of events or ideas.

▶ GENERAL-TO-SPECIFIC is a text structure that describes a general topic then provides details about a specific aspect of that topic.

▶ COMPARE-CONTRAST texts give the similarities and differences between two things.

Authors choose the organizational structure of their text according to their purpose. For example, an author who hopes to convince people to begin recycling might begin by talking about the problems that are caused by excessive waste and end by offering recycling as a reasonable solution. On the other hand, the author might choose to use a chronological structure for an article whose purpose is to give an impartial history of recycling.

EXAMPLE

For thirteen years, a spacecraft called *Cassini* was on an exploratory mission to Saturn. The spacecraft was designed not to return but to end its journey by diving into Saturn's atmosphere. This dramatic ending provided scientists with unprecedented information about Saturn's atmosphere and its magnetic and gravitational fields. First, however, *Cassini* passed Saturn's largest moon, Titan, where it recorded data on Titan's curious methane lakes, gathering information about potential seasons on the planet-sized moon. Then it passed through the unexplored region between Saturn itself and its famous rings. Scientists hope to learn how old the rings are and to directly examine the particles that make them up. *Cassini*'s mission ended in 2017, but researchers have new questions for future exploration.

7. Which of the following best describes the organization of this passage?
   A) general-to-specific
   B) compare-contrast
   C) chronological
   D) problem-solution

The Audience

The structure, purpose, main idea, and language of a text all converge on one target: the intended **AUDIENCE**. An author makes decisions about every aspect of a piece of writing based on that audience, and readers can evaluate the writing by considering who the author is writing for. By considering the probable reactions of an intended audience, readers can determine many things:

▶ whether they are part of that intended audience

▶ the author's purpose for using specific techniques or devices

▶ the biases of the author and how they appear in the writing

▶ how the author uses rhetorical strategies.

DID YOU KNOW?

When reading a persuasive text, students should maintain awareness of what the author believes about the topic.

The audience for a text can be identified by careful analysis of the text. First, the reader considers who most likely cares about the topic and main idea of the text: who would want or need to know about this topic? The audience may be **SPECIFIC** (e.g., biologists who study sharks) or more **GENERAL** (e.g., people with an interest in marine life).

Next, consider the language of the text. The author tailors language to appeal to the intended audience, so the reader can determine from the language who the author is speaking to. A **FORMAL** style is used in business and academic settings and can make the author seem more credible. Characteristics of a formal style include:

▶ third person perspective (i.e., no use of *I* or *you*)

▶ no use of slang or clichés

▶ follows a clear structure (e.g., an introduction, a body, and a conclusion)

▶ technically correct grammar and sentence structure

▶ objective language

An **INFORMAL** style is used to appeal to readers in a more casual setting, such as a magazine or blog. Using an informal style may make the author seem less credible, but it can help create an emotional connection with the audience. Characteristics of informal writing include:

▶ use of first or second person (e.g., *I* or *you*)

▶ use of slang or casual language

▶ follows an unusual or flexible structure

▶ bends the rules of grammar

▶ appeals to audience's emotions

EXAMPLE

What do you do with plastic bottles? Do you throw them away, or do you recycle or reuse them? As landfills continue to fill up, there will eventually be no place to put our trash. If you recycle or reuse bottles, you will help reduce waste and turn something old into a creative masterpiece!

8. Which of the following BEST describes the intended audience for this passage?

A) a formal audience of engineering professionals

B) an audience of English language learners

C) a general audience that includes children

D) a group of scientists at an environmental conference

Evaluating Arguments

An author selects details to help support the main idea. The reader must then evaluate these details for relevance and consistency. Though the author generally includes details that support the text's main idea, it's up to the reader to decide whether those details are convincing.

Readers should be able to differentiate between facts and opinions in order to more effectively analyze supporting details. **FACTS** are based in truth and can usually be proven. They are pieces of information that have been confirmed or validated. An opinion is a judgment, belief, or viewpoint that is not based on evidence. **OPINIONS** are often stated in descriptive, subjective language that is difficult to define or prove. While opinions can be included in informative texts, they are often of little impact unless they are supported by some kind of evidence.

QUICK REVIEW
Which of the following phrases would be associated with opinions? *for example, studies have shown, I believe, in fact, it's possible that*

Sometimes, the author's **BIAS**—an inclination towards a particular belief—causes the author to leave out details that do not directly support the main idea or that support an opposite idea. The reader has to be able to notice not only what the author says but also what the author leaves out. Discovering the author's bias and how the supporting details reveal that bias is also key to understanding a text.

Writers will often use specific techniques, or RHETORICAL STRATEGIES, to build an argument. Readers can identify these strategies in order to clearly understand what an author wants them to believe, how the author's perspective and purpose may lead to bias, and whether the passage includes any logical fallacies.

Common rhetorical strategies include the appeals to ethos, logos, and pathos. An author uses these to build trust with the reader, explain the logical points of his or her argument, and convince the reader that his or her opinion is the best option.

An ETHOS (ETHICAL) APPEAL uses balanced, fair language and seeks to build a trusting relationship between the author and the reader. An author might explain her or his credentials, include the reader in an argument, or offer concessions to an opposing argument.

QUICK REVIEW
Consider how different audiences would react to the same text.

A LOGOS (LOGICAL) APPEAL builds on that trust by providing facts and support for the author's opinion, explaining the argument with clear connections and reasoning. At this point, the reader should beware of logical fallacies that connect unconnected ideas and build arguments on incorrect premises. With a logical appeal, an author strives to convince the reader to accept an opinion or belief by demonstrating that not only is it the most logical option but that it also satisfies her or his emotional reaction to a topic.

A PATHOS (EMOTIONAL) APPEAL does not depend on reasonable connections between ideas; rather, it seeks to remind the reader, through imagery, strong language, and personal connections, that the author's argument aligns with her or his best interests.

EXAMPLE

Exercise is critical for healthy development in children. Today in the United States, there is an epidemic of poor childhood health; many of these children will face further illnesses in adulthood that are due to poor diet and lack of exercise now. This is a problem for all Americans, especially with the rising cost of health care.

It is vital that school systems and parents encourage children to engage in a minimum of thirty minutes of cardiovascular exercise each day, mildly increasing their heart rate for a sustained period. This is proven to decrease the likelihood of developmental diabetes, obesity, and a multitude of other health problems. Also, children need a proper diet, rich in fruits and vegetables, so they can develop physically and learn healthy eating habits early on.

9. Which of the following statements from the passage is a fact, not an opinion?

   A) Fruits and vegetables are the best way to help children be healthy.

   B) Children today are lazier than they were in previous generations.

   C) The risk of diabetes in children is reduced by physical activity.

   D) Children should engage in thirty minutes of exercise a day.

Drawing Conclusions

Reading text begins with making sense of the explicit meanings of information or a narrative. Understanding occurs as the reader draws conclusions and makes logical inferences. First, the reader considers the details or facts. He or she then comes to a **CONCLUSION**—the next logical point in the thought sequence. For example, in a Hemingway story, an old man sits alone in a cafe. A young waiter says that the cafe is closing, but the old man continues to drink. The waiter starts closing up, and the old man signals for a refill. Based on these details, the reader might conclude that the old man has not understood the young waiter's desire for him to leave.

An inference is distinguished from a conclusion drawn. An **INFERENCE** is an assumption the reader makes based on details in the text as well as his or her own knowledge. It is more of an educated guess that extends the literal meaning of a text. Inferences begin with the given details; however, the reader uses the facts to determine additional information. What the reader already knows informs what is being suggested by the details of decisions or situations in the text. Returning to the example of the Hemingway story, the reader might *infer* that the old man is lonely, enjoys being in the cafe, and therefore is reluctant to leave.

When reading fictional text, inferring character motivations is essential. The actions of the characters move the plot forward; a series of events is understood by making sense of why the characters did what they did. Hemingway includes contrasting details as the young waiter and an older waiter discuss the old man. The older waiter sympathizes with the old man; both men have no one at home and experience a sense of emptiness in life, which motivates them to seek the cafe.

Another aspect of understanding text is connecting it to other texts. Readers may connect the Hemingway story about the old man in the cafe to other Hemingway stories about individuals struggling to deal with loss and loneliness in a dignified way.

DID YOU KNOW?
When considering a character's motivations, the reader should ask what the character wants to achieve, what the character will get by accomplishing this, and what the character seems to value the most.

DID YOU KNOW?
Conclusions are drawn by thinking about how the author wants the reader to feel. A group of carefully selected facts can cause the reader to feel a certain way.

They can extend their initial connections to people they know or their personal experiences. When readers read a persuasive text, they often connect the arguments made to counterarguments and opposing evidence of which they are aware. They use these connections to infer meaning.

EXAMPLE

After World War I, political and social forces pushed for a return to normalcy in the United States. The result was disengagement from the larger world and increased focus on American economic growth and personal enjoyment. Caught in the middle were American writers, raised on the values of the prewar world and frustrated with what they viewed as the superficiality and materialism of postwar American culture. Many of them fled to Paris, where they became known as the "lost generation," creating a trove of literary works criticizing their home culture and delving into their own feelings of alienation.

10. Which conclusion about the effects of war is most likely true, according to the passage?

A) War served as an inspiration for literary works.

B) It was difficult to stabilize countries after war occurred.

C) Writers were torn between supporting war and their own ideals.

D) Individual responsibility and global awareness declined after the war.

Tone and Mood

The **TONE** of a passage describes the author's attitude toward the topic. In general, the author's tone can be described as positive, negative, or neutral. The **MOOD** is the pervasive feeling or atmosphere in a passage that provokes specific emotions in the reader. Put simply, tone is how the author feels about the topic. Mood is how the reader feels about the text.

DICTION, or word choice, helps determine mood and tone in a passage. Many readers make the mistake using the author's ideas alone to determine tone; a much better practice is to look at specific words and try to identify a pattern in the emotion they evoke. Does the writer choose positive words like *ambitious* and *confident*? Or does he describe those concepts with negative words like *greedy* and *overbearing*? The first writer's tone might be described as admiring, while the more negative tone would be disapproving.

When looking at tone, it's important to examine not just the literal definition of words. Every word has not only a literal meaning but also a **CONNOTATIVE MEANING**, which relies on the common emotions and experiences an audience might associate with that word. The following words are all synonyms: *dog, puppy, cur, mutt,*

DID YOU KNOW?
To decide the connotation of a word, the reader examines whether the word conveys a positive or negative association in the mind. Adjectives are often used to influence the feelings of the reader, such as in the phrase *an ambitious attempt to achieve*.

canine, *pet*. Two of these words—*dog* and *canine*—are neutral words, without strong associations or emotions. Two others—*pet* and *puppy*—have positive associations. The last two—*cur* and *mutt*—have negative associations. A passage that uses one pair of these words versus another pair activates the positive or negative reactions of the audience.

Table 4.1. Words That Describe Tone		
POSITIVE	NEUTRAL	NEGATIVE
admiring	casual	angry
approving	detached	annoyed
celebratory	formal	belligerent
earnest	impartial	bitter
encouraging	informal	condescending
excited	objective	confused
funny	questioning	cynical
hopeful	unconcerned	depressed
humorous		disrespectful
nostalgic		embarrassed
optimistic		fearful
playful		gloomy
poignant		melancholy
proud		mournful
relaxed		pessimistic
respectful		skeptical
sentimental		solemn
silly		suspicious
sympathetic		unsympathetic

EXAMPLES

Day had broken cold and grey, exceedingly cold and grey, when the man turned aside from the main Yukon trail and climbed the high earth-bank, where a dim and little-travelled trail led eastward through the fat spruce timberland. It was a steep bank, and he paused for breath at the top, excusing the act to himself by looking at his watch. It was nine o'clock. There was no sun nor hint of sun, though there was not a cloud in the sky. It was a clear day, and yet there seemed an intangible pall over the face of things, a subtle gloom that made the day dark, and that was due to the absence of sun. This fact did not worry the man. He was used to the lack of sun. It had been days since he had seen the sun, and he knew that a few more days must pass before that cheerful orb, due south, would just peep above the sky-line and dip immediately from view.

—from "To Build a Fire" by Jack London

11. Which of the following best describes the mood of the passage?
    A) exciting and adventurous
    B) unhappy and anxious
    C) bleak but accepting
    D) grim yet hopeful

12. The connotation of the words *intangible pall* is
    A) a death-like covering.
    B) a sense of familiarity.
    C) a feeling of communal strength.
    D) an understanding of the struggle ahead.

Meaning of Words and Phrases

When confronted with unfamiliar words, the passage itself can help clarify their meaning. Often, identifying the tone or main idea of the passage can help eliminate answer choices. For example, if the tone of the passage is generally positive, try eliminating the answer choices with a negative connotation. Or, if the passage is about a particular occupation, rule out words unrelated to that topic.

Passages may also provide specific context clues that can help determine the meaning of a word. One type of context clue is a DEFINITION, or DESCRIPTION, CLUE. Sometimes, authors use a difficult word, then include *that is* or *which is* to signal that they are providing a definition. An author also may provide a synonym or restate the idea in more familiar words:

> Teachers often prefer teaching students with intrinsic motivation; these students have an internal desire to learn.

The meaning of *intrinsic* is restated as *an internal desire*.

Similarly, authors may include an EXAMPLE CLUE, providing an example phrase that clarifies the meaning of the word:

> Teachers may view extrinsic rewards as efficacious; however, an individual student may not be interested in what the teacher offers. For example, a student who does not like sweets may not feel any incentive to work when offered a sugary reward.

Efficacious is explained with an example that demonstrates how an extrinsic reward may not be effective.

Another commonly used context clue is the CONTRAST, or ANTONYM, CLUE. In this case, authors indicate that the unfamiliar word is the opposite of a familiar word:

> In contrast to intrinsic motivation, <u>extrinsic</u> motivation is contingent on teachers offering rewards that are appealing.

The phrase *in contrast* tells the reader that extrinsic is the opposite of intrinsic.

EXAMPLES

13. Which of the following is the meaning of *incentivize* as used in the sentence?

One challenge of teaching is finding ways to incentivize, or to motivate, learning.

- **A)** encourage
- **B)** determine
- **C)** challenge
- **D)** improve

14. Which of the following is the meaning of *apprehensive* as used in the sentence?

If an extrinsic reward is extremely desirable, a student may become so apprehensive he or she cannot focus. The student may experience such intense pressure to perform that the reward undermines its intent.

- **A)** uncertain
- **B)** distracted
- **C)** anxious
- **D)** forgetful

Figurative Language

Figures of speech are expressions that are understood to have a nonliteral meaning. Rather than stating their ideas directly, authors use **FIGURATIVE LANGUAGE** to suggest meaning by speaking of a subject as if it were something else. For example, when Shakespeare says, "All the world's a stage,/ And all men and women merely players," he is speaking of the world as if it is a stage. Since the world is not literally a stage, the reader has to ask how the two are similar and what Shakespeare might be implying about the world through this comparison. Figures of speech extend the meaning of words by engaging the reader's imagination and adding emphasis to different aspects of their subject.

A **METAPHOR** is a type of figurative language that describes something that may be unfamiliar to the reader (the topic) by referring to it as though it were something else that is more familiar to the reader (the vehicle). A metaphor stands in as a synonym, interchangeable with its corresponding topic. As the reader reflects on the similarities between the topic and the vehicle, he or she forms a clearer understanding of the topic.

For example, in Shakespeare's *Romeo and Juliet*, Romeo says that "Juliet is the sun." By making this comparison, Romeo is comparing Juliet's energy to the brightness of the sun, which is familiar to readers.

A SIMILE is a type of figurative language that directly points to similarities between two things. As with a metaphor, the author uses a familiar vehicle to express an idea about a less familiar topic. Unlike a metaphor, however, a simile does not replace the object with a figurative description; it compares the vehicle and topic using "like," "as," or similar words. For example, in his poem "The Rime of the Ancient Mariner," Coleridge describes his ship as "idle as a painted ship/ Upon a painted ocean." He speaks about the boat as if it were painted (unlike Romeo above, who says explicitly that Juliet is the sun itself). The reader understands that paintings do not move, so Coleridge uses this comparison to show the reader that the ship in the poem is completely motionless.

IMAGERY is vivid description that appeals to the reader's sense of sight, sound, smell, taste, or touch. This type of figurative language allows readers to experience through their senses what is being described; as readers use their imaginations to visualize or recall sensory experience, they are drawn into the scene of the story or poem.

HYPERBOLE is an overstatement, an exaggeration intended to achieve a particular effect. Hyperbole can create humor or add emphasis to a text by drawing the reader's attention to a particular idea. For example, a character might say he or she is "so hungry, [he or she] could eat a horse." Though the character probably cannot literally eat a horse, the reader understands that he or she is extremely hungry.

PERSONIFICATION is a type of figurative language in which human characteristics are attributed to objects, abstract ideas, natural forces, or animals. For example, if a writer refers to "murmuring pine trees," he or she is attributing to the pine trees the human ability of murmuring. The writer is using the familiar vehicle of the sound of murmuring to help the reader understand the sound pine trees make in the wind.

SYMBOLISM is a literary device in which the author uses a concrete object, action, or character to represent an abstract idea. The significance of the symbol reaches beyond the object's ordinary meaning. Familiar symbols are roses representing beauty, light representing truth, and darkness representing evil. As readers notice an author's use of symbolism, they begin to make connections and to formulate ideas about what the author is suggesting.

An ALLUSION, not to be confused with illusion, is a reference to a historical person or event, a fictional character or event, a mythological or religious character or event, or an artist or artistic work. When a reader recognizes an allusion, he or she may make associations that contribute to his or her understanding of the text. For example, if a character is described as having a "Mona Lisa smile," an instant image will arise in the minds of most readers. Because allusions can be difficult to recognize, especially for young readers whose experiences are limited, teachers must provide instruction in how to recognize, research, and interpret unfamiliar references.

CLICHÉS are common sayings that lack originality but are familiar and relatable to an audience. Though clichés are not necessarily beneficial to the author who is trying to write a wholly original work, they can be helpful for a writer who is attempting to show that he or she can relate to the audience.

DIALECT and SLANG are linguistic qualities that an author might incorporate into his or her writing in order to develop characters or setting. A character's dialect may reveal where he or she is from, while the slang he or she uses may be an indication of social, economic, and educational status.

IRONY comes in different forms. VERBAL IRONY is used when a character or narrator says something that is the opposite of what he or she means. SITUATIONAL IRONY occurs when something happens that contradicts what the audience expected to happen. DRAMATIC IRONY occurs when the audience knows about something of which a character or characters are not aware.

EXAMPLE

Alfie closed his eyes and took several deep breaths. He was trying to ignore the sounds of the crowd, but even he had to admit that it was hard not to notice the tension in the stadium. He could feel 50,000 sets of eyes burning through his skin—this crowd expected perfection from him. He took another breath and opened his eyes, setting his sights on the soccer ball resting peacefully in the grass. One shot, just one last shot, between his team and the championship. He didn't look up at the goalie, who was jumping nervously on the goal line just a few yards away. Afterward, he would swear he didn't remember anything between the referee's whistle and the thunderous roar of the crowd.

15. Which of the following best describes the meaning of the phrase "he could feel 50,000 sets of eyes burning through his skin"?
    A) The 50,000 people in the stadium were trying to hurt Alfie.
    B) Alfie felt uncomfortable and exposed in front of so many people.
    C) Alfie felt immense pressure from the 50,000 people watching him.
    D) The people in the stadium are warning Alfie that the field is on fire.

Elements of Fiction

FICTION is a prose genre, made up of narratives whose details are not based in truth but are instead the creation of the author. Just as artists have the tools of color and shape to communicate ideas, so have writers their literary tools. These tools include point of view, plot, setting, character, tone, and figurative language. Each of these elements contributes to the overall idea that is developed in the text and, as such, can provide valuable insight into the theme of the work.

POINT OF VIEW is the perspective from which the action in a story is told. By carefully selecting a particular point of view, writers are able to control what their readers know. Most literature is written in either first person or third person point of view. With the **FIRST PERSON POINT OF VIEW**, the action is narrated by a character within the story, which can make it feel more believable and authentic to the reader. However, as a result of the first person point of view, the reader's knowledge and understanding are constrained by what the narrator notices and influenced by what the narrator thinks and values.

An author may, on the other hand, choose to tell the story from the **THIRD PERSON POINT OF VIEW**. A third person narrator is a voice outside the action of the story, an observer who shares what he or she knows, sees, or hears with the reader. A third person narrator might be **FULLY OMNISCIENT** (able to see into the minds of the characters and share what they are thinking and feeling), **PARTIALLY OMNISCIENT** (able to see into the minds of just one or a few characters), or **LIMITED** (unable to see into the minds of any of the characters and only able to share what can be seen and heard).

PLOT STRUCTURE is the way the author arranges the events of a narrative. In a conventional plot line, the story is structured around a central conflict, a struggle between two opposing forces. Conflicts in literature can be categorized in general terms as either internal or external, though most stories have a combination of both. Internal conflicts take place inside the main character's mind; he or she might be making a difficult decision, struggling with change, or sorting out priorities. External conflicts, on the other hand, occur when a character is in conflict with something or someone in the external world—the elements of nature, another character, supernatural forces, destiny, or society.

In a traditional plot structure, the author begins with **EXPOSITION**: important background information about the setting, the characters, and the current state of the world. Following the exposition, an **INCITING INCIDENT** introduces the antagonist and establishes the conflict. As the story progresses, the conflict becomes more complicated and tension increases, moving the story toward a **CLIMAX** or turning point, in which the conflict reaches a crisis point. Finally, there is a **RESOLUTION** to the conflict, followed by falling actions, events that move the characters away from the conflict and into a new life.

SETTING is the geographical and chronological location of events in a story. When considering setting, readers should examine how characters interact with their surroundings, how they are influenced by the societal expectations of that time and place, and how the location and time period impact the development of the story. Often, setting can seem inseparable from plot; therefore, a helpful question for beginning the discussion of setting is, How would this story change if it were set in a different time or place?

CHARACTER DEVELOPMENT is the process an author uses to create characters that are complex and, to some degree, believable. One way authors develop their characters is directly: they tell the reader explicitly what the character is like by describing traits and assigning values. Sometimes, authors might include the thoughts and feelings of the characters themselves, offering readers even more insight. Authors can also develop their characters indirectly by revealing their actions and interactions with others, sometimes including what one character says or thinks about another and allowing the reader to draw his or her own conclusions. Most authors use a combination of direct and indirect characterization; this ensures that readers know what they need to know while also providing opportunities for reflection and interpretation.

EXAMPLE

16. Which passage below from *A Mystery of Heroism* by Stephen Crane best demonstrates the third person omniscient point of view?

A) In the midst of it all Smith and Ferguson, two privates of A Company, were engaged in a heated discussion, which involved the greatest questions of the national existence.

B) An officer screamed out an order so violently that his voice broke and ended the sentence in a falsetto shriek.

C) The officer's face was grimy and perspiring, and his uniform was tousled as if he had been in direct grapple with an enemy. He smiled grimly when the men stared at him.

D) No, it could not be true. He was not a hero. Heroes had no shames in their lives, and, as for him, he remembered borrowing fifteen dollars from a friend and promising to pay it back the next day, and then avoiding that friend for ten months.

Answer Key

1. **D) is correct.** The art of the modern period reflects the new technologies and globalization possible through the internet.

2. **A) is correct.** According to the text, technology and the internet have "diversified the art world and brought it together simultaneously."

3. **B) is correct.** This option indicates both the main idea and what the reader will focus on while reading.

4. **D) is correct.** The phrase "no shortage of things to do or sights to see" suggests the writer is enthusiastic about the many interesting activities possible in California. There is no indication that the writer should do everything, though, or that one part is better than another.

5. **C) is correct.** The passage states that hiring subcontractors provides the advantage of "reduced legal responsibility to employees."

6. **D) is correct.** The text provides details on the experiment as well as its results.

7. **C) is correct.** The passage describes the journey of Cassini in chronological order: it passed by Titan, went through the region between Saturn and its rings, and ended its mission in 2017.

8. **C) is correct.** The informal tone and direct address of this passage suggest that the author is writing for a general audience that may include children. For instance, turning bottles into an art project could be a good activity for children.

9. **C) is correct.** Choice C is a simple fact stated by the author. It is introduced by the word *proven* to indicate that it is supported by evidence.

10. **D) is correct.** After the war, in the US there was a lack of focus on the world and greater focus on personal comforts, which writers viewed as superficiality and materialism.

11. **C) is correct.** The day is described as "cold and grey" with an "intangible pall," which creates a bleak mood. However, the man himself "did not worry" and knew that only "a few more days must pass" before he would see the sun again, suggesting he has accepted his circumstances.

12. **A) is correct.** Within the context of the sentence "It was a clear day, and yet there seemed an intangible pall over the face of things, a subtle gloom that made the day dark," the words *gloom* and *dark* are suggestive of death; the phrase *over the face* suggests a covering.

13. **A) is correct.** The word *incentivize* is defined immediately with the synonym *motivate*, or *encourage*.

14. **C) is correct.** The reader can infer that the *pressure to perform* is making the student anxious.

15. **C) is correct.** The metaphor implies that Alfie felt pressure from the people watching him to perform well. There is no indication that he is threatened physically.

16. **D) is correct.** The narrator is reporting the thoughts of the character, as the character's memory about not acting heroic in the past is revealed. The other choices only include descriptions of the characters words or actions.

PART III
Writing

CHAPTER FIVE
Language Skills

Parts of Speech

The **PARTS OF SPEECH** are the building blocks of sentences, paragraphs, and entire texts. Grammarians have typically defined eight parts of speech—nouns, pronouns, verbs, adverbs, adjectives, conjunctions, prepositions, and interjections—all of which play unique roles in the context of a sentence. Thus, a fundamental understanding of the parts of speech is necessary in order to form an understanding of basic sentence construction.

NOUNS and PRONOUNS

NOUNS are the words we use to give names to people, places, things, and ideas. Most often, nouns fill the position of subject or object within a sentence. The category of nouns has several subcategories: common nouns (*chair, car, house*), proper nouns (*Julie, David*), abstract nouns (*love, intelligence, sadness*), concrete nouns (*window, bread, person*), compound nouns (*brother-in-law, rollercoaster*), non-countable nouns (*money, water*), countable nouns (*dollars, cubes*), and verbal nouns (*writing, diving*). There is much crossover between these subcategories (for example, *chair* is common, concrete, and countable).

DID YOU KNOW?
Although some words fall easily into one category or another, many words can function as different parts of speech based on their usage within a sentence.

Sometimes, a word that is typically used as a noun will be used to modify another noun. The word then would be labeled as an adjective because of its usage within the sentence. In the following example, *cabin* is a noun in the first sentence and an adjective in the second:

The family visited the <u>cabin</u> by the lake.
Our <u>cabin</u> stove overheated during vacation.

PRONOUNS replace nouns in a sentence or paragraph, allowing a writer to achieve a smooth flow throughout a text by avoiding unnecessary repetition. The unique aspect of the pronoun as a part of speech is that the list of pronouns is finite: while there are innumerable nouns in the English language, the list of pronouns is rather limited in contrast. The noun that a pronoun replaces is called its **ANTECEDENT**.

Pronouns fall into several distinct categories. **PERSONAL PRONOUNS** act as subjects or objects in a sentence:

> She received a letter; I gave the letter to her.

POSSESSIVE PRONOUNS indicate possession:

> My coat is red; our car is blue.

REFLEXIVE (intensive) **PRONOUNS** intensify a noun or reflect back upon a noun:

> I myself made the dessert. I made the dessert myself.

DID YOU KNOW?
The subject performs the action of a sentence, while the object has the action performed on it.

Personal, possessive, and reflexive pronouns must all agree with the noun that they replace both in gender (male, female, or neutral), number (singular or plural), and person. **PERSON** refers to the point of view of the sentence. First person is the point of view of the speaker (I, me), second person is the person being addressed (you), and third person refers to a person outside the sentence (he, she, they).

Table 5.1. Personal, Possessive, and Reflexive Pronouns

CASE	FIRST PERSON		SECOND PERSON		THIRD PERSON	
	singular	plural	singular	plural	singular	plural
Subject	I	we	you	you (all)	he, she, it,	they
Object	me	us	you	you (all)	him, her, it	them
Possessive	my	our	your	your	his, her, its	their
Reflexive	myself	ourselves	yourself	yourselves	himself, herself, itself	themselves

RELATIVE PRONOUNS begin dependent clauses. Like other pronouns, they may appear in subject or object case, depending on the clause. Take, for example, the sentence below:

> Charlie, who made the clocks, works in the basement.

Here, the relative pronoun *who* is substituting for Charlie; that word indicates that Charlie makes the clocks, and so *who* is in the subject case because it is performing the action (*makes the clocks*).

In cases where a person is the object of a relative clause, the writer would use the relative pronoun *whom*. For example, read the sentence below:

My father, <u>whom</u> I care for, is sick.

Even though *my father* is the subject of the sentence, in the relative clause the relative pronoun *whom* is the object of the preposition *for*. Therefore that pronoun appears in the object case.

When a relative clause refers to a non-human, *that* or *which* is used. (*I live in Texas, which is a large state.*) The relative pronoun *whose* indicates possession. (*I don't know whose car that is.*)

Table 5.2. Relative Pronouns

Pronoun Type	Subject	Object
Person	who	whom
Thing	which, that	
Possessive	whose	

INTERROGATIVE PRONOUNS begin questions (*Who worked last evening?*). They request information about people, places, things, ideas, location, time, means, and purposes.

Table 5.3. Interrogative Pronouns

Interrogative Pronoun	Asks About	Example
who	person	<u>Who</u> lives there?
whom	person	To <u>whom</u> shall I send the letter?
what	thing	<u>What</u> is your favorite color?
where	place	<u>Where</u> do you go to school?
when	time	<u>When</u> will we meet for dinner?
which	selection	<u>Which</u> movie would you like to see?
why	reason	<u>Why</u> are you going to be late?
how	manner	<u>How</u> did the ancient Egyptians build the pyramids?

DEMONSTRATIVE PRONOUNS point out or draw attention to something or someone. They can also indicate proximity or distance.

		Table 5.4. Demonstrative Pronouns		
NUMBER	**SUBJECT/ PROXIMITY**	**EXAMPLE**	**OBJECT/ DISTANCE**	**EXAMPLE**
Singular	this (subject)	<u>This</u> is my apartment— please come in!	that (object)	I gave <u>that</u> to him yesterday.
	this (proximity)	<u>This</u> is the computer you will use right here, not the one in the other office.	that (distance)	<u>That</u> is the Statue of Liberty across the harbor.
Plural	these (subject)	<u>These</u> are flawless diamonds.	those (object)	Give <u>those</u> to me later.
	these (proximity)	<u>These</u> right here are the books we want, not the ones over there.	those (distance)	<u>Those</u> mountains across the plains are called the Rockies.

Indefinite pronouns simply replace nouns to avoid unnecessary repetition:

<u>Several</u> came to the party to see <u>both</u>.

Indefinite pronouns can be either singular or plural (and some can act as both depending on the context). If the indefinite pronoun is the subject of the sentence, it is important to know whether that pronoun is singular or plural so that the verb can agree with the pronoun in number.

	Table 5.5. Common Indefinite Pronouns		
SINGULAR		**PLURAL**	**SINGULAR OR PLURAL**
each	everybody	both	some
either	nobody	few	any
neither	somebody	several	none
one	anybody	many	all
everyone	everything		most
no one	nothing		more
someone	something		*These pronouns take their singularity or plurality from the object of the prepositions that follow: Some of the pies were eaten.*
anyone	anything		*Some of the pie was eaten.*
	another		

VERBS

VERBS express action (*run, jump, play*) or state of being (*is, seems*). The former are called action verbs, and the latter are linking verbs. Linking verbs join the subject of the sentence to the subject complement, which follows the verb and provides more information about the subject. See the sentence below:

> The dog is cute.

The dog is the subject, *is* is the linking verb, and *cute* is the subject complement.

Verbs can stand alone or they can be accompanied by **HELPING VERBS**, which are used to indicate tense. Verb tense indicates the time of the action. The action may have occurred in the past, present, or future. The action may also have been simple (occurring once) or continuous (ongoing). The perfect and perfect continuous tenses describe when actions occur in relation to other actions.

Table 5.6. Verb Tenses			
TENSE	**PAST**	**PRESENT**	**FUTURE**
Simple	I <u>answered</u> the question.	I <u>answer</u> your questions in class.	I <u>will answer</u> your question.
Continuous	I <u>was answering</u> your question when you interrupted me.	I <u>am answering</u> your question; please listen.	I <u>will be answering</u> your question after the lecture.
Perfect	I <u>had answered</u> all questions before class ended.	I <u>have answered</u> the questions already.	I <u>will have answered</u> every question before the class is over.
Perfect Continuous	I <u>had been answering</u> questions when the students started leaving.	I <u>have been answering</u> questions for 30 minutes and am getting tired.	I <u>will have been answering</u> students' questions for 20 years by the time I retire.
Helping Verbs: is/am/are/was/were, be/being/been, has/had/have, do/does/did, should, would, could, will			

Changing the spelling of the verb and/or adding helping verbs is known as **CONJUGATION**. In addition to being conjugated for tense, verbs are conjugated to indicate *person* (first, second, and third person) and *number* (whether they are singular or plural). The conjugation of the verb must agree with the subject of the sentence. A verb that has not be conjugated is called an infinitive and begins with *to* (*to swim, to be*).

Table 5.7. Verb Conjugation (Present Tense)		
PERSON	SINGULAR	PLURAL
First Person	I answer	we answer
Second Person	you answer	you (all) answer
Third Person	he/she/it answers	they answer

Verbs may be regular, meaning they follow normal conjugation patterns, or irregular, meaning they do not follow a regular pattern.

	SIMPLE PRESENT	PRESENT PARTICIPLE	SIMPLE PAST	PAST PARTICIPLE
Table 5.8. Regular and Irregular Verbs				
Regular	help	helping	helped	(have) helped
	jump	jumping	jumped	(have) jumped
Irregular	am	been	was	(have) been
	swim	swimming	swam	(have) swum
	sit	sitting	sat	(have) sat
	set	setting	set	(have) set
	lie	lying	lay	(have) lain
	lay	laying	laid	(have) laid
	rise	rising	rose	(have) risen
	raise	raising	raised	(have) raised

Verbs can be written in the active or passive voice. In the **ACTIVE** voice, the subject of the sentence performs the main action of the sentence. In the sentence below, Alexis is performing the action:

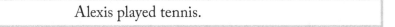

Alexis played tennis.

In the passive voice, the subject of the sentence is receiving the action of the main verb. In the sentence below, the subject is *tennis*, which receives the action *played*:

Tennis was played.

Note that, in the passive voice, there is no indication of who performed the action. For this reason, passive voice is used when the subject is unknown or unimportant. For example, in science, it is common to use the passive voice:

The experiment was performed three times.

At most other times, it is considered more appropriate to use the active voice because it is more dynamic and gives more information.

Finally, verbs can be classified by whether they take a **DIRECT OBJECT**, which is a noun that receives the action of the verb. Transitive verbs require a direct object. In the sentence below, the transitive verb *throw* has a direct object (ball):

> The pitcher will throw <u>the ball</u>.

Intransitive verbs do not require a direct object. Verbs like *run*, *jump*, and *go* make sense without any object:

> He will run.
> She jumped.

Many sets of similar verbs include one transitive and one intransitive verb, which can cause confusion. These troublesome verbs include combinations such as *lie* or *lay*, *rise* or *raise*, and *sit* or *set*.

Table 5.9. Intransitive and Transitive Verbs

INTRANSITIVE VERBS	TRANSITIVE VERBS	
lie – to recline	lay – to put	lay <u>something</u>
rise – to go or get up	raise – to lift	raise <u>something</u>
sit – to be seated	set – to put	set <u>something</u>
Hint: These intransitive verbs have *i* as the second letter. *Intransitive* begins with *i*.	Hint: The word *transitive* begins with a *t*, and it *TAKES* an object.	

ADJECTIVES and ADVERBS

ADVERBS take on a modifying or describing role and often take the ending *–ly*. These words can describe a number of different parts of speech and even phrases or clauses:

- verbs: *He <u>quickly</u> ran to the house next door.*
- adjectives: *Her <u>very</u> effective speech earned her a new job.*
- other adverbs: *Several puppies arrived <u>rather</u> happily after they had eaten dog treats.*
- entire sentences: *<u>Instead</u>, the owner kept his shop.*

Like adverbs, **ADJECTIVES** modify or describe, but they add to the meaning of nouns and pronouns only:

> <u>Five thoughtful</u> students came to work at the farm.

> The idea from the committee proved a <u>smart</u> one.

One very important note regarding the adjective is that any word used to describe a noun or pronoun will be classified as an adjective. *Her* could be used as a pronoun or an adjective depending on usage:

> <u>Her</u> dog barks until midnight. (adjective modifying *dog*)
> We gave several books to <u>her</u>. (pronoun)

Also note that *a*, *and*, and *the* (called articles) are always adjectives.

CONJUNCTIONS

Conjunctions join words into phrases, clauses, and sentences by use of three mechanisms. There are three main types of conjunctions. **Coordinating conjunctions** join together two independent clauses (i.e., two complete thoughts). These include *and*, *but*, *or*, *for*, *nor*, *yet*, *so* (FANBOYS). Note that some of these can also be used to join items in a series.

> I'll order lunch, <u>but</u> you need to go pick it up.
> Make sure to get sandwiches, chips, <u>and</u> sodas.

Correlative conjunctions (whether/or, either/or, neither/nor, both/and, not only/but also) work together to join items:

> <u>Both</u> the teacher <u>and</u> the students needed a break after the lecture.

Subordinating conjunctions join dependent clauses (thoughts that cannot stand alone as sentences) to the related independent clause. They usually describe some sort of relationship between the two parts of the sentence, such as cause/effect or order. They can appear at the beginning or in the middle of a sentence:

> We treat ourselves during football season to several orders <u>because</u> we love pizza.
> <u>Because</u> we love pizza, we treat ourselves during football season to several orders.

Table 5.10 Subordinating Conjunctions	
SUBORDINATING CONJUNCTIONS	
Time	after, as, as long as, as soon as, before, since, until, when, whenever, while
Manner	as, as if, as though
Cause	because

SUBORDINATING CONJUNCTIONS	
Condition	although, as long as, even if, even though, if, provided that, though, unless, while
Purpose	in order that, so that, that
Comparison	as, than

When using correlative conjunctions, be sure that the structure of the word, phrase, or clause that follows the first part of the conjunction mirrors the structure of the word, phrase, or clause that follows the second part.

> I will neither mow the grass nor pull the weeds today. (correct)
> I will neither mow the grass nor undertake the pulling of the weeds today.
> (incorrect)

PREPOSITIONS

PREPOSITIONS set up relationships in time (*after the party*) or space (*under the cushions*) within a sentence. A preposition will always function as part of a prepositional phrase, which includes the preposition along with the object of the preposition. If a word that usually acts as a preposition is standing alone in a sentence, the word is likely functioning as an adverb:

> She hid <u>underneath</u>.

Table 5.11 Common Prepositions

PREPOSITIONS	COMPOUND PREPOSITIONS
along, among, around, at, before, behind, below, beneath, beside, besides, between, beyond, by, despite, down, during, except, for, from, in, into, near, of, off, on, onto, out, outside, over, past, since, through, till, to, toward, under, underneath, until, up, upon, with, within, without	according to, as of, as well as, aside from, because of, by means of, in addition to, in front of, in place of, in respect to, in spite of, instead of, on account of, out of, prior to, with regard to

INTERJECTIONS

INTERJECTIONS have no grammatical attachment to the sentence itself other than to add expressions of emotion. These parts of speech may be punctuated with commas or exclamation points and may fall anywhere within the sentence itself:

DID YOU KNOW?
Interjections should generally be avoided in formal writing.

> <u>Ouch</u>! He stepped on my toe.
>
> She shopped at the stores after Christmas and, <u>hooray</u>, found many items on sale.
>
> I have seen his love for his father in many expressions of concern—<u>Wow</u>!

EXAMPLES

1. List all of the adjectives used in the following sentence:

    Her camera fell into the turbulent water, so her frantic friend quickly grabbed the damp item.

    A) turbulent, frantic, damp

    B) turbulent, frantic, quickly, damp

    C) her, turbulent, her, frantic, damp

    D) her, the, turbulent, her, frantic, the, damp

2. List all of the pronouns used in the following sentence:

    Several of the administrators who had spoken clearly on the budget increase gave both of the opposing committee members a list of their ideas.

    A) several, of, their

    B) several, who, both

    C) several, who, both, their

    D) several, both

3. List all of the conjunctions in the following sentence, and indicate after each conjunction whether the conjunctions are coordinating, correlative, or subordinating:

    The political parties do not know if the most popular candidates will survive until the election, but neither the voters nor the candidates will give up their push for popularity.

    A) if (subordinating), until (subordinating), but (coordinating), neither/nor (correlative), for (coordinating)

    B) if (subordinating), but (coordinating), neither/nor (correlative), for (coordinating)

    C) if (subordinating), but (coordinating), neither/nor (correlative)

    D) if (subordinating), until (subordinating), but (coordinating), neither/nor (correlative), up (subordinating), for (coordinating)

Constructing Sentences

SYNTAX is the study of how words are combined to create sentences. In English, words are used to build phrases and clauses, which, in turn, are combined to create sentences.

By varying the order and length of phrases and clauses, writers can create sentences that are diverse and interesting.

Phrases and clauses are made up of either a subject, a predicate, or both. The SUBJECT is what the sentence is about. It will be a noun that is usually performing the main action of the sentence, and it may be accompanied by modifiers. The PREDICATE describes what the subject is doing or being. It contains the verb(s) and any modifiers or objects that accompany it.

PHRASES

A PHRASE is a group of words that communicates a partial idea and lacks either a subject or a predicate. Several phrases may be strung together, one after another, to add detail and interest to a sentence.

> The animals crossed the large bridge to eat the fish on the wharf.

Phrases are categorized based on the main word in the phrase. A PREPOSITIONAL PHRASE begins with a preposition and ends with an object of the preposition; a VERB PHRASE is composed of the main verb along with its helping verbs; and a NOUN PHRASE consists of a noun and its modifiers.

> Prepositional phrase: The dog is hiding under the porch.
> Verb phrase: The chef would have created another soufflé, but the staff protested.
> Noun phrase: *The big, red barn* rests beside the vacant chicken house.

An APPOSITIVE PHRASE is a particular type of noun phrase that renames the word or group of words that precedes it. Appositive phrases usually follow the noun they describe and are set apart by commas.

> My dad, a clock maker, loved antiques.

VERBAL PHRASES begin with a word that would normally act as a verb but is instead filling another role within the sentence. These phrases can act as nouns, adjectives, or adverbs. GERUND PHRASES begin with gerunds, which are verbs that end in *–ing* and act as nouns. The word *gerund* has an *n* in it, a helpful reminder that the gerund acts as a noun. Therefore, the gerund phrase might act as the subject, the direct object, or the object of the preposition just as another noun would.

> Gerund phrase: Writing numerous Christmas cards occupies her aunt's time each year.

A PARTICIPIAL PHRASE is a verbal phrase that acts as an adjective. These phrases start with either present participles (which end in *–ing*) or past participles (which usually end in –*ed*). Participial phrases can be extracted from the sentence, and the sentence will still make sense because the participial phrase is playing only a modifying role:

> <u>Enjoying the stars that filled the sky</u>, Dave lingered outside for quite a while.

Finally, an **INFINITIVE PHRASE** is a verbal phrase that may act as a noun, an adjective, or an adverb. Infinitive phrases begin with the word *to*, followed by a simple form of a verb (to eat, to jump, to skip, to laugh, to sing).

> <u>To visit Europe</u> had always been her dream.

CLAUSES

CLAUSES contain both a subject and a predicate. They can be either independent or dependent. An **INDEPENDENT** (or main) **CLAUSE** can stand alone as its own sentence:

> The dog ate her homework.

Dependent (or subordinate) clauses cannot stand alone as their own sentences. They start with a subordinating conjunction, relative pronoun, or relative adjective, which will make them sound incomplete:

> <u>Because</u> the dog ate her homework

Table 5.12. Words That Begin Dependent Clauses	
SUBORDINATING CONJUNCTIONS	**RELATIVE PRONOUNS AND ADJECTIVES**
after, before, once, since, until, when, whenever, while, as, because, in order that, so, so that, that, if, even if, provided that, unless, although, even though, though, whereas, where, wherever, than, whether	who, whoever, whom, whom-ever, whose, which, that, when, where, why, how

TYPES of SENTENCES

Sentences can be classified based on the number and type of clauses they contain. A **SIMPLE SENTENCE** will have only one independent clause and no dependent clauses. The sentence may contain phrases, complements, and modifiers, but it will comprise only one independent clause, one complete idea.

> The cat under the back porch jumped against the glass yesterday.

A **COMPOUND SENTENCE** has two or more independent clauses and no dependent clauses:

> The cat under the back porch jumped against the glass yesterday, and he scared my grandma.

A **COMPLEX SENTENCE** has only one independent clause and one or more dependent clauses:

> The cat under the back porch, who loves tuna, jumped against the glass yesterday.

A **COMPOUND-COMPLEX SENTENCE** has two or more independent clauses and one or more dependent clause:

> The cat under the back porch, who loves tuna, jumped against the glass yesterday; he left a mark on the window.

Table 5.13. Sentence Structure and Clauses

SENTENCE STRUCTURE	INDEPENDENT CLAUSES	DEPENDENT CLAUSES
Simple	1	0
Compound	2 +	0
Complex	1	1 +
Compound-complex	2 +	1 +

Writers can diversify their use of phrases and clauses in order to introduce variety into their writing. Variety in **SENTENCE STRUCTURE** not only makes writing more interesting but also allows writers to emphasize that which deserves emphasis. In a paragraph of complex sentences, a short, simple sentence can be a powerful way to draw attention to a major point.

EXAMPLES

4. Identify the prepositional phrase in the following sentence:

   Wrapping packages for the soldiers, the kind woman tightly rolled the t-shirts to see how much space remained for the homemade cookies.

   A) Wrapping packages for the soldiers

   B) the kind woman

   C) to see how much space

   D) for the homemade cookies

5. Which sentence is correct in its sentence structure label?

A) The grandchildren and their cousins enjoyed their day at the beach. (compound)

B) Most of the grass has lost its deep color despite the fall lasting into December. (complex)

C) The members who had served selflessly were cheering as the sequestration ended. (simple)

D) Do as you please. (complex)

Punctuation

Many of the choices writers must make relate to **PUNCTUATION**. While creative writers have the liberty to play with punctuation to achieve their desired ends, academic and technical writers must adhere to stricter conventions. The main punctuation marks are periods, question marks, exclamation marks, colons, semicolons, commas, quotation marks, and apostrophes.

DID YOU KNOW?

Exclamation points should be used sparingly or not at all in formal writing.

There are three terminal punctuation marks that can be used to end sentences. The **PERIOD** is the most common and is used to end declarative (statement) and imperative (command) sentences. The **QUESTION MARK** is used to end interrogative sentences, and exclamation marks are used to indicate that the writer or speaker is exhibiting intense emotion or energy.

> Sarah and I are attending a concert.
> How many people are attending the concert?
> What a great show that was!

The **COLON** and the **SEMICOLON**, though often confused, have a unique set of rules surrounding their respective uses. While both punctuation marks are used to join clauses, the construction of the clauses and the relationship between them varies.

The **SEMICOLON** is used to show a general relationship between two independent clauses (IC; IC):

> The disgruntled customer tapped angrily on the <u>counter; she</u> had to wait nearly ten minutes to speak to the manager.

Coordinating conjunctions (FANBOYS) cannot be used with semi-colons. However, conjunctive adverbs can be used following a semi-colon:

> She may not have to take the course this <u>year; however,</u> she will eventually have to sign up for that specific course.

The **COLON**, somewhat less limited than the semicolon in its usage, is used to introduce a list, definition, or clarification. While the clause preceding the colon must be an independent clause, the clause that follows does not have to be one:

> The buffet offers three choices that include: ham, turkey, or roast. (incorrect)
> The buffet offers three choices: ham, turkey, or roast. (correct)
> The buffet offers three choices that include the following: ham, turkey, or roast. (correct)

Note that neither the semicolon nor the colon should be used to set off an introductory phrase from the rest of the sentence.

> After the trip to the raceway; we realized that we should have brought ear plugs. (incorrect)
> After the trip to the raceway: we realized that we should have brought ear plugs. (incorrect)
> After the trip to the raceway, we realized that we should have brought ear plugs. (correct)

The **COMMA** is a complicated piece of punctuation that can serve many different purposes within a sentence. Many times comma placement is an issue of style, not mechanics, meaning there is not necessarily one correct way to write the sentence. There are, however, a few important hard-and-fast comma rules to be followed.

1. Commas should be used to separate two independent clauses along with a coordinating conjunction.
   George ordered the steak, but Bruce preferred the ham.

2. Commas should be used to separate coordinate adjectives (two different adjectives that describe the same noun).
   The shiny, regal horse ran majestically through the wide, open field.

3. Commas should be used to separate items in a series. The comma before the conjunction is called the Oxford or serial comma, and is optional.
   The list of groceries included cream, coffee, donuts, and tea.

4. Commas should be used to separate introductory words, phrases, and clauses from the rest of the sentence.
   Slowly, Nathan became aware of his surroundings after the concussion.
   Within an hour, the authorities will descend on the home.
   After Alice swam the channel, nothing intimidated her.

5. Commas should be used to set off non-essential information and appositives.

DID YOU KNOW?
Many people are taught that a comma represents a pause for breath. While this trick is useful for helping young readers, it is not a helpful guide for comma usage when writing.

Estelle, our newly elected chairperson, will be in attendance.
Ida, my neighbor, watched the children for me last week.

6. Commas should be used to set off titles of famous individuals.
    Charles, Prince of Wales, visited Canada several times in the last ten years.

7. Commas should be used to set off the day and month of a date within a text.
    My birthday makes me feel quite old because I was born on February 16, 1958, in Minnesota.

8. Commas should be used to set up numbers in a text of more than four digits.
    We expect 25,000 visitors to the new museum.

QUOTATION MARKS are used for many purposes. First, quotation marks are used to enclose direct quotations within a sentence. Terminal punctuation that is part of the quotation should go inside the marks, and terminal punctuation that is part of the larger sentence goes outside:

> She asked him menacingly, "Where is my peanut butter?"
> What is the original meaning of the phrase "king of the hill"?

In American English, commas are used to set quotations apart from the following text and are placed inside the marks:

DID YOU KNOW?
If a quotation is within another quotation, then the inner quotation uses single quotation marks.

> "Although I find him tolerable," Arianna wrote, "I would never want him as a roommate."

Additionally, quotation marks enclose titles of short, or relatively short, literary works such as short stories, chapters, and poems. (The titles of longer works, like novels and anthologies, are italicized.) Writers also use quotation marks to set off words used in special sense or for a non-literary purpose:

> The shady dealings of his Ponzi scheme earned him the ironic name "Honest Abe."

APOSTROPHES, sometimes referred to as single quotation marks, show possession; replace missing letters, numerals, and signs; and form plurals of letters, numerals, and signs in certain instances.

1. To signify possession by a singular noun not ending in *s*, add *'s: boy → boy's.*

2. To signify possession by a singular noun ending in *s*, add *'s: class → class's.*

3. To signify possession by an indefinite pronoun not ending in *s*, add *'s: someone → someone's.*

4. To signify possession by a plural noun not ending in *s*, add *'s*: *children* → *children's*

5. To signify possession by a plural noun ending in *s*, add only the apostrophe: *boys* → *boys'*.

6. To signify possession by singular, compound words and phrases, add *'s* to the last word in the phrase: *everybody else* → *everybody else's*.

7. To signify joint possession, add *'s* only to the last noun: *John and Mary's house*.

8. To signify individual possession, add *'s* to each noun: *John's and Mary's houses*.

9. To signify missing letters in a contraction, place the apostrophe where the letters are missing: *do not* → *don't*.

10. To signify missing numerals, place the apostrophe where the numerals are missing: *1989* → *'89*.

11. There are differing schools of thought regarding the pluralization of numerals and dates, but be consistent within the document with whichever method you choose: *1990's/1990s*; *A's/As*.

Other marks of punctuation include:

▶ EN DASH (–) to indicate a range of dates

▶ EM DASH (—) to indicate an abrupt break in a sentence and emphasize the words within the em dashes

▶ PARENTHESES ( ) to enclose insignificant information

▶ BRACKETS [ ] to enclose added words to a quotation and to add insignificant information within parentheses

▶ SLASH (/) to separate lines of poetry within a text or to indicate interchangeable terminology

▶ ELLIPSES (…) to indicate information removed from a quotation, to indicate a missing line of poetry, or to create a reflective pause

EXAMPLES

6. Identify the marks of punctuation needed in the following sentence:
Freds brother wanted the following items for Christmas a red car a condo and a puppy.
   A) Fred's / Christmas; / car, /condo,
   B) Fred's / Christmas: / car, / condo,
   C) Fred's / Christmas: / red, / car,
   D) Fred's / items' / Christmas: / car, / condo,

Avoiding Common Usage Errors
ERRORS in AGREEMENT

Some of the most common grammatical errors are those involving agreement between subjects and verbs, and between nouns and pronouns. While it is impossible to cover all possible errors, the lists below include the most common agreement rules to look for on the test.

SUBJECT/VERB AGREEMENT

1. Single subjects agree with single verbs; plural subjects agree with plural verbs.
   ▷ The girl walks her dog.
   ▷ The girls walk their dogs.

2. Compound subjects joined by *and* typically take a plural verb unless considered one item.
   ▷ Correctness and precision are required for all good writing.
   ▷ Macaroni and cheese makes a great snack for children.

3. Compound subjects joined by *or* or *nor* agree with the nearer or nearest subject.
   ▷ Neither I nor my friends are looking forward to our final exams.
   ▷ Neither my friends nor I am looking forward to our final exams.

4. For sentences with inverted word order, the verb will agree with the subject that follows it.
   ▷ Where are Bob and his friends going?
   ▷ Where is Bob going?

DID YOU KNOW?
Ignore words between the subject and the verb to help make conjugation clearer:
The new library with its many books and rooms fills a long-felt need.

5. All single, indefinite pronouns agree with single verbs.
   ▷ Neither of the students is happy about the play.
   ▷ Each of the many cars is on the grass.
   ▷ Every one of the administrators speaks highly of Trevor.

6. All plural, indefinite pronouns agree with plural verbs.
   ▷ <u>Several</u> of the students <u>are</u> happy about the play.
   ▷ <u>Both</u> of the cars <u>are</u> on the grass.
   ▷ <u>Many</u> of the administrators <u>speak</u> highly of Trevor.

7. Collective nouns agree with singular verbs when the collective acts as one unit. Collective nouns agree with plural verbs when the collective acts as individuals within the group.
   ▷ The <u>band plans</u> a party after the final football game.
   ▷ The <u>band play</u> their instruments even if it rains.
   ▷ The <u>jury announces</u> its decision after sequestration.
   ▷ The <u>jury make</u> phone calls during their break time.

8. The linking verbs agree with the subject and the predicate.
   ▷ My <u>favorite is</u> strawberries and apples.
   ▷ My <u>favorites are</u> strawberries and apples.

9. Nouns that are plural in form but singular in meaning will agree with singular verbs.
   ▷ <u>Measles is</u> a painful disease.
   ▷ <u>Sixty dollars is</u> too much to pay for that book.

10. Singular verbs come after titles, business corporations, and words used as terms.
   ▷ <u>"Three Little Kittens" is</u> a favorite nursery rhyme for many children.
   ▷ <u>General Motors is</u> a major employer for the city.

PRONOUN/ANTECEDENT AGREEMENT

1. Antecedents joined by *and* typically require a plural pronoun.
   The <u>children and their dogs</u> enjoyed <u>their</u> day at the beach.

2. For compound antecedents joined by *or*, the pronoun agrees with the nearer or nearest antecedent.
   Either the resident mice <u>or the manager's cat</u> gets <u>itself</u> a meal of good leftovers.

3. When indefinite pronouns function in a sentence, the pronoun must agree with the number of the pronoun.
   ▷ <u>Neither</u> student finished <u>his or her</u> assignment.
   ▷ <u>Both</u> of the students finished <u>their</u> assignments.

4. When collective nouns function as antecedents, the pronoun choice will be singular or plural depending on the function of the collective.
   ▷ The <u>audience</u> was cheering as <u>it</u> rose to <u>its</u> feet in unison.
   ▷ Our <u>family</u> are spending <u>their</u> vacations in Maine, Hawaii, and Rome.

5. When *each* and *every* precede the antecedent, the pronoun agreement will be singular.

▷ <u>Each and every man, woman, and child</u> brings unique qualities to <u>his or her</u> family.

▷ <u>Every creative writer, technical writer, and research writer</u> is attending <u>his or her</u> assigned lecture.

ERRORS in SENTENCE CONSTRUCTION

ERRORS IN PARALLELISM occur when items in a series are not put in the same form. For example, if a list contains two nouns and a verb, the sentence should be rewritten so that all three items are the same part of speech. Parallelism should be maintained in words, phrases, and clauses:

> The walls were painted <u>green</u> and <u>gold</u>.
> Her home is <u>up the hill</u> and <u>beyond the trees</u>.
> <u>If we shop on Friday</u> and <u>if we have enough time</u>, we will then visit the aquarium.

SENTENCE ERRORS fall into three categories: fragments, comma splices (comma fault), and fused sentences (run-on). A FRAGMENT occurs when a group of words does not have both a subject and verb as needed to construct a complete sentence or thought. Many times a writer will mirror conversation and write down only a dependent clause, for example, which will have a subject and verb but will not have a complete thought grammatically.

> Why are you not going to the mall? Because I do not like shopping. (incorrect)
> Because I do not like shopping, I will not plan to go to the mall. (correct)

A COMMA SPLICE (comma fault) occurs when two independent clauses are joined together with only a comma to "splice" them together. To fix a comma splice, a coordinating conjunction should be added, or the comma can be replaced by a semicolon:

> My family eats turkey at Thanksgiving, we eat ham at Christmas. (incorrect)
> My family eats turkey at Thanksgiving, and we eat ham at Christmas. (correct)
> My family eats turkey at Thanksgiving; we eat ham at Christmas. (correct)

FUSED (run-on) sentences occur when two independent clauses are joined with no punctuation whatsoever. Like comma splices, they can be fixed with a comma and conjunction or with a semicolon:

> My sister lives nearby she never comes to visit. (incorrect)

My sister lives nearby, but she never comes to visit. (correct)
My sister lives nearby; she never comes to visit. (correct)

COMMONLY CONFUSED WORDS

A, AN: *a* is used before words beginning with consonants or consonant sounds; *an* is used before words beginning with vowels or vowel sounds.

AFFECT, EFFECT: *affect* is most often a verb; *effect* is usually a noun (*The experience affected me significantly* OR *The experience had a significant effect on me.*)

AMONG, AMONGST, BETWEEN: *among* is used for a group of more than two people; *amongst* is archaic and not commonly used in modern writing; *between* is reserved to distinguish two people, places, things, or groups.

AMOUNT, NUMBER: *amount* is used for non-countable sums; *number* is used with countable nouns (*She had a large amount of money in her purse, nearly fifty dollars.*)

CITE, SITE: *cite* is a verb used in documentation to credit an author of a quotation, paraphrase, or summary; *site* is a location.

ELICIT, ILLICIT: *elicit* means to draw out a response from an audience or a listener; *illicit* refers to illegal activity.

EVERY DAY, EVERYDAY: *every day* is an indefinite adjective modifying a noun—*each day* could be used interchangeably with *every day*; *everyday* is a one-word adjective to imply frequent occurrence (*Our visit to the Minnesota State Fair is an everyday activity during August.*)

FEWER, LESS: *fewer* is used with a countable noun; *less* is used with a non-countable noun (*Fewer parents are experiencing stress since the new teacher was hired; parents are experiencing less stress since the new teacher was hired.*)

FIRSTLY, SECONDLY: These words are archaic; today, *first* and *second* are more commonly used.

GOOD, WELL: *good* is always the adjective; *well* is always the adverb except in cases of health (*She felt well after the surgery.*)

IMPLIED, INFERRED: *implied* is something a speaker does; *inferred* is something the listener does after assessing the speaker's message (*The speaker implied something mysterious, but I inferred the wrong thing.*)

IRREGARDLESS, REGARDLESS: *irregardless* is non-standard usage and should be avoided; *regardless* is the proper usage of the transitional statement.

ITS, IT'S: *its* is a possessive case pronoun; *it's* is a contraction for *it is*.

MORAL, MORALE: *moral* is a summative lesson from a story or life event; *morale* is the emotional attitude of a person or group of people.

PRINCIPAL, PRINCIPLE: *principal* is the leader of a school in the noun usage; *principal* means *main* in the adjectival usage; *principle* is a noun meaning *idea* or *tenet* (*The principal of the school spoke on the principal meaning of the main principles of the school.*)

QUOTE, QUOTATION: *quote* is a verb and should be used as a verb; *quotation* is the noun and should be used as a noun.

REASON WHY: *reason why* is a redundant expression—use one or the other (*The reason we left is a secret. Why we left is a secret.*)

SHOULD OF, SHOULD HAVE: *should of* is improper usage, likely resulting from misunderstood speech—*of* is not a helping verb and can therefore cannot complete the verb phrase; *should have* is the proper usage. (*He should have driven.*)

THAN, THEN: *than* sets up a comparison of some kind; *then* indicates a reference to a point in time (*When I said that I liked the hat better than the gloves, my sister laughed; then she bought both for me.*)

THEIR, THERE, THEY'RE: *their* is the possessive case of the pronoun *they*. *There* is the demonstrative pronoun indicating location, or place. *They're* is a contraction of the words *they are*, the third-person plural subject pronoun and third-person plural, present-tense conjugation of the verb *to be*. These words are very commonly confused in written English.

TO LIE (TO RECLINE), TO LAY (TO PLACE): *to lie* is the intransitive verb meaning *to recline*, so the verb does not take an object; *to lay* is the transitive verb meaning *to place something*. (*I lie out in the sun; I lay my towel on the beach.*)

TO TRY AND: *to try and* is sometimes used erroneously in place of *to try to*. (*She should try to succeed daily.*)

UNIQUE: *unique* is an ultimate superlative. The word *unique* should not be modified technically. (*The experience was very unique.*)

WHO, WHOM: *who* is the subject relative pronoun. (*My son, who is a good student, studies hard.*) Here, the son is carrying out the action of studying, so the pronoun is a subject pronoun (*who*). *Whom* is the object relative pronoun. (*My son, whom the other students admire, studies hard.*) Here, *son* is the object of the other students' admiration, so the pronoun standing in for him, *whom*, is an object pronoun.

YOUR, YOU'RE: *your* is the possessive case of the pronoun *you*. *You're* is a contraction of the words *you are*, the second-person subject pronoun and the second-person singular, present-tense conjugation of the verb *to be*. These words are commonly confused in written English.

EXAMPLES

8. Which sentence does NOT contain an error?

   A)   My sister and my best friend lives in Chicago.

   B)   My parents or my brother is going to pick me up from the airport.

   C)   Neither of the students refuse to take the exam.

   D)   The team were playing a great game until the rain started.

9. Which sentence does NOT contain an error?

   A)   The grandchildren and their cousins enjoyed their day at the beach.

   B)   Most of the grass has lost their deep color.

   C)   The jury was cheering as their commitment came to a close.

   D)   Every boy and girl must learn to behave themselves in school.

10. Which of the following sentence errors is labeled correctly?

   A)   Since she went to the store. (fused)

   B)   The football game ended in a tie, the underdog caught up in the fourth quarter. (fragment)

   C)   The football game ended in a tie the underdog caught up in the fourth quarter. (fused)

   D)   When the players dropped their gloves, a fight broke out on the ice hockey rink floor. (comma splice)

Answer Key

1. A) is incorrect. This list is incomplete.

   B) is incorrect. This list is incomplete and inaccurate; *quickly* is an adverb.

   C) is incorrect. This list is incomplete.

   D) is correct. *Turbulent*, *frantic*, and *damp* are adjectives; *her* is modifying first *camera* and then *friend*; and *the* is always a limiting adjective—the definite article.

2. A) is incorrect. The word *of* is a preposition; the word *their* is being used as a possessive adjective.

   B) is correct. *Several* is an indefinite plural pronoun; *who* is a relative pronoun introducing the adjectival clause *who had spoken clearly on the budget increase*; *both* is an indefinite plural pronoun.

   C) is incorrect. The word *their* is being used as a possessive adjective.

   D) is incorrect. The list is missing the word *who* which is a relative pronoun introducing the adjectival clause *who had spoken clearly on the budget increase*.

3. A) is incorrect. *Until* and *for* in this sentence are acting as prepositions.

   B) is incorrect. *For* is acting as a preposition.

   C) is correct. *If* is acting as a subordinating conjunction; *but* is acting as a coordinating conjunction; and *neither/nor* is a correlative conjunction pair.

   D) is incorrect. *Up* is acting as an adverb.

4. A) is incorrect. This is a participial phrase that begins with the participle *wrapping*.

   B) is incorrect. This is a noun phrase that contains the noun *woman* and modifiers.

   C) is incorrect. This is an infinitive phrase that begins with the infinitive *to see*.

   D) is correct. This phrase begins with the preposition *for*.

5. A) is incorrect. This sentence is simple with only one independent clause.

   B) is incorrect. This sentence is simple with only one independent clause but several phrases.

   C) is incorrect. This sentence is complex, having only one independent clause and two dependent clauses.

   D) is correct. This sentence is complex because it has one independent clause (*Do*) and one dependent (*as you please*).

6. A) is incorrect. *Christmas* must have a colon after it and not a semicolon. A semicolon must have an independent clause that precedes and follows.

B) is correct. To be possessive, *Fred's* requires an apostrophe before the *s*. *Christmas* needs a colon to indicate the upcoming list, and *car* and *condo* should be followed by a comma since they are items in a series.

C) is incorrect. The correct comma placement for items in a series is a, b, and c. *Red* is an adjective modifying *car* and so does not require a comma; it is not an item in the series of nouns.

D) is incorrect. The word *items* is simply plural without showing possession.

7. A) is incorrect. The commas are used correctly in this series.

   B) is correct. This compound sentence requires a comma before the conjunction *but*.

   C) is incorrect. This complex sentence does not require a comma.

   D) is incorrect. The appositive phrase *who lives in Indiana* is appropriately set apart by commas.

8. A) is incorrect. Because the sentence reads <u>My</u> sister and <u>my</u> best friend, the subject is plural and needs a plural verb (*live*).

   B) is correct. The verb agrees with the closest subject—in this case, the singular *brother*.

   C) is incorrect. *Neither* is a singular, indefinite pronoun, so the agreement is singular. *Neither refuses...*

   D) is incorrect. In the context of a game, the *team* is functioning as a singular, so it should take a singular verb. *The team was...*

9. **A) is correct.** *Grandchildren and cousins/their*

   B) is incorrect. *Most of the grass has lost <u>its</u> deep color.*

   C) is incorrect. *The jury was cheering as <u>its</u> commitment came to a close.*

   D) is incorrect. *Every boy and girl must learn to behave himself or herself in school.*

10. A) is incorrect. The group of words in choice A) is not a complete thought and would, therefore, be classified as a fragment.

   B) is incorrect. The sentence in choice B) joins two complete thoughts with only a comma and would therefore be classified as a comma splice.

   C) is correct. These two independent clauses in choice C) are fused because there is no punctuation where the two clauses meet.

   D) is incorrect. The sentence in choice D) is punctuated properly and constructed correctly. The introductory, adverbial clause is punctuated with a comma; then an independent clause follows.

CHAPTER SIX
Writing

Regardless of the format or topic, a high-scoring essay can be written by following several simple rules. First, identify the type of essay to be written: if the essay doesn't correctly address the prompt, it will always receive a low score. Second, determine what the main point and organizational structure of the essay will be. It is much easier to write using a clear outline than to haphazardly organize along the way. Third, make sure that the essay uses sound evidence while maintaining a style that's appropriate to the test. A good essay doesn't have to be complicated; it just needs to have a clear, well-reasoned position. Finally, all of this must be accomplished within a limited time frame. Fortunately, the essay graders will understand that a first draft written under test conditions does not need to be as polished as a final essay in a classroom assignment.

Types of Essays

It is important to note that essays do not follow a single format. Rather, the format is determined by the intended purpose of each essay. For example, an essay may attempt to inform or persuade the reader, or perhaps describe or narrate a scene. It is important to use the appropriate type of essay for a given task.

PERSUASIVE

A **PERSUASIVE ESSAY** is meant to convince the reader of the author's point of view on a particular issue. Typically, such an essay will also include a call to action. Thus, a persuasive essay should cause the reader to feel and act in a particular way.

A persuasive essay can be written on any topic on which people can have a difference of opinion. For example, an essay may argue that social media is harmful to teenagers or that a noise ordinance should be adopted in a community. These both seek to sway the reader's opinion to that of the author's. In contrast, essays describing the social media habits of teenagers or telling the story of a neighborhood's attempt to pass local noise ordinances are not persuasive because they do not present a specific opinion.

In writing a persuasive essay, it is vital to take a clear stance on an issue. The reader should be left with no doubt as to which side of an issue the writer supports. In addition, a persuasive essay must include facts and logical reasoning to show that the ideas put forth by the author are superior to other ideas on the topic. This type of essay should be written with a specific audience in mind to tailor the arguments and language to the intended readers.

When writing persuasive essays in an exam setting, keep in mind that the actual stance taken in the essay is not important. The graders don't care about the specific opinion expressed in the essay; they only care that the opinion is well written and supported by logically relevant evidence.

PERSUASIVE ESSAY EXAMPLE

PROMPT: Technology has launched us into a new era and, with it, a new way of living with and relating to one another. It has opened doors and allowed us to accomplish things that would have been impossible in the past: we are able to keep up closely with a large number of people in an easy and comfortable way. As it continues to develop, social media technology will, time and again, offer us new and better ways of staying in touch with one another and, because of it, will make our lives and our relationships fuller and more meaningful.

Discuss the extent to which you agree or disagree with this opinion. Support your position with specific reasoning and examples from your experience, observations, and reading.

One would be foolish to argue that technology has not had a real and pervasive impact on our daily lives. Many of us rely daily on cell phones, tablets, and computers that allow us to reach family, friends, and business associates with little to no trouble. However, this ease of access does not necessarily mean our relationships are improving: the impersonal and anonymous nature of social media and other communication technologies make it even more difficult for us to make meaningful, lasting connections with the people around us.

Social media is, by nature, impersonal. Though we are able to build personal profiles that reflect whom we want the world to see, these profiles do little to improve our connection and communication with others. In fact, it is these very tools that are distancing us from our fellow humans. Birthday notifications, for example, remind social media users every day of the "friends" who are celebrating that day. While this tool seems, in theory, to be a great way to keep up with others, it actually desensitizes us. In truth, when I receive birthday notifications via social media, I end up either ignoring them altogether or sending an impersonal "Happy Birthday" just to be able to say I did. In fact, I never send birthday notes via social media to friends and family whose birthdays I actually care about because I do so in a more personal way—via a phone call or in person. Furthermore, I don't need an app to remember those birthdays. Though it may seem more useful or convenient to be able to stay in touch through social media, the relationships that rely on it are, in my experience, rarely very meaningful. By allowing us to stay in touch with larger numbers of people, social media also makes our connections shallower.

In addition to being impersonal, social media and other communication technologies can also be anonymous, creating a world of users that are disconnected from the things they post and read and, ultimately, from each other. Cyber bullying has been a significant concern of the twenty-first century, with numerous incidents leading to depressing outcomes, like teenage suicide. Through the lens of social media, bullies are able to disregard the humanity of the person on the other end and say things that they might never say in real life. A similar effect is clear during important political events: people post, with aggressive fervor, in favor of their own beliefs and respond, with equally aggressive insults, to anyone they disagree with. While this may, on the surface, seem to encourage open dialogue, social media and other communication technologies fail to have any effect on the quality of the conversation itself. Rather than learning to interact with one another respectfully, a tactic that may actually lead to increased understanding and greater acceptance of others, social media users learn that what they say has little to no consequence in real life.

The sense of community created by social media is deceptive. The ease with which people can "connect" often makes those connections meaningless. The friend who "Likes" a photo you post isn't putting any real energy into that friendship—he just clicked once and moved on. Similarly, people can use the anonymity of the internet to just as easily create enemies. One angry comment (that would never be said face-to-face) can launch a hundred nasty replies. These types of relationships don't make our lives fuller or more meaningful. They make our lives empty and shallow.

Writing a Thesis Statement

The thesis, or **THESIS STATEMENT**, is central to the structure and meaning of an essay: it presents the writer's argument or position on an issue. In other words, it tells readers specifically what the author is going to say in the essay. A strong, direct thesis statement is key to the organization of any essay. It introduces both the central idea of the essay and the main points that will be used to support that idea. Thus, the thesis will mirror the organization of the essay as a whole: each paragraph can elaborate on each supporting point.

In writing a thesis statement, it is important to respond to the prompt provided. The author must identify keywords in the prompt and think about what the prompt is asking. For example, the prompt may be asking for a clear stance to be taken a

DID YOU KNOW?

Find an op-ed article in the newspaper. Read it carefully and try to identify the thesis and supporting points.

particular issue, or it may require a detailed explanation of a topic. Once a clear understanding of the task is reached, the author must develop a central idea along with supporting points from relevant sources, including any provided documents and personal knowledge or experience. The central idea and supporting points can then be concisely packaged into a one or two sentence statement. Generally, a thesis statement is no more than two sentences.

THESIS STATEMENT EXAMPLES

PROMPT: Many high schools have begun to adopt 1:1 technology programs, meaning that each school provides every student with a computing device, such as a laptop or tablet. Educators who support these initiatives say that the technology allows for more dynamic collaboration and that students need to learn technology skills to compete in the job market. On the other hand, opponents cite increased distraction and the dangers of cyber-bullying or unsupervised internet use as reasons not to provide students with such devices.

In your essay, take a position on this question. You may write about either one of the two points of view given, or you may present a different point of view on this question. Use specific reasons and examples to support your position.

Possible thesis statements:

1. Providing technology to every student is good for education because it allows students to learn important skills such as typing, web design, and video editing, and it also gives students more opportunities to work cooperatively with their classmates and teachers.

2. I disagree with the idea that schools should provide technology to students because most students will simply be distracted by the free access to games and websites when they should be studying or doing homework.

3. By providing each student with a laptop or tablet, schools can help students apply technology to work more effectively with other students, communicate with teachers and classmates, and conduct research for class projects.

Structuring the Essay

There are a lot of different ways to organize an essay. In the limited timeframe of an exam, however, it is best to stick to a basic five-paragraph essay that includes an introduction, body, and conclusion. This structure can be used to discuss nearly any topic and will be easy for graders to follow.

INTRODUCTIONS

The purpose of an **INTRODUCTION** is to set the stage for the essay. This is accomplished by capturing the reader's interest, introducing and providing context for the topic, and stating the central idea and main points of the essay. Usually the introductory paragraph ends with a thesis statement, which clearly sets forth the position or point the essay will argue.

INTRODUCTION EXAMPLE

Technology has changed massively in recent years, but today's generation barely notices—high school students are already experienced with the internet, computers, apps, cameras, cell phones, and more. It's inevitable that these technologies will be begin to make their way into classrooms. Opponents of 1:1 technology programs might argue that students will be distracted or misuse the technology, but that is exactly why schools must teach them to use it. Students need to know how to navigate technology safely and effectively, and schools have a responsibility to ensure they learn these skills. By providing each student with a laptop or tablet, schools can help students learn how to apply technology to work more effectively with other students, communicate with teachers and classmates, and conduct research for class projects.

Explanation: This introduction *introduces* the topic in the first sentence. It then provides context by discussing why technology in the classroom is an important—and controversial—topic. The paragraph closes with a thesis statement that takes a firm stance and introduces the supporting ideas that the essay will be organized around.

THE BODY PARAGRAPHS

The body of the essay should consist of two to four paragraphs, each of which is focused on a single supporting idea. The body of an essay can be organized in a number of ways:

- ▶ Body paragraphs can explain each supporting detail given in the thesis statement.

- ▶ Body paragraphs can describe a problem then discuss the pros and cons of a solution in separate paragraphs.

- ▶ Body paragraphs can tell a story, with the story broken into two to four logical parts.

- ▶ Body paragraphs can compare and contrast the merits of two arguments, possibly drawing a conclusion about which is better at the end.

QUICK REVIEW

Which essay structure would be better suited to a persuasive essay? What about an expository essay?

Each paragraph should be structurally consistent, beginning with a topic sentence to introduce the main idea, followed by supporting ideas and examples. No extra ideas unrelated to the paragraph's focus should appear. Transition words and phrases can be used to connect body paragraphs and to improve the flow and readability of the essay.

BODY PARAGRAPH EXAMPLE

Technology can be a powerful tool for collaboration. When all of the students in a classroom have access to reliable laptops or tablets, they are able to more effectively share information and work together on projects. Students can communicate quickly via email, share files through a cloud service, and use a shared calendar for scheduling. They also have the opportunity to teach each other new skills since each student may bring to the group unique knowledge about particular apps or programs. When the availability of technology is limited or inconsistent, these opportunities are lost.

Explanation: This body paragraph discusses a supporting detail given the thesis (*schools can help students apply technology to work more effectively with other students*). It introduces the topic, then provides concrete examples of how technology makes it easier to work with other students. The final sentence reemphasizes the paragraph's main idea.

CONCLUSIONS

To end an essay smoothly, the author must compose a conclusion that reminds the reader of the importance of the topic and then restates the essay's thesis and supporting details. The writer should revisit the ideas in the introduction and thesis statement, but these ideas should not be simply repeated word-for-word. Rather, a well-written conclusion will reinforce the argument using wording that differs from the thesis statement but conveys the same idea. The conclusion should leave the reader with a strong impression of the essay's main idea and provide the essay with a sense of closure.

CONCLUSION EXAMPLE

As technology continues to change and become more incorporated into everyday life, students will need to adapt to it. Schools already teach young people a myriad of academic and life skills, so it makes sense that they would teach students how to use technology appropriately, too. When technology is incorporated into schoolwork, students will learn to collaborate, communicate, and research more effectively. Providing students with their own devices is one part of this important task, and schools that do so should be supported.

Explanation: This conclusion reminds the reader why the topic is important and then restates the thesis and supporting ideas. It ends with a strong, clear statement of the writer's stance on the issue.

Supporting Evidence

An essay's arguments are made up of claims, which in turn are backed by supporting evidence. This evidence can be drawn from a number of sources. Some essay prompts will include texts from which to draw supporting evidence. Other essays will require the writer to use his or her own background knowledge of the issue. For some essay prompts, it may be appropriate to use personal anecdotes and experiences. Regardless of the source of the evidence, it is important that it be conveyed in a clear, specific, and accurate manner.

PROVIDING SPECIFIC EXAMPLES

In body paragraphs, general statements should be followed with specific examples that will help to convince the reader that the argument has merit. These specific examples do not bring new ideas to the paragraph; rather, they explain or defend the general ideas that have already been stated. A poorly written essay will be full of general claims supported by little to no evidence or specific examples. Conversely, successful essays will use multiple specific examples to back up general claims.

EXAMPLES of GENERAL and SPECIFIC STATEMENTS

The following are some examples of general statements, followed by examples of specific statements that provide more detailed support of an idea.

General: Students may get distracted online or access harmful websites.

Specific: Some students spend too much time using chat features or social media, or they get caught up in online games. Others spend time reading websites that have nothing to do with an assignment.

Specific: Teens often think they are hidden behind their computer screens. However, providing personal information online can lead to danger in the real world.

General: Schools can teach students how to use technology appropriately and expose them to new tools.

Specific: Schools can help students learn how to use technology to work on class projects, communicate with classmates and teachers, and carry out research for classwork.

Specific: Providing students with laptops or tablets will allow them to get lots of practice using technology and programs at home, and only school districts can ensure that these tools are distributed widely, especially to students who may not have access to them otherwise.

INCORPORATING SOURCES

Providing evidence from outside sources is an excellent way to provide support for the claims in an essay. Some essay prompts will include texts that may be cited in the essay,

or writers may want to cite sources from memory. In either case, this supporting evidence should be incorporated smoothly into the essay. Context should be provided for the quote, and the quote should always be followed by a discussion of its importance or relevance to the essay.

When using outside sources, it is vital to credit the author or source within the text. Usually a full citation isn't needed—it can simply be sufficient to note the author's name in the text. And, as always, the writer must make sure to place direct quotations in quotation marks.

INCORPORATING SOURCES EXAMPLE

In addition to helping students work better with each other, technology can also help students communicate more effectively with teachers. A recent study from the University of Montana showed that over 75 percent of students have at some point been too intimidated to speak up in class, even if they thought they had something valuable to contribute (Higgins, 2015). But what if technology could provide a way to make speaking up easier? Private online messaging, comment boards for questions, and online tutorials are all made possible by introducing technology to the classroom. A well-trained teacher will be able to use these resources to encourage more effective classroom communication. In my personal experience, I have seen numerous students respond effectively when given the chance to communicate in the privacy of an online interaction.

Explanation: This first-person paragraph incorporates two sources: a scientific study and a personal anecdote from the author.

Writing Well

Although the content of an essay is of primary importance, the writing itself will also factor into the essay's final score. Writing well means that the language and tone are appropriate for the purpose and audience of the essay, the flow of ideas and the relationships among them are logical and clear, and the sentences are varied enough to keep the reader interested.

TRANSITIONS

Transitions are words, phrases, and ideas that help connect ideas throughout a text both between sentences and between paragraphs. Transitions can be used to imply a range of relationships, including cause and effect, sequence, contradictions, and continuance of an idea. Consistent and creative use of transitions will help the essay flow logically from one idea to the next and will make the essay easy for the reader to follow.

Transitions between paragraphs can also be polished by starting paragraphs with references to ideas mentioned in previous paragraphs or by ending them with a transition to the next topic. Such guideposts will guide the reader from one paragraph to the next.

EXAMPLES OF TRANSITIONS

Teens often think they are hidden behind their computer screens. <u>However,</u> providing personal information online can lead to danger in the real world.

<u>In addition to</u> helping students work better with each other, technology can also help students communicate more effectively with teachers.

They <u>also</u> have the opportunity to teach each other new skills.

SYNTAX

A variety of well-written sentences will help maintain the reader's interest in the essay. To create this theme, a writer can use sentences that differ in length and that begin with varying words, rather than repeating the same word at the start of each new sentence. It is also important for the writer to use a mix of different sentence structures, including simple, complex, compound, and compound-complex sentences.

SYNTAX EXAMPLE

Technology can be a powerful tool for collaboration. When all of the students in a classroom have access to reliable laptops or tablets, they are able to more effectively share information and work together on projects. Students can communicate quickly via email, share files through a cloud service, and use a shared calendar for scheduling. They also have the opportunity to teach each other new skills since each student may bring to the group unique knowledge about particular apps or programs. When the availability of technology is limited or inconsistent, these opportunities are lost.

WORD CHOICE and TONE

The words a writer chooses influence the reader's assessment of the essay. When writing essays, it is always necessary to choose words that are appropriate to the task.

For instance, a formal essay on an academic topic may benefit from complex sentences and an expansive vocabulary. However, a first-person essay on a personal topic may use a more causal vocabulary and organization. In general, when writing for exam graders, it is best to use clear, direct vocabulary and avoid using vague, general words such as good, bad, very, or a lot. Showing variety in word choice can also help improve an essay's score. However, it is better to use more familiar vocabulary than to try to impress the exam grader with unfamiliar words or words that do not fit the context of the essay.

WORD CHOICE EXAMPLES

Technology has changed massively in recent years, but today's generation barely notices—high school students are already experienced with the internet, computers, apps, cameras, cell phones, and more. It is inevitable that these technologies will be begin to make their way into classrooms. Opponents of 1:1 technology programs might argue that students will be distracted or misuse the technology, but that is exactly why schools must teach them to use it. Students need to know how to navigate technology safely and effectively, and schools have a responsibility to ensure they learn these skills. By providing each student with a laptop or tablet, schools can help students apply technology to work more effectively with other students, communicate with teachers and classmates, and conduct research for class projects.

Technology is everywhere in modern life. We've all walked into a coffee shop full of laptops or have seen people walking with their phones in front of their faces. I know I've often looked up from my tablet to realize I've missed a whole conversation. With technology everywhere, it seems obvious that we would start using it in classrooms. Opponents of 1:1 technology programs say that technology will be too distracting or will be abused by students, but it seems like that's an even more important reason for students to learn how to use it. Schools are where students learn all kinds of life skills, and technology is just another skill to learn. By giving students laptops or tablets, schools can help students work better with each other, work better with teachers, and learn to do better research.

Explanation: The two paragraphs above discuss the same topic. The first has a word choice and tone for an academic essay; the second is written in a more relaxed, personal style.

MANAGING TIME

When working on an essay under time constraints, it is important to manage time wisely. Simply launching into the introduction will likely result in a hurried, unorganized essay and a low score. Instead, the writer should take a few minutes to plan. As a first step, the writer should thoroughly read the prompt and any accompanying texts, and then determine the type of essay that is required. Next, the writer must decide on a thesis and what kind of supporting evidence to use. Once the thesis is clear, it is a good idea for the writer to create a brief outline of the essay. This whole process should only take a few minutes, leaving the bulk of the time for writing. However, it is always a good idea to leave a few minutes at the end to proofread and revise as necessary.

DID YOU KNOW?
Underline key words in the prompt so you can refer to them while writing the essay. This can help keep you and your essay focused.

Example Essays

PROMPT: The rise in popularity of e-cigarettes has reduced the overall smoking rate according to the Centers for Disease Control and Prevention. Many hail the new technology for helping smokers quit traditional tobacco cigarettes. However, others raise concerns about the appeal of e-cigarettes to young people and advocate FDA regulation of e-cigarettes to prevent negative side effects of their use on a new generation of smokers.

In your essay, take a position on this question. You may write about either one of the two points of view given, or you may present a different point of view on this question. Use specific reasons and examples to support your position.

EXAMPLE ESSAY ONE

For decades, youth smoking was a major concern for both parents and public health advocates. With education campaigns informing youth of the dangers of smoking and legal action taken against tobacco producers for their advertising tactics, the number of youth smoking traditional cigarettes has never been lower. But new technology is threatening to overturn that progress as electronic (e-cigarettes) have skyrocketed in popularity among both adults and youth. E-cigarettes should be regulated by the FDA to prevent youth from smoking since the long-term effects of e-cig use are unknown, youth are still becoming addicted to nicotine, and e-cigs could be a gateway to traditional smoking.

Smoking has long been a way for young people to feel cool or sophisticated. Popular culture, including film and television, glamorized smoking and led generations of Americans to pick up the habit. Although traditional smoking is no longer considered cool, the use of e-cigarettes, or vaping, threatens to take the same position in popular culture. Companies which produce traditional cigarettes have long been banned from advertising their products on television, but because e-cigarettes are not regulated by the FDA, there are no restrictions on their advertisement. This allows e-cig companies to reach youth through a wide range of media. Furthermore, the gadget-like design of e-cigs and the variety of candy-like flavors make them especially appealing to youth—a tactic that seems designed to hook a new generation on smoking.

This is particularly concerning as the long-term effects of vaping are not yet known for either adults or youth. The technology is too new to have been studied adequately. The FDA must study a drug for years before it can become available to the general public. Yet a device that delivers a highly-addictive substance remains unregulated. It is true that e-cigarettes are healthier for smokers than traditional cigarettes, but we cannot yet know the impact on youth who would have otherwise not smoked but for the easy access to these drug-delivery devices.

In addition, we do know that nicotine is a highly-addictive drug and that once this habit is established, it is very difficult to quit. If nothing else, this is a wasteful way for young people to spend their money. But even more concerning is the danger that nicotine use could alter the brain chemistry of young people and potentially make them prone to other addictions. Even if vaping does not become a gateway to hard drug use, it does make the leap to traditional smoking much more likely, and we know how harmful cigarettes have been.

The FDA has a responsibility to protect the public's health, and it is clear that regulation is needed to stop the momentum of the e-cigarette industry from getting youth addicted to their products. Although long-term health effects of vaping are unknown at this time, we must be cautious and err on the side of safety. At the very least, youth can be spared from an expensive, addictive habit; at best, an entire generation can live longer, healthier lives.

Explanation: This response provides good context for the discussion of the topic and takes a clear stance on the issue raised in the prompt. Strong examples and sound reasoning support the thesis. The essay is cohesive, and strong transitions connect ideas. Vocabulary and tone are appropriate, and the conclusion leaves the reader with a sense of the importance of the issue. Overall, this response would receive a high score.

EXAMPLE ESSAY TWO

Everyone knows smoking is bad for you. So, it's good that lots of people are quitting, and I think e-cigarettes, or vapes as they are also called, are helping people quit. Even though I don't use them, I know some people who use vapes, and they seem pretty healthy. It may be true that e-cigarettes have harmful side-effects, but it will be too far into the future before we know. The FDA should be studying this so that we do know if vapes are safe to use, especially for kids. No one wants kids to get hooked on drugs or to be unhealthy.

If they do start smoking, it is better for the kids to use e-cigarettes. They are less harmful because they don't use real tobacco or produce the terrible smelling smoke that normal cigarettes do. Some of my friends vape, and I don't even mind being in the same room. They actually smell pretty sweet. I don't think it's good to vape too much, but once in a while is fine, and I hope people make good choices about smoking.

Explanation: This response does not sufficiently address the prompt. The writer seems to disagree with the position of FDA regulation of e-cigarettes but does not develop this into a clear thesis. The writer's position is further confused by stating that the FDA should be studying the matter. The response is short and lacks adequate supporting detail. Although some personal examples are used, they are weak and a divergence from the main point. Although free of most errors, the language is simplistic, personal pronouns are overused, and the tone is not appropriate for academic writing. Overall, this response would receive a low score.

PART IV
Test Your Knowledge

CHAPTER SEVEN

Mathematics Practice Test

Arithmetic

Choose the best answer.

1. Which of the following has the greatest value?
   - **A)** −4(3)(−2)
   - **B)** −16 − 17 + 31
   - **C)** 18 − 15 + 27
   - **D)** −20 + 10 + 10

2. A teacher has 50 notebooks to hand out to students. If she has 16 students in her class, and each student receives 2 notebooks, how many notebooks will she have left over?
   - **A)** 2
   - **B)** 16
   - **C)** 18
   - **D)** 32

3. What is the remainder when 397 is divided by 4?
   - **A)** 0
   - **B)** 1
   - **C)** 2
   - **D)** 4

4. A high school cross country team sent 25 percent of its runners to a regional competition. Of these, 10 percent won medals. If 2 runners earned medals, how many members does the cross country team have?
   - **A)** 8
   - **B)** 80
   - **C)** 125
   - **D)** 1250

5. What is the value of 17.38 − 19.26 + 14.2?
   - **A)** 12.08
   - **B)** 12.32
   - **C)** 16.08
   - **D)** 16.22

6. 40% of what number is equal to 17?
   - **A)** 2.35
   - **B)** 6.8
   - **C)** 42.5
   - **D)** 680

7. What is the value of $\frac{7}{8} - \frac{1}{10} - \frac{2}{3}$?

A) $\frac{1}{30}$

B) $\frac{13}{120}$

C) $\frac{4}{21}$

D) $\frac{4}{105}$

8. Which of the following is closest in value to 129,113 + 34,602?

A) 162,000

B) 163,000

C) 164,000

D) 165,000

9. Convert 3.28 to a fraction.

A) $3\frac{1}{25}$

B) $3\frac{1}{50}$

C) $3\frac{7}{25}$

D) $3\frac{7}{50}$

10. If a student answers 42 out of 48 questions correctly on a quiz, what percentage of questions did she answer correctly?

A) 82.5%

B) 85%

C) 87.5%

D) 90%

11. Michael is making cupcakes. He plans to give $\frac{1}{2}$ of the cupcakes to a friend and $\frac{1}{3}$ of the cupcakes to his coworkers. If he makes 48 cupcakes, how many will he have left over?

A) 8

B) 10

C) 16

D) 24

12. If an employee who makes $37,500 per year receives a 5.5% raise, what is the employee's new salary?

A) $35,437.50

B) $35,625

C) $39,375

D) $39,562.50

13. What is the value of 14.25 + 6.38 + 12.54?

A) 32.17

B) 32.07

C) 33.07

D) 33.17

14. The population of a town was 7,250 in 2014 and 7,375 in 2015. What was the percent increase from 2014 to 2015 to the nearest tenth of a percent?

A) 1.5%

B) 1.6%

C) 1.7%

D) 1.8%

15. Which of the following is listed in order from least to greatest?

A) $-0.95, 0, \frac{2}{5}, 0.35, \frac{3}{4}$

B) $-1, -\frac{1}{10}, -0.11, \frac{5}{6}, 0.75$

C) $-\frac{3}{4}, -0.2, 0, \frac{2}{3}, 0.55$

D) $-1.1, -\frac{4}{5}, -0.13, 0.7, \frac{9}{11}$

16. What is 498,235 rounded to the nearest thousands?

A) 498,000

B) 498,200

C) 499,000

D) 500,000

17. Allison used $2\frac{1}{2}$ cups of flour to make a cake, and $\frac{3}{4}$ of a cup of flour to make a pie. If she started with 4 cups of flour, how many cups of flour does she have left?

A) $\frac{3}{4}$

B) $\frac{5}{2}$

C) $\frac{13}{4}$

D) $\frac{16}{4}$

18. Which of the following is not a negative value?

A) $(-3)(-1)(2)(-1)$

B) $14 - 7 + (-7)$

C) $7 - 10 + (-8)$

D) $-5(-2)(-3)$

19. What is the value of 15.32×4.76?

A) 60.2432

B) 72.9232

C) 602.432

D) 729.232

20. Juan plans to spend 25% of his workday writing a report. If he is at work for 9 hours, how many hours will he spend writing the report?

A) 2.25

B) 2.50

C) 2.75

D) 4.00

Quantitative Reasoning, Algebra, and Statistics

Choose the best answer.

1. A company interviewed 21 applicants for a recent opening. Of these applicants, 7 wore blue and 6 wore white, while 5 applicants wore both blue and white. What is the number of applicants who wore neither blue nor white?

    A) 1
    B) 6
    C) 12
    D) 13

2. A worker was paid $15,036 for 7 months of work. If he received the same amount each month, how much was he paid for the first 2 months?

    A) $2,148
    B) $4,296
    C) $6,444
    D) $8,592

3. The average speed of cars on a highway (s) is inversely proportional to the number of cars on the road (n). If a car drives at 65 mph when there are 250 cars on the road, how fast will a car drive when there are 325 cars on the road?

    A) 50 mph
    B) 55 mph
    C) 60 mph
    D) 85 mph

4. Which of the following is equivalent to $z^3(z + 2)^2 - 4z^3 + 2$?

    A) 2
    B) $z^5 + 4z^4 + 4z^3 + 2$
    C) $z^6 + 4z^3 + 2$
    D) $z^5 + 4z^4 + 2$

5. What is the value of $10^2 - 7(3 - 4) - 25$?

    A) −12
    B) 2
    C) 68
    D) 82

6. Which of the following is a solution of the given equation?
    $4(m + 4)^2 - 4m^2 + 20 = 276$

    A) 3
    B) 6
    C) 12
    D) 24

7. Rectangular water tank A is 5 feet long, 10 feet wide, and 4 feet tall. Rectangular tank B is 5 feet long, 5 feet wide, and 4 feet tall. If the same amount of water is poured into both tanks and the height of the water in Tank A is 1 foot, how high will the water be in Tank B?

    A) 1 foot
    B) 2 feet
    C) 3 feet
    D) 4 feet

8. Which of the following is the *y*-intercept of the given equation?

$$7y - 42x + 7 = 0$$

A) $(0, \frac{1}{6})$

B) $(6,0)$

C) $(0,-1)$

D) $(-1,0)$

9. The pie graph below shows how a state's government plans to spend its annual budget of $3 billion. How much more money does the state plan to spend on infrastructure than education?

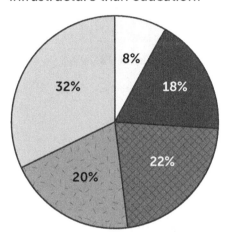

Employees   Education

Healthcare   Pension

Infrastructure

A) $60,000,000

B) $120,000,000

C) $300,000,000

D) $600,000,000

10. What is the value of *z* in the following system?

$$z - 2x = 14$$
$$2z - 6x = 18$$

A) −7

B) 3

C) 5

D) 24

11. The mean of 13 numbers is 30. The mean of 8 of these numbers is 42. What is the mean of the other 5 numbers?

A) 5.5

B) 10.8

C) 16.4

D) 21.2

12. *W*, *X*, *Y*, and *Z* lie on a circle with center *A*. If the diameter of the circle is 75, what is the sum of $\overline{AW}$, $\overline{AX}$, $\overline{AY}$, and $\overline{AZ}$?

A) 75

B) 300

C) 150

D) 106.5

13. If a person reads 40 pages in 45 minutes, approximately how many minutes will it take her to read 265 pages?

A) 202

B) 236

C) 265

D) 298

14. If angles *a* and *b* are congruent, what is the measurement of angle *c*?

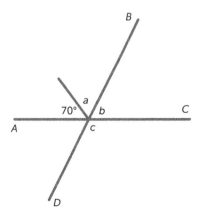

A) 70°

B) 125°

C) 110°

D) 55°

15. According to the graph below, New York had the fewest months with less than 3 inches of rain in every year except which of the following?

Number of Months with 3 or Fewer Than 3 Inches of Rain

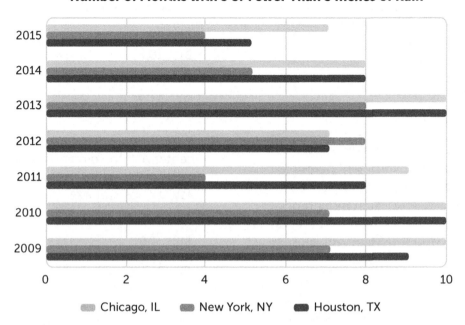

A) 2012

B) 2013

C) 2014

D) 2015

16. What is the value of
$-(3^2) + (5 - 7)^2 - 3(4 - 8)$?

A) −17

B) −1

C) 7

D) 25

17. Fifteen DVDs are to be arranged on a shelf. 4 of the DVDs are horror films, 6 are comedies, and 5 are science fiction. In how many ways can the DVDs be arranged if DVDs of the same genre must be placed together?

A) 2,073,600

B) 6,220,800

C) 12,441,600

D) 131,216,200

18. In a class of 20 students, how many conversations must be had so that every student talks to every other student in the class?

A) 190

B) 380

C) 760

D) 6840

19. A bag contains 6 blue, 8 silver, and 4 green marbles. Two marbles are drawn. What is the probability that the second marble drawn will be green if there is no replacement?

A) $\frac{2}{9}$

B) $\frac{4}{17}$

C) $\frac{11}{17}$

D) $\frac{7}{9}$

20. If one leg of a right triangle has a length of 40, which of the following could be the lengths of the two remaining sides?

A) 50 and 41

B) 9 and 41

C) 9 and 30

D) 50 and 63

Advanced Algebra and Functions

Choose the best answer.

1. If $\dfrac{4x-5}{3} = \dfrac{\frac{1}{2}(2x-6)}{5}$, what is the value of x?

   A) $-\dfrac{2}{7}$

   B) $-\dfrac{4}{17}$

   C) $\dfrac{16}{17}$

   D) $\dfrac{8}{7}$

2. Which of the following is the solution set to the given inequality?

   $2x + 4 \geq 5(x - 4) - 3(x - 4)$

   A) $(-\infty,\infty)$

   B) $(-\infty,6.5]$

   C) $[6.5,-\infty)$

   D) $(-\infty,6.5) \cup (6.5,\infty)$

3. Cone A is similar to cone B with a scale factor of 3:4. If the volume of cone A is 54π, what is the volume of cone B?

   A) 72π

   B) 128π

   C) 162π

   D) 216π

4. What are the real zero(s) of the following polynomial?

   $2n^2 + 2n - 12 = 0$

   A) $\{2\}$

   B) $\{-3,2\}$

   C) $\{2,4\}$

   D) There are no real zeros of n.

5. If the volume of a cube is 343 cubic meters, what is the cube's surface area?

   A) 49 m²

   B) 84 m²

   C) 196 m²

   D) 294 m²

6. Which of the following are the vertical asymptotes of the given function?

   $f(x) = \dfrac{x^3 - 16x}{-4x^2 + 4x + 24}$

   A) $x = -4$ and $x = 4$

   B) $x = -3$ and $x = 2$

   C) $x = -2$ and $x = 3$

   D) $x = 0$ and $x = 4$

7. Find $(f - g)(x)$ if $f(x) = x^2 + 16x$ and $g(x) = 5x^2 + 4x + 25$.

   A) $-4x^2 + 12x - 25$

   B) $-4x^2 - 12x - 25$

   C) $-4x^2 - 20x + 25$

   D) $4x^2 - 20x - 25$

8. If the smallest angle in a non-right triangle is 20° and the shortest side is 14, what is the length of the largest side if the largest angle is 100°?

   A) 12.78

   B) 34.31

   C) 40.31

   D) 127.81

9. What transformation is created by the −3 in the graph of $y = -3|x - 2| + 2$?

A) The −3 moves the vertex down 3 and reflects the graph over the *x*-axis.

B) The −3 moves the vertex to the left 3 and widens the graph.

C) The −3 makes the graph wider and reflects it over the *x*-axis.

D) The −3 makes the graph narrower and reflects the graph over the *x*-axis.

10. Which inequality is represented by the following graph?

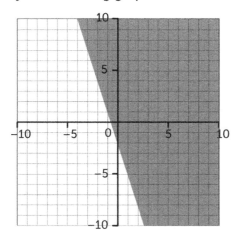

A) $y \geq -3x - 2$

B) $y \geq 3x - 2$

C) $y > -3x - 2$

D) $y \leq -3x - 2$

11. What is the domain of the inequality $\left|\frac{x}{8}\right| \geq 1$?

A) $(-\infty, \infty)$

B) $[8, \infty)$

C) $(-\infty, -8]$

D) $(-\infty, -8] \cup [8, \infty)$

12. Find the approximate value of *x* in the triangle below.

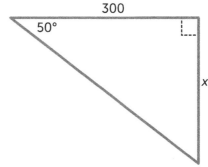

A) 229

B) 300

C) 357

D) 400

13. Which expression is equivalent to $\log_6\left(\frac{36}{x}\right)$?

A) $2 - x$

B) $6 - \log x$

C) $2 - \log_6 x$

D) $\log_6 x - 2$

14. What are the zeros of $\left(\frac{g}{h}\right)(k)$ if $g(k) = -3k^2 - k$ and $h(k) = -2k - 4$?

A) $\left\{0, \frac{1}{3}\right\}$

B) $\{-2\}$

C) $\{0\}$

D) $\left\{-2, 0, \frac{1}{3}\right\}$

15. 50 shares of a financial stock and 10 shares of an auto stock are valued at $1,300. If 10 shares of the financial stock and 10 shares of the auto stock are valued at $500, what is the value of 50 shares of the auto stock?

A) $30

B) $20

C) $1,300

D) $1,500

16. If $\triangle ABD \sim \triangle DEF$ and the similarity ratio is 3:4, what is the measure of DE if $AB = 12$?

A) 9

B) 16

C) 96

D) 12

17. Simplify: $\dfrac{3+\sqrt{3}}{4-\sqrt{3}}$

A) $\dfrac{13}{15}$

B) $\dfrac{15+7\sqrt{3}}{13}$

C) $\dfrac{15}{19}$

D) $\dfrac{15+7\sqrt{3}}{19}$

18. The line $f(x)$ is shown on the graph below. If $g(x) = f(x-2) + 3$, which of the following points lies on $g(x)$?

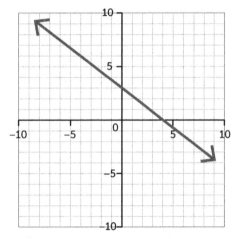

A) $(1,2)$

B) $(2,3)$

C) $(6,3)$

D) $(7,2)$

19. If $j = 4$, what is the value of $2(j-4)^4 - j + \frac{1}{2}j$?

A) 0

B) -2

C) 2

D) 4

20. If $\triangle ABC$ is rotated counterclockwise 180° about point A, what are the coordinates of the new triangle?

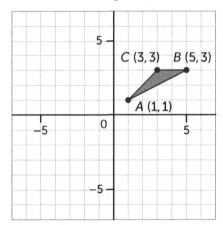

A) $A'\,(1,1),\ B'\,(-3,-1),\ C'\,(-1,-1)$

B) $A'\,(-1,-1),\ B'\,(-5,-1),\ C'\,(-3,-3)$

C) $A'\,(1,1),\ B'\,(-5,-1),\ C'\,(-3,-3)$

D) $A'\,(-1,-1),\ B'\,(-3,-1),\ C'\,(-1,-1)$

Answer Key
ARITHMETIC

1. **C)** Evaluate to find greatest value.

   $-4(3)(-2) = 24$

   $-16 - 17 + 31 = -2$

   $18 - 15 + 27 = \mathbf{30}$

   $-20 + 10 + 10 = 0$

2. **C)** If each student receives 2 notebooks, the teacher will need $16 \times 2 = 32$ notebooks. After handing out the notebooks, she will have $50 - 32 = \mathbf{18}$ notebooks left.

3. **B)** Find the highest possible multiple of 4 that is less than or equal to 397, and then subtract to find the remainder.

   $99 \times 4 = 396$

   $397 - 396 = \mathbf{1}$

4. **B)** Work backwards to find the number of runners in the competition (c) and then the number of runners on the team (r).

   $\frac{2}{c} = \frac{10}{100}$

   $c = 20$

   $\frac{20}{r} = \frac{25}{100}$

   $\boldsymbol{r = 80}$

5. **B)** Align the decimals and add/subtract from left to right.

   $17.38 - 19.26 + 14.2 =$

   $(-1.88) + 14.2 = \mathbf{12.32}$

6. **C)** Use the equation for percentages.

   $\text{whole} = \frac{\text{part}}{\text{percent}} = \frac{17}{0.4} = \mathbf{42.5}$

7. **B)** Convert each fraction to the LCD and subtract the numerators.

   $\frac{7}{8} - \frac{1}{10} - \frac{2}{3}$

   $= \frac{7}{8}\left(\frac{15}{15}\right) - \frac{1}{10}\left(\frac{12}{12}\right) - \frac{2}{3}\left(\frac{40}{40}\right)$

   $= \frac{105}{120} - \frac{12}{120} - \frac{80}{120} = \mathbf{\frac{13}{120}}$

8. **C)** Round each value and add.

   $129{,}113 \approx 129{,}000$

   $34{,}602 \approx 35{,}000$

   $129{,}000 + 35{,}000 = \mathbf{164{,}000}$

9. **C)** Place the decimal over 100 and simplify.

   $\frac{28}{100} = \frac{7}{25}$

   $3.28 = \mathbf{3\frac{7}{25}}$

10. **C)** Use the formula for percentages.

    $\text{percent} = \frac{\text{part}}{\text{whole}} = \frac{42}{48}$

    $= 0.875 = \mathbf{87.5\%}$

11. **A)** Add the number of cupcakes he will give to his friend and to his coworkers, then subtract that value from 48.

    # of cupcakes for his friend:

    $\frac{1}{2} \times 48 = 24$

    # of cupcakes for his coworkers:

    $\frac{1}{3} \times 48 = 16$

    $48 - (24 + 16) = \mathbf{8}$

12. **D)** Find the amount of change and add to the original amount.

    amount of change = original amount × percent change

    $= 37{,}500 \times 0.055 = 2{,}062.50$

    $37{,}500 + 2{,}062.50 = \mathbf{\$39{,}562.50}$

13. **D)** Align the decimal points and add.

14.25

6.38

+ 12.54

33.17

14. **C)** Use the formula for percent change.

percent change = $\frac{\text{amount of change}}{\text{original amount}}$

$= \frac{(7,375 - 7,250)}{7,250} = 0.017 =$ **1.7%**

15. **D)** Write each value in decimal form and compare.

$-0.95 < 0 < 0.4 < 0.35 < 0.75$ FALSE

$-1 < -0.1 < -0.11 < 0.8\overline{3} < 0.75$ FALSE

$-0.75 < -0.2 < 0 < 0.\overline{66} < 0.55$ FALSE

$-1.1 < -0.8 < -0.13 < 0.7 < 0.\overline{81}$ **TRUE**

16. **A)** The 8 is in the thousands place. Because the value to the right of the 8 is less than 5, the 8 remains the same and all values to its right become zero. The result is **498,000**.

17. **A)** Add the fractions and subtract the result from the amount of flour Allison started with.

$2\frac{1}{2} + \frac{3}{4} = \frac{5}{2} + \frac{3}{4} = \frac{10}{4} + \frac{3}{4} = \frac{13}{4}$

$4 - \frac{13}{4} = \frac{16}{4} - \frac{13}{4} = \frac{3}{4}$

18. **B)** Evaluate to find the non-negative value.

$(-3)(-1)(2)(-1) = -6$

$14 - 7 + (-7) = \mathbf{0}$

$7 - 10 + (-8) = -11$

$-5(-2)(-3) = -30$

19. **B)** Multiply the values without the decimal points, then move the decimal so that the final answer has 4 values to the right of the decimal.

$1532 \times 476 = 729,232 \rightarrow$ **72.9232**

20. **A)** Use the equation for percentages.

part = whole × percentage =

$9 \times 0.25 =$ **2.25**

QUANTITATIVE REASONING, ALGEBRA, and STATISTICS

1. D) Set up an equation to find the number of people wearing neither white nor blue. Subtract the number of people wearing both colors so they are not counted twice.

$21 = 7 + 6 + neither - 5$

$neither = \mathbf{13}$

2. B) Write a proportion and then solve for x.

$\frac{15{,}036}{7} = \frac{x}{2}$

$7x = 30{,}072$

$x = \mathbf{4{,}296}$

3. A) Use the formula for inversely proportional relationships to find k and then solve for s.

$sn = k$

$(65)(250) = k$

$k = 16{,}250$

$s(325) = 16{,}250$

$s = \mathbf{50}$

4. D) Simplify using PEMDAS.

$z^3(z + 2)^2 - 4z^3 + 2$

$z^3(z^2 + 4z + 4) - 4z^3 + 2$

$z^5 + 4z^4 + 4z^3 - 4z^3 + 2$

$\mathbf{z^5 + 4z^4 + 2}$

5. D) Simplify using PEMDAS.

$10^2 - 7(3 - 4) - 25$

$= 10^2 - 7(-1) - 25$

$= 100 + 7 - 25$

$= 107 - 25 = \mathbf{82}$

6. B) Plug each value into the equation.

$4(3 + 4)^2 - 4(3)^2 + 20 = 180 \neq 276$

$4(6 + 4)^2 - 4(6)^2 + 20 = \mathbf{276}$

$4(12 + 4)^2 - 4(12)^2 + 20 = 468 \neq 276$

$4(24 + 4)^2 - 4(24)^2 + 20 = 852 \neq 276$

7. B) Calculate the volume of water in tank A.

$V = l \times w \times h$

$5 \times 10 \times 1 = 50 \text{ ft}^3$

Find the height this volume would reach in tank B.

$V = l \times w \times h$

$50 = 5 \times 5 \times h$

$h = \mathbf{2 \text{ ft}}$

8. C) Plug 0 in for x and solve for y.

$7y - 42x + 7 = 0$

$7y - 42(0) + 7 = 0$

$y = -1$

The y-intercept is at **(0,−1)**.

9. A) Find the amount the state will spend on infrastructure and education, and then find the difference.

$infrastructure =$
$0.2(3{,}000{,}000{,}000) = 600{,}000{,}000$

$education = 0.18(3{,}000{,}000{,}000) =$
$540{,}000{,}000$

$600{,}000{,}000 - 540{,}000{,}000 =$
$60,000,000

10. D) Solve the system using substitution.

$z - 2x = 14 \rightarrow z = 2x + 14$

$2z - 6x = 18$

$2(2x + 14) - 6x = 18$

$4x + 28 - 6x = 18$

$-2x = -10$

$x = 5$

$z - 2(5) = 14$

$z = \mathbf{24}$

11. **B)** Find the sum of the 13 numbers whose mean is 30.

$13 \times 30 = 390$

Find the sum of the 8 numbers whose mean is 42.

$8 \times 42 = 336$

Find the sum and mean of the remaining 5 numbers.

$390 - 336 = 54$

$\frac{54}{5} = \mathbf{10.8}$

12. **C)** All the points lie on the circle, so each line segment is a radius. The sum of the 4 lines will be 4 times the radius.

$r = \frac{75}{2} = 37.5$

$4r = \mathbf{150}$

13. **D)** Write a proportion and then solve for x.

$\frac{40}{45} = \frac{265}{x}$

$40x = 11{,}925$

$x = 298.125 \approx \mathbf{298}$

14. **B)** Use the two sets of linear angles to find b and then c.

$a = b$

$a + b + 70 = 180$

$2a + 70 = 180$

$a = b = 55°$

$b + c = 180°$

$55 + c = 180$

$c = \mathbf{125°}$

15. **A)** In 2012, New York had more months with less than 3 inches of rain than either Chicago or Houston.

16. **C)** Simplify using PEMDAS.

$-(3^2) + (5 - 7)^2 - 3(4 - 8)$

$= -(3^2) + (-2)^2 - 3(-4)$

$= -9 + 4 - 3(-4)$

$= -9 + 4 + 12 = \mathbf{7}$

17. **C)** Use the fundamental counting principle to determine how many ways the DVDs can be arranged within each category and how many ways the 3 categories can be arranged.

ways to arrange horror $= 4! = 24$

ways to arrange comedies $= 6!$

$= 720$

ways to arrange science fiction $= 5! = 120$

ways to arrange categories $=$

$3! = 6$

$(24)(720)(120)(6) = \mathbf{12{,}441{,}600}$

18. **A)** Use the combination formula to find the number of ways to choose 2 people out of a group of 20.

$C(20,2) = \frac{20!}{2!\,18!} = \mathbf{190}$

19. **A)** Find the probability that the second marble will be green if the first marble is blue, silver, or green, and then add these probabilities together.

P(first blue and second green) $=$ *P(blue)* $\times$ *P(green|first blue)* $=$

$\frac{6}{18} \times \frac{4}{17} = \frac{4}{51}$

P(first silver and second green) $=$ *P(silver)* $\times$ *P(green|first silver)* $=$

$\frac{8}{18} \times \frac{4}{17} = \frac{16}{153}$

P(first green and second green) $=$ *P(green)* $\times$ *P(green|first green)* $=$

$\frac{4}{18} \times \frac{3}{17} = \frac{2}{51}$

P(second green) $= \dfrac{4}{51} + \dfrac{16}{153} + \dfrac{2}{51}$

$= \dfrac{2}{9}$

20. **B)** Use the Pythagorean theorem to determine which set of values forms a right triangle.

$40^2 + 41^2 = 50^2$

$3{,}281 \neq 2{,}500$

$9^2 + 40^2 = 41^2$

$1{,}681 = 1{,}681$

$9^2 + 30^2 = 40^2$

$981 \neq 1{,}600$

$40^2 + 50^2 = 63^2$

$4{,}100 \neq 3{,}969$

ADVANCED ALGEBRA and FUNCTIONS

1. **C)** Cross multiply and solve for x.

$$\frac{4x - 5}{3} = \frac{\frac{1}{2}(2x - 6)}{5}$$

$$5(4x - 5) = \frac{3}{2}(2x - 6)$$

$$20x - 25 = 3x - 9$$

$$17x = 16$$

$$x = \frac{16}{17}$$

2. **A)** Simplify the inequality.

$$2x + 4 \geq 5x - 20 - 3x + 12$$

$$2x + 4 \geq 2x - 8$$

$$4 \geq -8$$

Since the inequality is always true, the solution is all real numbers, **$(-\infty, \infty)$**.

3. **B)** Set up a proportion. Cube the scale factor when calculating volume.

$$\frac{54\pi}{x} = \frac{3^3}{4^3}$$

$$x = 128\pi$$

4. **B)** Factor the trinomial and set each factor equal to 0.

$$2n^2 + 2n - 12 = 0$$

$$2(n^2 + n - 6) = 0$$

$$2(n + 3)(n - 2) = 0$$

$$n = -3 \text{ and } n = 2$$

5. **D)** Use the volume to find the length of the cube's side.

$$V = s^3$$

$$343 = s^3$$

$$s = 7 \text{ m}$$

Find the area of each side and multiply by 6 to find the total surface area.

$$7(7) = 49 \text{ m}$$

$$49(6) = \mathbf{294 \text{ m}^2}$$

6. **C)** Make sure there are no factors that cancel, and then set the denominator equal to 0.

$$\frac{x^3 - 16x}{-4x^2 + 4x + 24} = \frac{x(x^2 - 16)}{-4(x^2 - x - 6)}$$

$$= \frac{x(x + 4)(x - 4)}{-4(x - 3)(x + 2)}$$

The graph has no holes.

$$-4(x - 3)(x + 2) = 0$$

$$x = 3 \text{ and } x = -2$$

7. **A)** Subtract $g(x)$ from $f(x)$.

$$x^2 + 16x - (5x^2 + 4x + 25) =$$

$$x^2 + 16x - 5x^2 - 4x - 25 =$$

$$\mathbf{-4x^2 + 12x - 25}$$

8. **C)** Use the law of sines.

$$\frac{\sin 20°}{14} = \frac{\sin 100°}{x}$$

$$x = \frac{14(\sin 100°)}{\sin 20°}$$

$$x = 40.31$$

9. **D)** For the function $y = a|x - h| + k$:

When $|a| > 1$, the graph will narrow.

When a is negative, the graph is reflected over the x-axis.

10. **A)** Eliminate answer choices that don't match the graph.

A) Correct.

B) The graph has a negative slope while this inequality has a positive slope.

C) The line on the graph is solid, so the inequality should include the "or equal to" symbol.

D) The shading is above the line, meaning the inequality should be "y is greater than."

11. **D)** Split the absolute value inequality into two inequalities and simplify. Switch the inequality when making one side negative.

$$\frac{x}{8} \geq 1$$

$$x \geq 8$$

$$-\frac{x}{8} \geq 1$$

$$\frac{x}{8} \leq -1$$

$$x \leq -8$$

$x \leq -8$ or $x \geq 8 \rightarrow$ **(−∞,−8] ∪ [8,∞)**

12. **C)** Use the equation for tangent.

$$\tan 50° = \frac{x}{300}$$

$$x = 300(\tan 50°)$$

x ≈ 357

13. **C)** Expand the original expression using the properties of logarithms.

$$\log_6\left(\frac{36}{x}\right) = \log_6(36) - \log_6(x) =$$

2 − log₆x

14. **A)** Set the numerator of the resulting rational function equal to 0 to find the zeros.

$$\left(\frac{g}{h}\right)(k) = \frac{(-3k^2 - k)}{(-2k - 4)}$$

$$0 = 3k^2 - k$$

$$0 = k(3k - 1)$$

$$k = 0, \frac{1}{3}$$

15. **D)** Set up a system of equations and solve using elimination.

f = the cost of a financial stock

a = the cost of an auto stock

$$50f + 10a = 1300$$

$$10f + 10a = 500$$

$$50f + 10a = 1300$$

$$+ \ -50f - 50a = -2500$$

$$-40a = -1,200$$

$$a = 30$$

$$50(30) = \mathbf{1,500}$$

16. **B)** Set up a proportion and solve.

$$\frac{AB}{DE} = \frac{3}{4}$$

$$\frac{12}{DE} = \frac{3}{4}$$

$$3(DE) = 48$$

DE = 16

17. **B)** Multiply by the complex conjugate and simplify.

$$\frac{3 + \sqrt{3}}{4 - \sqrt{3}}\left(\frac{4 + \sqrt{3}}{4 + \sqrt{3}}\right)$$

$$= \frac{12 + 4\sqrt{3} + 3\sqrt{3} + 3}{16 - 4\sqrt{3} + 4\sqrt{3} - 3} = \frac{\mathbf{15 + 7\sqrt{3}}}{\mathbf{13}}$$

18. **C)** The function $g(x) = f(x − 2) + 3$ is a translation of $\langle 2,3 \rangle$ from $f(x)$. Test each possible point by undoing the transformation and checking if the point lies on $f(x)$.

$(1,2) \rightarrow (−1,−1)$: This point is not on $f(x)$.

$(2,3) \rightarrow (0,0)$: This point is not on $f(x)$.

$(6,3) \rightarrow (4,0)$: **This point is on f(x).**

$(7, 2) \rightarrow (5, −1)$: This point is not on $f(x)$.

19. **B)** Plug 4 in for j and simplify.

$$2(j - 4)^4 - j + \frac{1}{2}j$$

$$2(4 - 4)^4 - 4 + \frac{1}{2}(4) = \mathbf{-2}$$

20. **A)** A rotation of 180° is found by performing the transformation $(x,y) \rightarrow (−x,−y)$. Since this rotation is around the point A, treat point A as the origin.

A remains **(1,1)**.

B is 4 units right and 2 units up from A, so count 4 units left and 2 units down from A to find B': $(5,3) \rightarrow$ **(−3,−1)**

C is 2 units right and 2 units up from A, so count 2 units left and 2 units down from A to find C':

$(3,3) \rightarrow (-1,-1)$

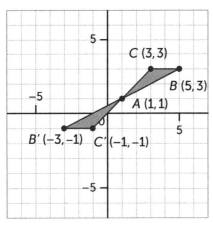

CHAPTER EIGHT

Reading Practice Test

Read the passage(s) below and answer the question based on what is stated or implied in the passage(s) and in any introductory material that may be provided.

The following passage provides an overview of the purpose and applications of social psychology. Information was drawn from Dr. Eliot Aronson's acclaimed book The Social Animal.

In his treatise *Politics*, Aristotle wrote, "Man is by nature a social animal; an individual who is unsocial naturally and not accidentally is either beneath our notice or more than human. Society is something in nature that precedes the individual. Anyone who either cannot lead the common life or is so self-sufficient as not to need to, and therefore does not partake of society, is either a beast or a god." For centuries, philosophers have been examining the relationship between man and his social world. It is no wonder, then, that a field of study has arisen to examine just that; the field is referred to as social psychology.

Social psychologists have been studying the effect of societal influences on human behavior for decades, and a number of fascinating findings have been the result. Together, these discoveries have shed light on one clear truth—that human behavior cannot be understood in a vacuum; that is, our daily behaviors are inextricably linked with the social context in which they occur.

Why is this important? According to social psychologist Eliot Aronson, it's important because it helps us to understand that the behaviors we witness in others may be as much a result of social influence as they are of the individual's disposition. For example, if you have ever been cut off in the middle of bad city traffic, you may have immediately assumed that the offender was inconsiderate or incompetent. While this may be true, it may be equally likely that the person is dealing with an emergency situation or that they simply did not see you. According to Aronson, this tendency to attribute behaviors, especially negative behaviors, to disposition is risky and can ultimately be detrimental to us and to the other person.

Take, for example, Philip Zimbardo's famous prison experiment, conducted at Stanford University in 1971. At the beginning of the experiment, the participants, all healthy, stable, intelligent male Stanford University students, were classified as either guards or prisoners and told they would be acting their parts in a simulated prison environment for two weeks. However, after just six days, Zimbardo had to terminate the experiment because of the extreme behaviors he was witnessing in both groups: prisoners had become entirely submissive to and resentful of the guards, while the guards had become cruel and unrelenting in their treatment of the prisoners. The otherwise healthy, well-adjusted students had experienced dramatic transformations as a result of their assigned roles. Zimbardo's conclusion? Even giving individuals temporary power over others was enough to completely alter the way they viewed and behaved toward each other; indeed, the behaviors he witnessed in each of the groups were not a result of the dispositions of the participants but of the situation in which they had been placed.

Today, social psychologists study the effect of social influence on a number of different behaviors: conformity, obedience, aggression, prejudice, and even attraction and love. The insights these researchers have gained have laid the foundation for further examination of human social behavior and, ultimately, for a refined approach to legal and social policy.

1. The author most likely uses the Aristotle quote in the first paragraph in order to—
   A) illustrate the seriousness with which social psychology should be treated.
   B) support his/her claim that curiosity about man's relationship with the social world is not a quality unique to modern thinking.
   C) encourage introverts to build stronger relationships with those around them.
   D) compare the social environment of beasts with the social environment of man.

2. The author indicates that making assumptions about people based on isolated actions is—
   A) a prudent way to draw conclusions about one's social world.
   B) recommended when no other information is available.
   C) the most accurate way to assess various personality strengths.
   D) unwise and potentially harmful to all involved.

3. The author most likely includes the example of the Stanford Prison Experiment in order to—

  A) encourage the reader to participate in social psychology studies

  B) challenge the reader to question how he or she would behave in the same situation

  C) illustrate the extent to which social context can influence behavior

  D) undermine the reader's assumption that the quality of one's education can influence his or her behavior

4. The author most likely includes the statement in the last paragraph about legal and social policy in order to—

  A) mention one possible application for the findings of social psychologists.

  B) advocate for prison reform.

  C) criticize the work of social psychologists.

  D) dispel doubts regarding the reliability of the research of social psychologists.

Passage One

In the field of veterinary medicine, the inquiry into whether animals experience pain the same way humans do is especially important in the context of pain management. Although many advancements have been made in research sciences, and pain management is widely accepted as a necessary job of practitioners, a number of myths about animal pain still plague the field of veterinary medicine and prevent practitioners from making pain management a priority. According to veterinarian and writer Debbie Grant, three myths are especially detrimental to the cause.

The first of these is the myth that animals do not feel pain at all or that they feel it less intensely than humans; in fact, according to Grant, the biological mechanisms by which we experience pain are the very same mechanisms by which animals experience pain. Even the emotional reaction to a painful experience, like being afraid to return to the dentist after an unpleasant visit, is mirrored in animals.

The second myth that prevents the advancement of pain management practices is the myth that pain is a necessary part of an animal's recovery. While some veterinarians believe that pain may prevent a healing dog, for example, from playing too vigorously, Grant says this is simply not the case. In fact, restlessness and discomfort may even lead to unusually high levels of agitation and may consequently slow the recovery process even further.

Finally, contrary to the third myth, animals do not necessarily tolerate pain any better than humans do, though they may handle their pain differently. Grant emphasizes that veterinarians must be aware that a lack of obvious signs does not necessarily suggest that pain is not present: in fact, many animals are likely to conceal their pain out of an instinct to hide weaknesses that may make them easy targets for predators.

PASSAGE TWO

Unlike doctors, who typically have the benefit of discussing their patients' concerns, veterinarians cannot ask their patients whether and where they are experiencing discomfort. Additionally, veterinarians must be aware of the survival instinct of many animals to mask pain in response to stressful experiences or foreign environments. For these reasons, diagnostic tools and strategies are instrumental in the effective practice of veterinary medicine.

Veterinarians have a unique challenge when it comes to diagnosing their patients. In 2014, researchers of veterinary medicine at the University of Perugia in Italy completed a review of the diagnostic tools and strategies available to today's practitioners and found a number of them to be effective. Presumptive diagnosis, the first of these strategies, involves making a prediction about the animal's pain based on the observable damage to the body or body part. In addition to presumptive diagnosis, veterinarians can use close observation to assess changes in the animal's behavior.

The most common tool for performing diagnosis is the clinical exam, which can include both a physical exam and laboratory testing. As part of this process, a veterinarian might make use of an objective pain scale, by which he or she could assess the animal's condition according to a number of criteria. This tool is especially useful throughout the course of treatment, as it provides the practitioner with a quantitative measure for evaluating the effectiveness of various treatment options.

5. The author of Passage 1 most likely includes the example of the unpleasant dentist visit in order to—

    A) provide a relatable example of how pain can influence a person's emotions.

    B) challenge the reader to overcome his or her natural, emotional response to painful experiences.

    C) question a popular perception about the experience of going to the dentist.

    D) highlight a similarity in the way humans and animals respond to pain.

6. The author of Passage 1 indicates that despite advancements in veterinary sciences—

    A) many veterinarians do not see the value in pain management practices for their patients.

    B) many veterinarians still employ outdated methods of pain management.

    C) many veterinarians still believe that pain management is a responsibility of the pet owner.

    D) many veterinarians still have misguided beliefs and practices related to pain management in animals.

7. The author of Passage 2 indicates that veterinarians can improve their pain management practices by—

    A) attempting to communicate with their patients about the pain they are experiencing.

    B) employing the best diagnostic practices in their field.

    C) encouraging pet owners to keep careful watch over their animals.

    D) inventing novel ways to assess and treat pain in animals.

8. Both authors indicate that veterinarians—

    A) must be aware that a lack of obvious symptoms does not necessarily suggest an absence of pain.

    B) should make pain management for their patients a priority.

    C) ought to be familiar with the misguided assumptions that exist in their field.

    D) need to conduct a thorough examination before releasing an animal back to its owner.

9. The author of Passage 2 indicates that objective pain measures are useful because—

    A) they allow the veterinarian to compare an animal's pain level to the pain levels of other animals.

    B) they challenge the veterinarian to devise a treatment plan as quickly as possible.

    C) they discount the assumption that pain cannot be measured on an objective scale.

    D) they provide the veterinarian with a quantitative method for tracking pain levels over the course of an animal's treatment.

10. Which of the following best describes the relationship between the two passages?

    A) The first passage makes the claim that pain management should be a priority for veterinarians, while the second passage rejects this claim.

    B) The first passage emphasizes the veterinarian's responsibility to prioritize pain management in animals, while the second passage explores the tools by which veterinarians can execute this responsibility.

    C) The first passage seeks to dispel myths about pain management in animals, while the second passage denies that they are myths.

    D) The first passage sheds light on the shortcomings of veterinary sciences as they currently exist, while the second passage provides insight into how these shortcomings might be overcome.

The social and political discourse of America continues to be permeated with idealism. An idealistic viewpoint asserts that the ideals of freedom, equality, justice, and human dignity are the truths that Americans must continue to aspire to. Idealists argue that truth is what should be, not necessarily what is. In general, they work to improve things and to make them as close to ideal as possible.

11. The main purpose of the passage is to

    A) advocate for freedom, equality, justice, and human rights

    B) explain what an idealist believes in

    C) explain what's wrong with social and political discourse in America

    D) persuade readers to believe in certain truths

Alexander Hamilton and James Madison called for the Constitutional Convention to write a constitution as the foundation of a stronger federal government. Madison and other Federalists like John Adams believed in separation of powers, republicanism, and a strong federal government. Despite the separation of powers that would be provided for in the US Constitution, anti-Federalists like Thomas Jefferson called for even more limitations on the power of the federal government.

12. According to the passage, which of the following would most likely NOT support a strong federal government?

    A) Alexander Hamilton

    B) James Madison

    C) John Adams

    D) Thomas Jefferson

We've been told for years that the recipe for weight loss is fewer calories in than calories out. In other words, eat less and exercise more, and your body will take care of the rest. As many of those who've tried to diet can attest, this edict doesn't always produce results. If you're one of those folks, you might have felt that you just weren't doing it right—that the failure was all your fault.

However, several new studies released this year have suggested that it might not be your fault at all. For example, a study of people who'd lost a high percentage of their body weight (>17%) in a short period of time found that they could not physically maintain their new weight. Scientists measured their resting metabolic rate and found that they'd need to consume only a few hundred calories a day to meet their metabolic needs. Basically, their bodies were in starvation mode and seemed to desperately hang on to each and every calorie. Eating even a single healthy, well-balanced meal a day would cause these subjects to start packing back on the pounds.

Other studies have shown that factors like intestinal bacteria, distribution of body fat, and hormone levels can affect the manner in which our bodies process calories. There's also the fact that it's actually quite difficult to measure the number of calories consumed during a particular meal and the number used while exercising.

13. Which of the following would weaken the author's argument?

A) a new diet pill from a pharmaceutical company that promises to help patients lose weight by changing intestinal bacteria

B) the personal experience of a man who was able to lose a significant amount of weight by taking in fewer calories than he used

C) a study showing that people in different geographic locations lose different amounts of weight when on the same diet

D) a study showing that people often misreport their food intake when part of a scientific study on weight loss

In Greek mythology, two gods, Epimetheus and Prometheus, were given the work of creating living things. Epimetheus gave good powers to the different animals. To the lion he gave strength; to the bird, swiftness; to the fox, sagacity; and so on. Eventually, all of the good gifts had been bestowed, and there was nothing left for humans. As a result, Prometheus returned to heaven and brought down fire, which he gave to humans. With fire, human beings could protect themselves by making weapons. Over time, humans developed civilization and superiority.

14. Which of the following is the meaning of the word *bestowed* as it is used in the passage?

A) purchased

B) forgotten

C) accepted

D) given

I deny that Ireland has ever been really conquered; and even should the most sanguinary suggestions proposed in a nineteenth-century serial be carried out, I am certain she could not be. Ireland has never been permanently subdued by Dane or Norman, Dutchman or Saxon; nor has she ever been really united to England. A man is surely not united to a jailer because he is bound to him by an iron chain which his jailer has forged for his safe keeping. This is not union; and the term "United Kingdom" is in fact a most miserable misnomer. Unity requires something more than a mere material approximation.

15. The function of the second sentence of the passage is to

A) elaborate on the idea that Ireland once engaged in a bloody war with northern countries.

B) provide historical evidence that Ireland has never been entirely controlled by another country.

C) describe the central problem of the Irish people.

D) make an allusion to the many people who have settled in Ireland.

Alfie closed his eyes and took several deep breaths. He was trying to ignore the sounds of the crowd, but even he had to admit that it was hard not to notice the tension in the stadium. He could feel 50,000 sets of eyes burning through his skin—this crowd expected perfection from him. He took another breath and opened his eyes, setting his sights on the soccer ball resting peacefully in the grass. One shot, just one last shot, between his team and the championship. He didn't look up at the goalie, who was jumping nervously on the goal line just a few yards away. Afterward, he would swear he didn't remember anything between the referee's whistle and the thunderous roar of the crowd.

16. Which of the following conclusions is best supported by the passage?
    A) Alfie passed out on the field and was unable to take the shot.
    B) The goalie blocked Alfie's shot.
    C) Alfie scored the goal and won his team the championship.
    D) The referee declared the game a tie.

The greatest changes in sensory, motor, and perceptual development happen in the first two years of life. When babies are first born, most of their senses operate in a similar way to those of adults. For example, babies are able to hear before they are born; studies show that babies turn toward the sound of their mothers' voices just minutes after being born, indicating they recognize the mother's voice from their time in the womb.

The exception to this rule is vision. A baby's vision changes significantly in its first year of life; initially it has a range of vision of only 8 – 12 inches and no depth perception. As a result, infants rely primarily on hearing; vision does not become the dominant sense until around the age of 12 months. Babies also prefer faces to other objects. This preference, along with their limited vision range, means that their sight is initially focused on their caregiver.

17. Which of the following is a accurate summary of the passage?
    A) Babies have no depth perception until 12 months, which is why they focus only on their caregivers' faces.
    B) Babies can recognize their mothers' voices when born, so they initially rely primarily on their sense of hearing.
    C) Babies have senses similar to those of adults except for their sense of sight, which doesn't fully develop until 12 months.
    D) Babies' senses go through many changes in the first year of their lives.

Taking a person's temperature is one of the most basic and common health care tasks. Everyone from nurses to emergency medical technicians to concerned parents should be able to grab a thermometer to take a patient or loved one's temperature. But what's the best way to get an accurate reading? The answer depends on the situation.

The most common way people measure body temperature is orally. A simple digital or disposable thermometer is placed under the tongue for a few minutes, and the task is done. There are many situations, however, when measuring temperature orally isn't an option. For example, when a person can't breathe through his nose, he won't be able to keep his mouth closed long enough to get an accurate reading. In these situations, it's often preferable to place the thermometer in the rectum or armpit. Using the rectum also has the added benefit of providing a much more accurate reading than other locations can provide.

It's also often the case that certain people, like agitated patients or fussy babies, won't be able to sit still long enough for an accurate reading. In these situations, it's best to use a thermometer that works much more quickly, such as one that measures temperature in the ear or at the temporal artery. No matter which method is chosen, however, it's important to check the average temperature for each region, as it can vary by several degrees.

18. According to the passage, why is it sometimes preferable to take a person's temperature rectally?

A) Rectal readings are more accurate than oral readings.

B) Many people cannot sit still long enough to have their temperatures taken orally.

C) Temperature readings can vary widely between regions of the body.

D) Many people do not have access to quick-acting thermometers.

To know psychology, therefore, is absolutely no guarantee that we shall be good teachers. To advance to that result, we must have an additional endowment altogether, a happy tact and ingenuity to tell us what definite things to say and do when the pupil is before us. That ingenuity in meeting and pursuing the pupil, that tact for the concrete situation, though they are the alpha and omega of the teacher's art, are things to which psychology cannot help us in the least.

19. Which of the following statements most closely identifies the characteristics of "good teaching" that James describes in the passage?

A) Good teaching involves presenting information in clever ways and providing plenty of practice.

B) Good teaching involves sensitivity to students, concrete examples, and engaging students.

C) Good teaching is the art of making material interesting and engaging the students' attention.

D) Good teaching is an art that can be improved with the study of psychology.

In the eleven years that separated the Declaration of the Independence of the United States from the completion of that act in the ordination of our written Constitution, the great minds of America were bent upon the study of the principles of government that were essential to the preservation of the liberties which had been won at great cost and with heroic labors and sacrifices. Their studies were conducted in view of the imperfections that experience had developed in the government of the Confederation, and they were, therefore, practical and thorough.

20. The author suggests which of the following about the writers of the Constitution?

A) The writers studied principles of government in relation to the government of the Confederation; their goal was to write a Constitution that would secure liberty in America.

B) The writers worked to make sure that Americans would never lose the freedom that they fought to achieve.

C) The writers of the Constitution were both thorough and practical as they wrote the Constitution.

D) The writers studied the government of the Confederation and worked very hard to take into account the imperfections of this government.

Answer Key

1. A) is incorrect. The author does not imply that social psychology requires a serious approach.

    B) is correct. The author writes, "For centuries, philosophers have been examining the relationship between man and his social world. It is no wonder, then, that a field of study has arisen to examine just that[...]"

    C) is incorrect. The author does not advocate for relationship building in the first paragraph.

    D) is incorrect. The author does not provide information about the social environment of animals.

2. A) is incorrect. The author writes that "human behavior cannot be understood in a vacuum; that is, our daily behaviors are inextricably linked with the social context in which they occur."

    B) is incorrect. The author does not recommend that the reader make assumptions about people based on isolated incidents; he indicates that the "tendency to attribute behaviors, especially negative behaviors, to disposition is risky and can ultimately be detrimental to us and the other person."

    C) is incorrect. The author writes that "human behavior cannot be understood in a vacuum; that is, our daily behaviors are inextricably linked with the social context in which they occur."

    D) is correct. The author writes that "the behaviors we witness in others may be as much a result of social influence as they are of the individual's disposition" and that the "tendency to attribute behaviors, especially negative behaviors, to disposition is risky and can ultimately be detrimental to us and to the other person."

3. A) is incorrect. The author does not suggest that the reader participate in social psychology studies.

    B) is incorrect. The author does not necessarily encourage the reader to empathize with the students, only to recognize the impact of social roles on behavior.

    C) is correct. The author writes, "Even giving individuals temporary power over others was enough to completely alter the way they viewed and behaved toward each other; indeed, the behaviors he witnessed in each of the groups were not a result of the dispositions of the participants but of the situation in which they had been placed."

    D) is incorrect. The author does not indicate that she is challenging assumptions about education.

4. **A) is correct.** The author implies that the findings of social psychologists have practical, meaningful applications.

    B) is incorrect. Though the reader might infer this from the statement, the author does not specifically advocate for prison reform.

C) is incorrect. The author does not criticize the work of social psychologists but highlights the importance of this work.

D) is incorrect. The author does not discuss the reliability of social psychology research.

5. A) is incorrect. The author does not seek to make the experience of animals relatable, only to indicate that it is similar to the way humans experience pain and that it should be considered during the course of treatment.

B) is incorrect. The author does not seek to change the behavior of the reader.

C) is incorrect. The author does not challenge popular perceptions about the experience of going to the dentist; she only suggests that the experience is similar to that of animals in pain at the veterinarian's office.

D) is correct. The author writes that "[e]ven the emotional reaction to a painful experience (like being afraid to return to the dentist after an unpleasant visit) is mirrored in animals."

6. A) is incorrect. The author writes that "pain management is widely accepted as a necessary job of practitioners."

B) is incorrect. The author does not indicate that veterinarians employ outdated methods of pain management.

C) is incorrect. The author writes that "pain management is widely accepted as a necessary job of practitioners."

D) is correct. The author writes, "Though many advancements have been made in research sciences [...] a number of myths about animal pain still plague the field of veterinary medicine and prevent practitioners from making pain management a priority."

7. A) is incorrect. The author does not suggest that veterinaries attempt to communicate with animals about their pain.

B) is correct. The author writes that "veterinarians must be aware of the survival instinct of many animals to mask pain in response to stressful experiences or foreign environments. For these reasons, diagnostic tools and strategies are instrumental in the effective practice of veterinary medicine."

C) is incorrect. The author suggests that veterinarians have a responsibility that extends beyond informing pet owners of the importance of close observation.

D) is incorrect. The author indicates that veterinarians should rely on existing "diagnostic tools and strategies available to today's practitioners" that have been found "to be effective." She does not indicate that veterinarians should invent their own methods for assessing and treating pain.

8. **A) is correct.** The first author writes, "Grant emphasizes that veterinarians must be aware that a lack of obvious signs does not necessarily suggest that pain is not present: in fact, many animals, especially those that are prey animals in the wild, are likely to conceal their pain out of an instinct to hide

weaknesses that may make them easy targets for predators." The second author agrees, saying that "veterinarians must be aware of the survival instinct of many animals to mask pain in response to stressful experiences or foreign environments."

B) is incorrect. While the first author indicates that pain management should be priority for veterinarians, the second author does not discuss the prioritization of pain management in relation to other responsibilities.

C) is incorrect. The first author seeks to dispel myths that exist in the world of veterinary medicine; the second author does not.

D) is incorrect. The second author indicates that thorough examinations must be conducted; the first author does not.

9. A) is incorrect. The author does not indicate that objective pain scales are used to compare pain levels in different animals but that they are useful for "evaluating the effectiveness of various treatment options" in one animal.

B) is incorrect. The author does not indicate that this is an application of the objective pain scale.

C) is incorrect. The author does not indicate that objective pain scales are useful for this reason.

D) is correct. The author writes that to diagnose pain in animals, "a veterinarian might make use of an objective pain scale, by which he or she could assess the animal's condition according to a number of criteria. This tool is especially useful throughout the course of treatment, as it provides the practitioner with a quantitative measure for evaluating the effectiveness of various treatment options.

10. A) is incorrect. The second passage does not reject the claim that pain management should be a priority of veterinarians.

B) is correct. The author of the first passage writes that "a number of myths about animal pain still plague the field of veterinary medicine and present practitioners from making pain management a priority." This implies that the author believes pain management should be a priority of veterinarians. The second author writes that "diagnostic tools and strategies are instrumental in the effective practice of veterinary medicine" and then goes on to describe some of these tools.

C) is incorrect. The author of the second passage does not contradict that the myths in the first passage are untrue.

D) is incorrect. The authors do not discuss shortcomings of veterinary medicine in broad terms; they only address the issue of pain management.

11. A) is incorrect. The author identifies the ideals associated with idealism but does not offer an opinion on or advocate for them.

B) is correct. The purpose of the passage is to explain what an idealist believes in. The author does not offer any opinions or try to persuade readers about the importance of certain values.

C) is incorrect. The author states that social and political discourse are "permeated with idealism" but does not suggest that this is destructive or wrong.

D) is incorrect. The author provides the reader with information but does not seek to change the reader's opinions or behaviors.

12. A) is incorrect. The author states that "Alexander Hamilton...called for the Constitutional Convention to write a constitution as the foundation of a stronger federal government."

B) is incorrect. The author states that "James Madison called for the Constitutional Convention to write a constitution as the foundation of a stronger federal government."

C) is incorrect. The author states that "Federalists like John Adams believed in... a strong federal government."

D) is correct. In the passage, Thomas Jefferson is defined as an anti-Federalist, in contrast with Federalists who believed in a strong federal government.

13. A) is incorrect. A new diet pill would have no effect on the existing studies and would not prove anything about conventional dieting wisdom.

B) is incorrect. A single anecdotal example would not be enough to contradict the results of well-designed studies; if anything, the account would provide another example of how complex the topics of dieting and weight loss are.

C) is incorrect. This answer choice would strengthen the author's argument by highlighting the complexity of the topic of dieting.

D) is correct. People misreporting the amount of food they ate would introduce error into studies on weight loss and might make the studies the author cites unreliable.

14. A) is incorrect. According to the passage, gifts were assigned by Epimetheus and Prometheus, not purchased.

B) is incorrect. The passage gives no indication that gifts were forgotten.

C) is incorrect. The passage gives no indication that gifts were accepted by the animals, only that they were given by Epimetheus and Prometheus.

D) is correct. The word given best describes the idea that the gifts have been handed out: "to the lion [Epimetheus] gave strength; to the bird, swiftness; to the fox, sagacity; and so on."

15. A) is incorrect. The second sentence mentions several countries that at least partially conquered Ireland, but there is no mention of a war that led to that.

B) is correct. The sentence identifies the countries that have conquered but not permanently subdued Ireland. It provides supporting information for the main point, the first sentence that states Ireland cannot be fully conquered.

C) is incorrect. Although Ireland has experienced the attempts of other countries to conquer and subdue her, there is no mention of that being a central problem.

D) is incorrect. Several countries are listed, but they are identified as conquerors, not settlers.

16. A) is incorrect. Tough Alfie does not remember what happened, the phrase "doesn't remember anything between the referee's whistle and the thunderous roar of the crowd" indicates that he was able to take the shot.

B) is incorrect. The crowd "expected perfection from him [Alfie,]" so the reader can imply that the "thunderous roar" was a result of a successful goal.

C) is correct. The crowd's support for Alfie and their collective roar after the shot implies that Alfie scored the goal and won the championship.

D) is incorrect. The crowd "expected perfection from him [Alfie]," so the reader can imply that the "thunderous roar" was a result of a successful goal and a winning performance.

17. A) is incorrect. The passage is about babies' senses in general; therefore this answer choice is too specific.

B) is incorrect. The passage is about babies' senses in general; therefore this answer choice is too specific.

C) is correct. The passage states that babies' senses are much like those of their adult counterparts with the exception of their vision, which develops later.

D) is incorrect. The passage indicates that a baby's vision "changes significantly in its first year of life[,]" but suggests that other senses are relatively well-developed at birth.

18. **A) is correct.** The second paragraph of the passage states that "[u]sing the rectum also has the added benefit of providing a much more accurate reading than other locations can provide."

B) is incorrect. In the final paragraph, the author suggests that "certain people, like agitated patients or fussy babies" might have a difficult time sitting still but does not suggest that this is a problem for "many" people.

C) is incorrect. In the final paragraph, the author writes that "it's important to check the average temperature for each region, as it can vary by several degrees" but does not cite this as a reason to use a rectal thermometer.

D) is incorrect. The author does not mention access to thermometers as a consideration.

19. A) is incorrect. This option does not take into account the importance of concern for the student's needs and interests, although the part about presenting in interesting ways, "ingenuity," is correct.

B) is correct. The author mentions the qualities of "happy tact," "ingenuity," and use of the concrete.

C) is incorrect. This option does not take "tact" into consideration, which is explained as "a happy tact and ingenuity to tell us what definite things to say and do when the pupil is before us."

D) is incorrect. The passage indicates exactly the opposite: that the study of psychology cannot help teachers relate to students. It says, "To know psychology, therefore, is absolutely no guarantee that we shall be good teachers" and "That ingenuity in meeting and pursuing the pupil, that tact for the concrete situation, though they are the alpha and omega of the teacher's art, are things to which psychology cannot help us in the least."

20. **A) is correct.** The suggested idea is how thorough and practical the writers were as they studied the principles of government and analyzed their experience with government of the Confederation.

B) is incorrect. This option is too general; it does not mention the specifics of the work of the writers (studying government in view of the government of the Confederation).

C) is incorrect. This option offers no indication of what they were thorough and practical about.

D) is incorrect. This is only partially accurate. It omits the writers' study of the principles of government and the focus of their work, a Constitution that would protect freedom.

CHAPTER NINE
Writing Practice Test

Selected-Response

Read the following early draft of an essay and then choose the best answer to the question or the best completion of the statement.

(1) For centuries, artists and philosophers have long debated about the relationship between life and art. (2) While some argue that art is an imitation of life, others believe that, just as often, life ends up imitating art. (3) In no other genre is the impact of art on our real lives more visible than in the realm of science fiction. (4) Great minds of science fiction such as Jules Verne, Gene Roddenberry, H. G. Wells, and Stanley Kubrick have introduced ideas that, though fantastical at the time of their inception, eventually became reality. (5) Many of these artists were dead before they ever saw their ideas come to life.

(6) Some of humanity's biggest accomplishments were achieved first in science fiction. (7) Jules Verne wrote about humanity traveling to the moon over a century before it happened. (8) Scientists Robert H. Goddard and Leo Szilard both credit his work—on liquid-fueled rockets and atomic power, respectively—to H. G. Wells and his futuristic novels. (9) Gene Roddenberry, the creator of *Star Trek*, dreamed up replicators long before 3-D printers were invented.

(10) Jules Verne's work, for example, was the inspiration for both the submarine and the modern-day helicopter. (11) H. G. Wells wrote about automatic doors long before they began to turn up in almost every grocery store in America. (12) Roddenberry's *Star Trek* is even credited as the inspiration for the creation of the mobile phone. (13) Kubrick's HAL from *2001: A Space Odyssey* represented voice control at its finest, long before virtual assistants were installed in all the new smartphone models.

1. In context, which is the best version of the underlined portion of sentence 1 (reproduced below)?

   For centuries, <u>artists and philosophers have long debated about the relationship between life and art.</u>

   A) artists and philosophers have examined the facts and debated about the relationship between life and art.

   B) artists and philosophers have hemmed, hawed, and debated about the relationship between life and art.

   C) artists and philosophers have debated about the relationship between life and art.

   D) artists and philosophers have hemmed and hawed about the relationship between life and art.

2. Which of the following introductory phrases should be inserted at the beginning of sentence 6 (reproduced below)?

   Some of humanity's biggest accomplishments were achieved first in science fiction.

   A) Therefore,

   B) In fact,

   C) However,

   D) In addition,

3. In context, which revision to sentence 8 (reproduced below) is most needed?

   Scientists Robert H. Goddard and Leo Szilard both credit his work—on liquid-fueled rockets and atomic power, respectively—to H. G. Wells and his futuristic novels.

   A) delete the sentence

   B) insert *always* after the word *both*

   C) change *his* to *their*

   D) delete the phrase inside the dashes

4. In context, which of the following would provide the best introduction to the final paragraph?

   A) Transportation was of particular concern to science fiction writers, who dreamed up new ways for humanity to get around the world.

   B) These same authors had other interesting ideas as well.

   C) Sometimes science fiction is so much like life it is incredible.

   D) Many of the ideas life borrows from science fiction have infiltrated our everyday lives and our world to an even greater degree.

5. In context, which revision to sentence 5 (reproduced below) is most needed?

Many of these artists were dead before they ever saw their ideas come to life.

   A) delete the sentence

   B) change *many* to *most*

   C) change *dead* to *deceased*

   D) change *saw* to *witnessed*

6. In context, which of the following would provide the best conclusion to the essay?

   A) Science fiction will, no doubt, continue to influence our technology and our world for many years to come.

   B) These men are important figures in history for their ideas, and they should be respected as such.

   C) It is unfair that these creative individuals did not receive any money or rewards in exchange for their ideas.

   D) Science fiction is really an interesting topic, with many ideas and influential people to study and understand.

(1) Since its birth, humanity has sought explanations for the unexplainable. (2) In ancient cultures, mythology explained the weather, the elements of nature, and even the creation of the universe. (3) More recently, as recently as the last two centuries, many cultures have turned to folklore and superstition to explain odd occurrences and behaviors. (4) In the folk traditions of European countries, one creature in particular takes the blame when individuals, especially children, begin acting strangely, the changeling.

(5) According to many folk traditions, changelings were the children of fairies or elves, left in the places of human children who had been stolen from their families by the creatures. (6) If an individual's family began to notice strange behaviors in the individual, they would assume he or she had been kidnapped and replaced with a changeling. (7) This provided, at least, some answers to families whose children suffered from unexplained ailments or disabilities.

(8) Many families believed there were specific actions that would encourage the changeling to leave and return the human child. (9) In Germany, Ireland, and Wales, for example, it was thought that brewing egg shells would surprise the changeling into admitting his or her true identity. (10) Unfortunately, however, the belief that changelings could be convinced to leave was not just an innocuous superstition. (11) On some occasions, harm came to the individual who was thought to be a changeling. (12) Sometimes, parents would frighten the child with the hope of forcing the fairy or elf child out.

7. Which of the following is the best way to introduce sentence 3 (reproduced below)?

More recently, as recently as the last two centuries, many cultures have turned to folklore and superstition to explain odd occurrences and behaviors.

A) More recently,

B) These days,

C) Therefore,

D) On the other hand,

8. Which revision to sentence 7 (reproduced below) is most needed?

This provided, at least, some answers to families whose children suffered from unexplained ailments or disabilities.

A) delete the sentence

B) insert *explanation* after *this* and before *provided*

C) change *families* to *family's*

D) change *whose* to *who's*

9. Which is the best revision for the underlined portion of sentence 4 (reproduced below)?

In the folk traditions of European countries, <u>one creature in particular takes the blame when individuals, especially children, begin acting strangely, the changeling.</u>

A) one creature in particular takes the blame when individuals, especially children, begin acting strangely, the changeling.

B) one creature in particular takes the blame when individuals, especially children, begin acting strangely: the changeling.

C) one creature in particular takes the blame when individuals—especially children, begin acting strangely—the changeling.

D) one creature in particular takes the blame when individuals especially children begin acting strangely. The changeling.

10. Which is the best way to revise and combine sentences 10 and 11 (reproduced below) at the underlined point?

Unfortunately, however, the belief that changelings could be convinced to leave was not just <u>an innocuous superstition. On some occasions,</u> harm came to the individual who was thought to be a changeling.

A) an innocuous superstition, on some occasions,

B) an innocuous superstition, so on some occasions,

C) an innocuous superstition, but on some occasions,

D) an innocuous superstition: on some occasions,

11. Which of the following would NOT be an acceptable revision of the underlined portion of sentence 5 (reproduced below)?

According to many folk traditions, changelings were the children of fairies or elves, left in the places of human children who had been stolen from their families by the creatures.

- **A)** changelings were the children of fairies or elves, who were left in the places of human children who had been stolen from their families by the creatures.
- **B)** changelings were the children of fairies or elves; they were left in the places of human children who had been stolen from their families by the creatures.
- **C)** changelings were the children of fairies or elves, they were left in the places of human children who had been stolen from their families by the creatures.
- **D)** changelings were the children of fairies or elves—left in the places of human children who had been stolen from their families by the creatures.

12. What is the best placement for sentence 8 (reproduced below)?

Many families believed there were specific actions that would encourage the changeling to leave and return the human child.

- **A)** where it is now
- **B)** at the end of the second paragraph
- **C)** after sentence 9
- **D)** after sentence 10

(1) The relationship between humanity and the rest of the animal kingdom is a complicated one. (2) Leaning on its superior intelligence, humanity has sought to remain at the top of the food chain by asserting its control over the animal kingdom. (3) As is true with anything, though, things do occasionally go wrong. (4) While these incidents sometimes end in funny or heartwarming stories, other times they end in fear and destruction. (5) Either way, though, one thing is clear: we are not as in control as we like to think we are.

(6) Sometimes, escaped animal stories end happily and leave us feeling even more affection for our furry neighbors. (7) In the 1980s, for example, the world fell in love with Ken Allen, an orangutan who escaped three times from his supposedly escape-proof enclosure at the San Diego Zoo; when he escaped, Ken Allen would go for peaceful walks around the park because he liked observing the other animals and zoo patrons with fascination. (8) Hercules, a trained grizzly bear who escaped from the set of a television commercial, found similar fame during his twenty-four-days of freedom; news audiences fell in love with the bear who, despite his hunger, refused to hunt and kill the various wildlife he encountered.

(9) Other times, though, escaped animals can pose a threat to the safety of humans and other animals. (10) Goldie, for example, a male golden eagle, escaped from the London Zoo in 1965 and went on to attack two terriers who were at a park with their owner; fortunately, the owner was able to drive the predatory bird away, and zookeepers finally caught Goldie. (11) In 2007, a male gorilla named Bokito became infamous when he escaped his enclosure at a Netherlands zoo and promptly abducted, and caused severe injury to, a female zoo visitor. (12) It was reported that the visitor, who visited Bokito at the zoo multiple times each week, ignored numerous warnings by zookeepers to avoid making eye contact and smiling with the large gorilla, nonverbal cues that they worried he would interpret as aggressive. (13) In 1994 during a circus performance, Tyke, a female African elephant, killed her trainer and attacked two other circus employees before escaping the arena and running free for nearly half an hour; police fired numerous shots at the animal, eventually killing her.

13. Which is the best way to revise and combine sentences 3 and 4 (reproduced below) at the underlined point?

As is true with anything, though, things do <u>occasionally go wrong. While these incidents</u> sometimes end in funny or heartwarming stories, other times they end in fear and destruction.

A) They should not be combined.

B) occasionally go wrong, while these incidents

C) occasionally go wrong; however, while these incidents

D) occasionally go wrong while these incidents

14. Which of the following, if added to the end of sentence 5 (reproduced below), would clarify the author's meaning?

Either way, though, one thing is clear: we are not as in control as we like to think we are.

A) all the time

B) on a regular basis

C) day in and day out

D) of the animals around us

15. Which of the following provides the best introduction to the second paragraph?

A) Sometimes, escaped animal stories end happily and leave us feeling even more affection for our furry neighbors. (as it is now)

B) People love animals, especially animals who are smart and crazy.

C) Many animals that are portrayed as aggressive are not as scary as they are made out to be by experts.

D) Some animals just can't get enough fun.

16. Which is the best revision of the underlined portion of sentence 7 (reproduced below)?

In the 1980s, for example, the world fell in love with Ken Allen, an orangutan who escaped three times from his supposedly escape-proof enclosure at the San Diego Zoo; when he escaped, Ken Allen would go for peaceful walks around the <u>park because he liked observing the other animals and zoo patrons with fascination.</u>

A) as it is now

B) park, observing the other animals and zoo patrons with fascination.

C) park; observing the other animals and zoo patrons with fascination.

D) park, he observed the other animals and zoo patrons with fascination.

17. Which is the best revision for sentence 12 (reproduced below)?

It was reported that the visitor, who visited Bokito at the zoo multiple times each week, ignored numerous warnings from zookeepers to avoid making eye contact and smiling with the large gorilla, nonverbal cues that they worried he would interpret as aggressive.

A) delete the sentence

B) change *who* to *whom*

C) change *from* to *through*

D) change *they* to *zookeepers* and *he* to *Bokito*

18. Which of the following provides the best conclusion for this passage?

A) These stories are sad, but they are important moments in history and should be studied as such.

B) Tyke's story, fortunately, has led to many changes in circuses around the world, which have begun to minimize their use of animals in their acts.

C) These stories, both the happy and the sad, should serve as a clear warning to any human who encounters an animal: you are not in control.

D) Today, circus companies like Cirque du Soleil achieve equally stunning effects without the use of animal performers.

(1) Becoming president of the United States is a privilege few people will ever get to experience. (2) Since its founding in 1776, <u>many years ago,</u> the country has seen only forty-four presidents in office. (3) Most of them have since left office and have gone on to lead lives of comfort and influence. (4) <u>However,</u> they may never again experience the power or the excitement of their former office, retired presidents continue to enjoy many benefits as a result of their service as president of the United States.

(5) Presidents receive a number of benefits upon retirement, many of which are afforded by the Former Presidents Act of 1958. (6) First and foremost, they receive an <u>annual pension payment. (7) The amount of the pension</u> has been reviewed and

changed a number of times, most recently to reflect the salary of a high-level government executive (roughly $200,000 in the 2010s). (8) In addition to their pension, retired presidents and their families are also entitled to ongoing Secret Service protection, which lasts until the death of the president.

(9) In addition to the assurances of safety and stability, retired presidents continue to enjoy some of the influence that accompanies their former office and a few have even gone on to accomplish great work in their post-presidency years. (10) Particularly notable are the careers of William Howard Taft and Jimmy Carter. (11) In 1921, eight years after leaving office, William Howard Taft was appointed Chief Justice of the Supreme Court by President Warren G. Harding, an office he filled until just before his death; to this day, he is the only individual to ever fill both offices. (12) Jimmy Carter went on to become an enthusiastic and impactful campaigner for human rights. (13) He started the Carter Center in 1982 to advance his efforts and, in 2002, was granted the Nobel Peace Prize for his work.

19. Which of the following replacements for the underlined phrase in sentence 2 (reproduced below) most impactfully communicates the amount of time that has passed since 1776?

Since its founding in 1776, many years ago, the country has seen only forty-four presidents in office.

A) as it is now

B) long before any of our grandparents were born,

C) which no one alive can remember,

D) almost 250 years ago,

20. In context, which of the following replacements for the underlined portion would best begin sentence 4 (reproduced below)?

However, they may never again experience the power or the excitement of their former office, retired presidents continue to enjoy many benefits as a result of their service as president of the United States.

A) Therefore,

B) Consequently,

C) Though

D) Still,

21. Which of the following would NOT be an acceptable replacement for the underlined portion of sentence 10 (reproduced below)?

Particularly notable are the careers of William Howard Taft and Jimmy Carter.

A) Exceptionally outstanding are

B) Of particular interest are

C) Especially noteworthy are

D) Of particular interest were

22. Which of the following would NOT be an acceptable way to revise and combine sentences 6 and 7 (reproduced below) at the underlined point?

First and foremost, they receive an <u>annual pension payment. The amount of the pension</u> has been reviewed and changed a number of times, most recently to reflect the salary of a high-level government executive (roughly $200,000 in the 2010s).

A) as it is now

B) annual pension payment, the amount of which

C) annual pension payment; the amount of the pension

D) annual pension payment, the amount of the pension

23. Which of the following would provide the most logical conclusion to the second paragraph?

A) Interestingly, Richard Nixon was the only president ever to relinquish his right to ongoing Secret Service security.

B) However, spouses who remarry after the president has left office become ineligible for Secret Service security.

C) The Secret Service is a special security task force that is responsible for protecting the president, the vice president, and their families.

D) These measures ensure that retired presidents, as thanks for their years of demanding service, continue to live lives of safety and security.

24. Which of the following is the best version of the underlined portion of sentence 9 (reproduced below)?

In addition to the assurances of safety and stability, retired presidents continue to enjoy some of the influence <u>that accompanies their former office and a few have even gone on</u> to accomplish great work in their post-presidency years.

A) as it is now

B) that accompanies their former office; however, a few have even gone on

C) that accompanies their former office; a few have even gone on

D) that accompanies their office—a few have even gone on

25. Which of the following would be the most effective introductory phrase for sentence 12 (reproduced below)?

Jimmy Carter went on to become an enthusiastic and impactful campaigner for human rights.

A) Eventually,

B) After his own presidency,

C) When he was not in office,

D) However,

The Essay

On these essays, you must effectively express and develop your ideas in writing. Read a short passage; an assignment question follows about an important issue. Develop your own point of view on the issue in an essay. Be sure to support your argument with examples and reasoning. Your perspective on the issue will not influence your score.

ESSAY ONE

O judgment! Thou art fled to brutish beasts, and men have lost their reason.

– William Shakespeare, *Julius Caesar*

Don't judge a book by its cover.

– George Eliot, *The Mill on the Floss*

ASSIGNMENT: Can we be too quick to judge the actions of another person?

ESSAY TWO

It is said that a crowd, proportionately to its size, magnifies all that in its units pertains to the emotions, and diminishes all that in them pertains to thought. The group's passion for Zuleika was so intense precisely because of its size. This rule might apply to large groups of people gathered together, or even to whole nations of individuals with shared interests.

– Adapted from Max Beerbohm, *Zuleika Dobson*

ASSIGNMENT: Is it possible for a large group of people to remain rational and thoughtful when confronted with an emotional situation?

Answer Key

1. A) is incorrect. This choice is unnecessarily wordy, as examined the facts is implied in debated.

   B) is incorrect. This choice is unnecessarily wordy, as *hemmed* and *hawed* have a similar meaning as *debate*; they are also colloquial and do not share a tone with the rest of the passage.

   C) is correct. This is the clearest, most concise choice for communicating this idea.

   D) is incorrect. *Hemmed and hawed* is a colloquial saying, which does not match the tone of the rest of the passage.

2. A) is incorrect. *Therefore* does not fit in the context of this sentence, as no cause-and-effect relationship exists.

   B) is correct. *In fact* can be used correctly in this instance to draw attention to interesting information that builds on the previous sentence.

   C) is incorrect. *However* does not fit in the context of this sentence, as no contradictory relationship exists.

   D) is incorrect. *In addition* does not fit in the context of this sentence, as this sentence builds on the previous one and does not introduce a new idea.

3. A) is incorrect. The sentence provides important information about two scientists who point to science fiction as the inspiration for their work.

   B) is incorrect. *Always* is unnecessary to the reader's understanding of the sentence.

   C) is correct. *His* should become *their* because the work belongs to two people (Goddard and Szilard).

   D) is incorrect. The phrase inside the dashes is not grammatically necessary, but it is helpful to the reader's understanding of the sentence.

4. A) is incorrect. This choice is too specific, as only one sentence of the final paragraph relates to transportation.

   B) is incorrect. This sentence adds very little to the meaning of the paragraph.

   C) is incorrect. The tone of this sentence is conversational, and it does not fit with the rest of the passage.

   D) is correct. This choice provides a brief but interesting overview of the information to come.

5. **A) is correct.** This information is unnecessary and detracts from the point of the passage.

   B) is incorrect. *Many* and *most* have similar meanings and are both grammatically correct in this case.

   C) is incorrect. *Deceased* is a more formal word for *dead*, but neither is incorrect.

   D) is incorrect. *Witnessed* is a more formal word for *saw*, but neither is incorrect.

6. **A) is correct.** This sentence relates directly to the overall idea of the passage—that science fiction has a natural influence on real life.

   B) is incorrect. This sentence does not relate to the overall topic of the passage—the relationship between science fiction and reality.

C) is incorrect. This sentence is inappropriately argumentative when compared with the rest of the passage, and it detracts from the main idea of the passage.

D) is incorrect. This sentence is too general and provides no additional insight to the reader.

7. **A) is correct.** As it is written, *more recently* provides the reader with information about the time period being referred to as well as its relationship to the time period that was discussed in the previous sentence.

B) is incorrect. *These days* in a colloquial expression used to refer to the present day; it does not agree with the meaning the author hopes to convey.

C) is incorrect. *Therefore* incorrectly suggests a cause-and-effect relationship between this sentence and the preceding sentence.

D) is incorrect. *On the other hand* incorrectly suggests a contradictory relationship between this sentence and the preceding sentence.

8. A) is incorrect. This choice provides a meaningful conclusion to the paragraph by explaining why people may have been invested in the changeling legend.

B) is correct. *Explanation* adds an important detail about what the demonstrative pronoun *this* refers to.

C) is incorrect. *Families* is used correctly in the sentence to signify

multiple families and does not need to be changed.

D) is incorrect. *Whose* is used correctly in the sentence to signify possession (the children *of* the families) and does not need to be changed.

9. A) is incorrect. The final phrase *the changeling* is incorrectly set off from its descriptor with only a comma.

B) is correct. The final phrase *the changeling* is appropriately set off from the rest of the sentence—its descriptor—with a colon.

C. Incorrect. The dashes in this sentence incorrectly set off information that is essential to the meaning.

D. Incorrect. This choice creates a fragment by placing *the changeling* in its own sentence.

10. A) is incorrect. This choice creates a comma splice by combining two independent clauses with a comma.

B) is incorrect. This choice combines the independent clauses correctly with a comma and a conjunction; however, the meaning of the conjunction *so* suggests a cause-and-effect relationship, which does not exist here.

C) is incorrect. This choice combines the independent clauses correctly with a comma and a conjunction; however, the meaning of the conjunction *but* suggests a contradictory relationship, which does not exist here.

D) is correct. The choice correctly joins the independent clauses with a colon, signifying that the information in the second clause somehow builds or expands on the first.

11. A) is incorrect. This choice correctly turns the second clause into a subordinate clause by adding *who* and joins it to an independent clause with a comma.

B) is incorrect. This choice correctly joins two related independent clauses with a comma.

C) is correct. This choice incorrectly joins two independent clauses with a comma (*changelings were...* and *they were left...*).

D) is incorrect. The dash correctly joins the subordinate clause (*left in the places...*) to the main sentence.

12. **A) is correct.** As written, the sentence acts appropriately as an introductory sentence, providing a summary of the topic that will be discussed; additionally, it gives meaning to the phrase *for example* in sentence 9.

B) is incorrect. The content of the sentence is better aligned with the content of the third paragraph, as encouraging the changelings to leave was not an idea that was discussed in paragraph 2.

C) is incorrect. In this placement, the sentence above is notably vague compared to the sentences around it; as such, it works best as an introductory statement that summarizes the similarities between the various examples.

D) is incorrect. In this placement, the sentence above is notably vague compared to the sentences around it; as such, it works best as an introductory statement

that summarizes the similarities between the various examples.

13. **A) is correct.** The information in the two clauses is equally significant and both ideas require stand-alone sentences.

B) is incorrect. This choice incorrectly combines two complete sentences with only a comma, resulting in a comma splice.

C) is incorrect. Though the sentences are correctly combined with a semicolon, the transition word *however* suggests a contradiction where one does not exist.

D) is incorrect. This choice combines the two complete sentences with no punctuation, resulting in a run-on sentence.

14. A) is incorrect. *All the time* is vague and does not provide any more information about what the author is referring to with the final clause.

B) is incorrect. *On a regular basis* provides specific information but does not convey any more detail about what the author is referring to with the final clause.

C) is incorrect. *Day in and day out* is vague and does not convey any more detail about what the author is referring to with the final clause.

D) is correct. *Of the animals around us* provides the reader with specific information about what the author meant by *not as in control as we like to think we are.*

15. **A) is correct.** This choice is appropriately specific in introducing the topic of the paragraph.

B) is incorrect. This choice is too vague to be useful as an introduction, as it would not prepare the reader for the information in the paragraph.

C) is incorrect. This choice is irrelevant and detracts from the main idea of the paragraph.

D) is incorrect. This choice is overly conversational and only somewhat related to the subject of the paragraph.

16. A) is incorrect. While grammatically correct, this sentence assumes Ken Allen's behavior (walking around the park) was a result of his enjoyment of the zoo; this cannot be proven.

B) is correct. *Observing*, preceded by a comma, correctly sets off the participial phrase that gives more information about Ken Allen.

C) is incorrect. This choice incorrectly joins an independent clause (*Ken Allen would go...*) and a dependent clause (*observing*) with a semicolon.

D) is incorrect. This choice incorrectly joins two independent clauses (*Ken Allen would go...* and *he observed the other animals...*) with a comma, creating a comma splice.

17. **A) is correct.** Though it is interesting information, the details in this sentence are unnecessary, and they detract from the overall meaning of the paragraph.

B) is incorrect. *Who*, a subjective pronoun, correctly refers to the subject *visitor*.

C) is incorrect. *From* is the appropriate preposition to complete the prepositional idiom *warnings from*.

D) is incorrect. *They* (a plural pronoun) and *he* (a singular pronoun) each have clear antecedents.

18. A) is incorrect. This sentence is vague and does little to contribute to the reader's understanding of the author's purpose.

B) is incorrect. This sentence includes interesting information but is too specific to provide a strong conclusion.

C) is correct. This sentence provides an appropriate amount of detail and reminds the audience of the author's overall purpose—to communicate that humans are not in control of animals.

D) is incorrect. This sentence is too specific to the outcome of Tyke's story and does not provide a strong overall conclusion.

19. A) is incorrect. *Many years ago* is too vague to be impactful and leaves the interpretation entirely to the reader.

B) is incorrect. This choice, though true, is irrelevant and detracts from the topic of the passage.

C) is incorrect. This choice, also true, is too vague to be impactful and leaves too much room for interpretation.

D) is correct. This choice provides specific information, making it impactful and memorable.

20. A) is incorrect. *Therefore* incorrectly suggests a cause-and-effect relationship between this sentence and the previous one.

B) is incorrect. *Consequently* incorrectly suggests a cause-and-effect relationship between this sentence and the previous one.

C) is correct. *Though* signifies an important contradiction between the two clauses in this sentence.

D) is incorrect. *Still* incorrectly suggests an additive relationship between this sentence and the previous one.

21. A) is incorrect. *Are* is a plural verb that agrees with its subject *careers*; *exceptionally outstanding* suggests careers that were not only unusual but extremely unusual.

B) is incorrect. *Are* is a plural verb that agrees with its subject *careers*; *of particular interest* suggests careers that are especially applicable to the author's point.

C) is incorrect. *Are* is a plural verb that agrees with its subject *careers*; *especially noteworthy* suggests careers that were not only unusual but extremely unusual.

D) is correct. *Were* is a plural verb that agrees with the plural subject *careers*; however, *of particular interest* suggests relevance to the author's point, which should be referred to in present tense.

22. A) is incorrect. This choice correctly forms two complete sentences.

B) is incorrect. This choice makes the second clause subordinate and appropriately joins the clauses with a comma.

C) is incorrect. This choice correctly joins two complete sentences with a semicolon.

D) is correct. This choice creates two complete sentences but joins them incorrectly with a comma, creating a comma splice.

23. A) is incorrect. This choice provides unnecessary information that detracts from the main idea of the paragraph.

B) is incorrect. This choice provides unnecessary information that detracts from the main idea of the paragraph.

C) is incorrect. This choice provides unnecessary information that is too specific to be an effective conclusion.

D) is correct. This choice is appropriately specific and provides a brief summary of the information mentioned in the paragraph.

24. A) is incorrect. This choice incorrectly joins two complete sentences without punctuation, creating a run-on sentence.

B) is incorrect. This choice correctly joins two complete sentences with a semicolon, but the transition word *however* suggests a contradiction where one does not exist.

C) is correct. This choice correctly joins two related complete sentences with a semicolon.

D) is incorrect. This choice incorrectly joins two complete sentences with a dash.

25. A) is incorrect. *Eventually* is too vague to be effective, as it does not tell the reader when Jimmy Carter was working.

B) is correct. *After his own presidency* provides an appropriate amount of detail to describe when the action took place—immediately following his retirement.

C) is incorrect. *When he was not in office* is too vague to be effective, as it suggests anytime other than when Jimmy Carter was president.

D) is incorrect. *However* suggests a contradiction, but one does not exist in this context.

THE ESSAY
Sample Essay One — Score of 8

All people make mistakes, and it is easy to judge them from the outside. However, sometimes people behave in harmful ways as a result of unseen hardships. People should refrain from judgment until they have the full story. Still, an unusual challenge does not absolve someone from all responsibilities. Even those at a disadvantage are accountable for their responsibilities, but they may be forgiven for certain harms as long as they take steps to rectify them.

For instance, my parents do not get along with their neighbor because he has a messy yard, which brings down their property value. He also has a dog which he lets wander on the streets. My parents' dog, on the other hand, must stay in the house and is only allowed to run freely behind the fence in the yard or at a dog park. However, everyone in the area has approximately the same income. Furthermore, the neighbor is seemingly in good physical health and works normal hours. There seems to be no reason that he cannot spend a little time each week on yard work and keep his dogs in his yard like everyone else. However, he does have one unique characteristic: allergies.

The neighbor's health situation presents a dilemma. While he is responsible for cleaning his yard, he struggles with yardwork because his allergies prevent him from spending too much time among shrubs, bushes, and trees. In addition, it is hard for him to keep his dog in his house for long periods of time, as pet dander makes his allergies worse, but the more time the dog spends in the yard, the messier the yard gets. And on top of all that, he lives alone, with no one to help with chores. Meanwhile, both of my parents enjoy outdoor activity, have no allergies, and can tackle yardwork together quite easily. They are able to keep their dog inside without any health concerns and can take turns walking him. Taking these differences into account, it becomes clearer why the neighbor's yard is in disarray and why his dog is often out. These issues may be less about his character than his circumstances.

Still, the neighbor has a responsibility to those around him. First, he should not have a dog if he cannot properly care for it or keep it in his home. Not only is a dog roaming the streets a nuisance to other neighbors, but it is unsafe for the dog, which could be hit by a car or injured in some other way. Next, he should find a way to properly care for his yard. Perhaps he could pursue medical treatment for his allergies, hire workers to assist periodically, or even ask a friend, family member, or neighbor for assistance if his budget is tight. Even if he is struggling to care for his yard, as a homeowner he is responsible for it.

In this case, the neighbor could be forgiven if he took steps to fix the situation, because he is clearly at a disadvantage when it comes to yardwork and pet care due to his allergies, which are not his fault. However, if he does not take responsibility and make amends, his disadvantages do not matter, and he should not be forgiven. At that point, he could be judged as a poor neighbor or as a person of poor character because he has chosen to remain a nuisance in the neighborhood despite other options.

ANSWER EXPLANATION

This essay received an 8 because it demonstrates outstanding critical thinking, developing a nuanced argument even while answering the question (*Even those at a disadvantage are accountable for their responsibilities, but they may be forgiven for certain harms as long as they take steps to rectify them*). The writer supports the argument with one anecdotal example, but the level of detail in the scenario is sufficient to illustrate the author's argument that some disadvantages may be hidden and so one should not be quick to judge: *There seems to be no reason that he cannot spend a little time each week on yard work… However, he does have one unique characteristic: allergies.* The author offers possible solutions to the harms the neighbor brings on the neighborhood, which would allow him to be forgiven ("he could pursue medical treatment…hire workers to assist…or even ask a friend, family member, or neighbor for assistance" in cleaning the yard). The writing and organization is clear and coherent; the thesis is presented in the introduction, and the anecdotal scenario is fully developed. The writer uses varied sentence structure, strong vocabulary, and transition words. There are few, if any, mechanical errors.

SAMPLE ESSAY — SCORE OF 8

History provides countless examples of crowds that have become unruly, dangerous, even deadly. However, a commanding leader can make a difference. When a charismatic leader harnesses the emotions of the crowd, he or she can stir it up or calm it down with thoughtful and evocative words and actions. During the Great Depression, US President Franklin D. Roosevelt's speeches and "Fireside Chats" calmed Americans fearful of losing their savings and quelled financial panic. However, powerful speakers have the power to trigger violence. In the 1930s, Adolf Hitler's nationalist speeches in Germany inspired anti-Semitism, racism, and violent acts like Kristallnacht. A large crowd can remain calm in an emotional situation, but only with the right leadership.

Consumer panic makes an economic crisis into a catastrophe when people withdraw their funds from banks all at once, and social unrest can soon follow. FDR's public speeches and radio addresses, known as "Fireside Chats," were intended to calm the public while allowing bank reform and economic recovery to occur. Famously, in describing emergency measures to close the banks, he explained economic policy in plain language, reassuring Americans that their money would still be available when banks reopened. He also stayed positive and optimistic, using euphemisms like "bank holiday" and "inconvenience." His word choice and demeanor encouraged people to stay calm and cooperate with financial reforms. In fact, in his inaugural address, he proclaimed that there was "nothing to fear but fear itself," inspiring faith rather than panic in a time of national crisis when social unrest was feared.

On the other hand, Adolf Hitler rose to power in Germany on a platform of nationalism and discrimination. At the time, much like the United States, Germany was suffering from an economic depression and struggling to rebuild following the First World War. Unlike FDR, Hitler used negative language and scapegoated minority groups, especially Jewish people. He encouraged violence among his followers such as book-burnings, property damage, and deadly acts against Jewish people and other minority groups. As the Nazis became more powerful, Jewish people were subject to discriminatory laws and oppressive treatment. Jewish businesses were attacked and looted on Kristallnacht. Hitler's harsh rhetoric had contributed to a social and political environment where this abuse was acceptable, and it led to the Holocaust.

Overall, crowds are driven by emotion, and even people who remain rational within them cannot take control. Some people helped the Jews and other persecuted people in Nazi Germany, but they did so in secret, no match for the power of Hitler and Nazi ideology over the nation. Yet, as shown by FDR's leadership during the Great Depression, it is possible for a huge group—an entire nation—to stave off irrational, panicky behavior even with something as important as money. A crowd, despite its essential emotional nature, can be rendered rational and calm by the right leader.

ANSWER EXPLANATION

This essay received an 8 because it demonstrates outstanding critical thinking, developing a nuanced argument even while answering the question (*A large crowd can remain calm in an emotional situation, but only with the right leadership*). The writer uses two strong examples—FDR's speeches and "Fireside Chats" and Hitler's negative language and scapegoating—contrasting them and developing the examples with specific details. Organization is clear; the thesis is presented in the introduction, a paragraph is devoted to each example, and the conclusion compares the two, highlighting FDR's calming abilities and supporting the argument. The writer uses varied sentence structure, strong vocabulary, and transition words. There are few, if any, mechanical errors.

Made in the USA
Coppell, TX
22 December 2020

46940219R00131